THE CONSTITUTIONAL CORPORATION

The Constitutional Corporation
Rethinking Corporate Governance

STEPHEN BOTTOMLEY
ANU College of Law
The Australian National University, Australia

Routledge
Taylor & Francis Group

LONDON AND NEW YORK

First published 2007 by Ashgate Publishing

Published 2016 by Routledge
2 Park Square, Milton Park, Abingdon, Oxfordshire OX14 4RN
711 Third Avenue, New York, NY 10017, USA

First issued in paperback 2016

Routledge is an imprint of the Taylor & Francis Group, an informa business

British Library Cataloguing in Publication Data
Bottomley, Stephen
  The constitutional corporation : rethinking corporate
  governance. - (Applied legal philosophy)
  1. Corporate governance
  I. Title
  658.4

Library of Congress Cataloging-in-Publication Data
Bottomley, Stephen.
  The constitutional corporation : rethinking corporate governance / by Stephen
Bottomley.
      p. cm. -- (Applied legal philosophy)
  Includes index.
  ISBN: 978-0-7546-2418-9 1. Corporate governance--Law and
legislation--United States. I. Title.
  KF1422.B68 2007
  346.73'0664--dc22

                                                              2006031598

ISBN 13: 978-1-138-24835-9 (pbk)
ISBN 13: 978-0-7546-2418-9 (hbk)

Contents

List of Cases

List of Statutes

Preface

This book has had a long gestation (far too long, for those who have been closely involved in its production). What sparked it off was the decision of the Australian High Court in *Gambotto v WCP Ltd* in 1995, which upheld the claim of a minority shareholder not to have his shares compulsorily bought from him by the majority shareholder in the corporation. My sense was that the High Court had made an important contribution to corporate jurisprudence, although one that required more explanation and justification than could be found in the pages of the judgements. But I was also struck by the speed with which the many critics of that case were able to muster their counter-attack (and I don't think that 'attack' overstates the nature of some of the responses). Several articles, books, and conference papers appeared within a short period after the decision was handed down. Without wanting to down-play the diversity of those responses, it is accurate to say that most of the criticisms were anchored, one way or another, in a law and economics framework. It occurred to me that these critics had something of a strategic advantage — the well-established law and economics framework supplied them with a ready-made conceptual model which could be used to respond quickly to the High Court's decision. On the other hand, those corporate law scholars who found something of value in the decision, and who were troubled by some of the criticisms, were largely (but not entirely) silent, myself included. Perhaps, I thought, a competing conceptual framework was needed, from which to mount a response to the issues raised by that case and future developments.

This book is the outcome of my attempt to develop such a framework. As the work continued, the specific issues raised by the *Gambotto* decision ceased to be my central concern (indeed, the case is mentioned only occasionally in what follows). But my wish to develop a conceptual framework for analysing corporate law issues, that could work as an alternative to the widely accepted law and economics model, persisted. Whether the ideas presented in this book are successful in achieving this goal is, of course, for readers to decide.

The book draws on a number of previously published articles, book chapters and conference papers. It is not, however, a simple compilation of that work. In attempting to integrate that work I found that my ideas had changed at many points. Also, the task of 'putting it all together' for the purposes of the book revealed inconsistencies and conceptual gaps, forcing me to re-think, develop and (I hope) clarify my arguments.

Over the years many people have helped me in the process of organising my thoughts for this book. Given the passage of time, it is quite likely that some have forgotten their contribution, but every argument and idea presented here has been assisted by the questions, comments and gentle critique of others. Here, at last, is the chance to acknowledge and thank John Braithwaite, Angus Corbett, Christine

Parker, Philip Pettit, Colin Scott, Peta Spender (who read through many of the chapters in their near final form), Daniel Stewart, the late Michael Whincop, and John Williams. Thanks also to Tom Campbell for urging some last minute revisions. I have listened to their ideas and suggestions, although I confess that I have not always acted on them. In line with customary practice, I absolve them from any responsibility for what lies between the covers of this book, although I don't see why I should. After all, they encouraged me to continue with the project.

Thanks also to Jenna Bottomley for her work in compiling the tables of statutes and cases, and to Vera Joveska for formatting and preparing the text for publication.

The real driving force behind this book, however, has been my wife, Sheri. She has the good sense not to be engrossed in corporate law, but nevertheless she has continually challenged, urged and encouraged me to write this book (occasionally enlisting the aid of our daughters, Kristen, Sarah, Taryn and Jenna). Moreover — and here is my greatest debt — she has made space for me to do so. Acknowledging her support and patience in this, the final product, seems to be both an appropriate and a perverse way of thanking her.

Finally, the long period during which this book was being written witnessed the untimely and unexpected deaths of two corporate law scholars whose work is referred to on a number of occasions in the following chapters. Michael Whincop (Professor of Law at Griffith University) died in June 2003. I knew Michael, and his death was a great shock. John Parkinson (Professor of Law at Bristol University) died in February 2004, and although I didn't know him (we were to have met at a conference I was organising, but he died shortly before this), the news of his death was nevertheless saddening. They were scholars of different theoretical persuasions, but I have great admiration for their contributions to corporate law scholarship. I hope that this book might be regarded as being in the same company as theirs.

Stephen Bottomley

Acknowledgements

In parts this book draws upon previously published work. I thank the editors of the following publications for permission to use material from the following articles:

'From Contractualism to Constitutionalism: A Framework for Corporate Governance' (1997) *Sydney Law Review* 277.

'The Birds, The Beasts and The Bat: Developing a Constitutionalist Theory of Corporate Regulation' (1999) 27 *Federal Law Review* 243.

The book also refers to my research into company general meetings. This research was funded by a grant from the Australian Research Council, which I acknowledge with thanks.

Chapter 1

Corporations and Shareholders

It's a Corporate World

The renowned English legal scholar William Twining demonstrates the pervasiveness of law to his first year students by asking them to read a daily newspaper and to mark all the passages that they think are 'law-related'.[1] He finds that students frequently have difficulty deciding what to leave out. I suspect that the exercise would be only marginally less difficult if the assignment was to mark all the passages that relate to corporations.

We live in a corporate world.[2] Corporations are so much a part of our lives that their role is usually taken for granted, going unnoticed until the occurrence of some dramatic event brings it to our attention (all too often, that event is a corporation's seemingly unheralded descent into insolvency).[3] Principally it is corporations that supply or control our access to goods and services, work and leisure, knowledge and information. Indeed, most of what we know about the corporate world is communicated to us through media that are controlled by corporations. The activities of corporations shape or influence national economies, they affect the quality of the environment, and they influence the actions of nation states.[4] Corporations are increasingly called upon to contribute to the provision of social welfare and national development, either in partnership with or by taking over from the work of governments.[5] Corporations, especially transnational corporations, have a major impact on, and thus are called upon to

---

[1] W Twining, *Law in Context: Enlarging a Discipline* (1997) 210-213; *Globalisation and Legal Theory* (2000) 1-2.

[2] For a readable history of the rise of the corporation, see J Micklethwait and A Wooldridge, *The Company - A Short History of a Revolutionary Idea* (2003).

[3] Well known examples in the United States are the Enron Corporation in late 2001 and WorldCom Inc in mid-2002. In Australia One.Tel Ltd in May 2001, and HIH Insurance Ltd in March 2001 have a similar significance.

[4] This is not to say that interaction between corporations and states is all one-way. Corporations frequently have to adjust or structure their own activities to meet the demands of state agencies or court rulings, as in monopoly or anti-trust actions.

[5] For example, in 1998 the Australian Prime Minister John Howard called on the Australian corporate sector to contribute more to community welfare – Keynote Address to the Australian Council of Social Service National Congress, Adelaide, November 1998.

accept responsibility for the protection of, human rights.[6] Corporations work behind the scenes (and increasingly on centre-stage) to influence many aspects of national government policy and legislative action. Corporate donations are a major source of funding for political parties.[7] It is large corporations that determine the formulation of a wide array of regulatory standards on issues ranging from air safety to pharmaceutical products and telecommunications.[8]

This corporate influence is not always the product of deliberate lobbying or planned political pressure. More often it is simply the product of ordinary commercial activity. A corporation's decision to 'downsize', relocate, or expand its operations can have a significant impact on local and national economies and on social policy. Consequently, the mere threat of a major corporate restructuring can often produce governmental responses that individual citizens are unable to achieve.[9]

The significance of corporations in modern society is not confined to the private business sector. Corporate forms of organisation are now commonplace in the non-business and non-profit sectors, including social groups and religious organisations, sports and recreational clubs, educational institutions, professional firms, and welfare organisations.[10] There are many reasons behind this spread of the corporate form, including the perceived attractions of limited legal liability, perceptions (accurate or otherwise) about the efficiency of corporate styles of management, and the risk-assessments of lenders and grant-giving bodies about

---

[6]   See United Nations Sub-Commission on the Promotion and Protection of Human Rights, *Norms On The Responsibilities of Transnational Corporations and Other Business Enterprises With Regard to Human Rights*, August 2003; also M Addo (ed), *Human Rights and the Responsibility of Transnational Corporations* (1999); S Bottomley and D Kinley (eds), *Commercial Law and Human Rights* (2002).

[7]   I Ramsay, G Stapledon, and J Vernon, 'Political Donations by Australian Companies' (2001) 29 *Federal Law Review* 117 (also referring to the situation in the United Kingdom).

[8]   See generally J Braithwaite and P Drahos, *Global Business Regulation* (2000); C Scott, 'Private Regulation of the Public Sector: A Neglected Facet of Contemporary Governance' (2002) 29 *Journal of Law and Society* 56.

[9]   A recent example in Australia concerned the closure by Mitsubishi Motors Australia of its car assembly operations in the State of South Australia. With the prospect of losing an estimated 22,000 jobs and $2 billion gross state product, the South Australian Treasurer and the Federal Industry Minister flew to Japan to negotiate with the parent corporation: 'South Australia must drive its own future', *Australian Financial Review* (Sydney), 29 April 2004, 62; Brendan Pearson 'Mitsubishi on brink after crisis talks' *Australian Financial Review* (Sydney), 18 May 2004, 1. In June 2004, the Australian Government announced a $10 million subsidy for Mitsubishi workers.

[10] In some jurisdictions there are specialised forms or methods of incorporation for these types of corporations. See, for example, the associations incorporation legislation in Australian States and Territories (for example the *Associations Incorporation Act* 1991 (ACT)). In the United Kingdom there is a recommendation that there should be a separate form of incorporation specifically for charities: Company Law Review Steering Group, *Modern Company Law For a Competitive Economy: Final Report* (2001), para 4.63.

what constitutes an acceptable organisational structure. Governments have also been attracted to corporate forms of management, not only modelling their departmental structures along corporate lines ('corporatisation') but, increasingly, creating government-owned corporations to do the work of government.[11] Failing that, governments around the globe have demonstrated a fascination for 'outsourcing' areas of public administration to private sector corporations, or simply 'privatising' whole aspects of governmental operations. The range of activities that has been given over to private sector corporations includes power and water supplies, telecommunications, banking, roads, transport and shipping, and prisons.

In summary, corporations now feature in all aspects of social, political and economic life — private and public, business and non-business, large and small enterprise.

Related to this spread of the corporate form is the rise and spread of share ownership in the general population of many countries as a form of investment, savings, and retirement planning. This is particularly noticeable in Australia where since the late 1990s share ownership has become a significant feature of economic and political life. This trend has been driven by factors such as the compulsory superannuation requirement which has operated in Australia since 1992,[12] the full or partial privatization of large government-owned businesses such as Telstra and the Commonwealth Bank,[13] and the demutualisation of some corporations that have had 'icon' status (for example, the Australian Mutual Provident Society and the National Roads and Motorists Association). According to the Australian Stock Exchange (the ASX), Australia has one of the highest levels of direct and indirect share ownership in the world.[14] Data published by the ASX shows that the proportion of the Australian adult population holding shares either directly or indirectly (eg through managed investment schemes) rose from 34 per cent in 1997 to 55 per cent in 2004; 44 per cent of adults held shares directly. Similar figures are found in other countries. In New Zealand, for example, 39 per cent of adult investors had some form of share ownership in 2005, although only 23 per cent had

---

[11]   S Bottomley, 'Regulating Government-owned Corporations' (1994) 53 *Australian Journal of Public Administration* 521; S Bottomley, 'Corporatisation and Accountability: the Case of Commonwealth Government Companies' (1997) 7 *Australian Journal of Corporate Law* 156; B Collier and S Pitkin (eds), *Corporatisation and Privatisation in Australia* (1999).

[12]   The *Superannuation Guarantee (Administration) Act 1992* (Cth) requires employers to provide a prescribed minimum level of superannuation support for employees. Superannuation schemes are operated by private and public sector funds rather than a central government operated fund. See G Stapledon, 'Share Ownership and Control in Listed Australian Companies' (1999) 2 *Corporate Governance International* 17, 21.

[13]   Telstra, the Federal Government-owned telecommunications corporation, was partially privatised in 1997 with the public float of 33 per cent of its shares. A further 16 per cent was sold in 1999. The sale of the remaining 51 per cent continues to be a topic of political debate. The Commonwealth Bank was fully privatised in 1991.

[14]   Australian Stock Exchange, *Australian Share Ownership Study 2004* (2005).

direct shareholdings.[15] In the United States 49.5 per cent of households owned equities as at January 2002.[16] In 2003 shares had become the second most popular form of personal investment in Australia, ranking only behind superannuation. The value of individual share portfolios has also increased, from an average of $29,000 in 2000, to $41,400 in 2004. In that year 38 per cent of investors had less than $10,000 invested directly in shares, while 35 per cent had more than $50,000 invested.[17]

Of course, high levels of share ownership do not necessarily mean high levels of direct investor participation in the corporate economy or in the processes of corporate governance. Despite the high level of share ownership in Australia, many investors are relatively passive in their direct share holdings — this is one of the concerns of this book. The 2004 ASX survey found that about half of all direct share owners had not traded in the twelve months prior to the survey. Looking at another aspect of shareholder passivity, a survey of 217 Australian listed corporations in 2002 found that in 98 per cent of annual general meetings shareholders attending in person or by proxy represented no more than 20 per cent of all shareholders in the corporation. In the same group of corporations none of the 203 extraordinary general meetings held between 2001 and 2003 were called by shareholders.[18]

At the same time, the connection between citizens and their national and global communities is increasingly mediated through the financial and securities markets and, therefore, through the activities of corporations. A nation's state of well-being is judged as much by stock-market indices and corporate profit announcements as by non-economic factors. Perhaps this is why so much of the nightly television news bulletin is taken up with information about share price movements, shifts in various market performance indexes, currency fluctuations, and corporate reporting. When governments announce new policies or abandon old ones, when major national and international events take place, we are as likely to find that expert commentary is sought from an economist or a financial analyst as from a political or a social commentator.

This book takes this corporate world (for better or for worse) as its starting point. The book does not yearn for a return to some bygone era — if it ever

---

[15]　New Zealand Stock Exchange, *Press Release: More New Zealanders are investing in the share market*, (15 July 2005) <http://www.nzx.com/aboutus/news/press/research_15jul/view> at 3 January 2006.

[16]　Investment Company Institute/Securities Industry Association, *Equity Ownership in America 2002* (2002) <http://www.ici.org/shareholders/dec/1rpt_02_equity_owners.pdf> at 13 May 2004. Not all countries reveal the same trend. A survey in the United Kingdom, for example, found that in June 2002 only 22 per cent of private investors held stocks or shares: Proshare, *Private Share Ownership in Britain in 2002* (2002) <http://www.proshare.org/Research/bso2002.pdf> at 13 May 2004.

[17]　Australian Stock Exchange, *Australian Share Ownership Study 2004* (2005).

[18]　S Bottomley, The Role of Shareholders' Meetings in Improving Corporate Governance (Research Report, Centre for Commercial Law, Australian National University, 2003) vi-vii.

existed — in which corporations knew their place, and when the word 'share' was as likely to make one think of cooperative or altruistic behaviour as of a device for individual wealth accumulation. The purpose of this book is, however, to challenge some of the assumptions and practices that have come to define this corporate world. In particular, the book challenges the idea that the only, or the best, way in which shareholders should relate to corporations is as investors. It challenges the idea that the only, or the best, way in which corporations can relate to shareholders is through a short or medium term focus on profits and dividend returns. It challenges the idea that the only, or the best, criteria for assessing the relationship between shareholders and corporations are efficiency and wealth-maximisation. And, lastly, it challenges the sometimes explicit, but mostly implicit claim of economics to be the pre-eminent discipline for making real sense of these developments, and the capacity of economics to provide an over-arching metatheory for all things corporate.[19]

Focusing on Shareholders

As the previous paragraph indicates, the argument in this book is concerned with the relationship between a corporation's shareholders and its board of directors. This follows the standard legal model of the corporation that underpins corporate law regimes in many Western legal systems, whereby directors' actions must be oriented towards the best interests of the corporation's shareholders.[20] This book adopts this legal model, not because the model presents an organisational ideal to which corporations should necessarily aspire, and certainly not because the model is an accurate description of the way in which all corporations actually operate. Instead, the formal legal model is used because, regardless of the diversity in corporate structures, it does provide a common and resilient reference point and language for all corporations that operate in corporate law systems such as those found in Australia, the United Kingdom, and North America.

In the context of the literature on corporate governance, much of which urges a shift away from a shareholder primacy model of the corporation, this might be thought to be a narrow and legalistic focus, and so it requires further explanation. Many writers urge a much wider view than this. For example:

> Corporate governance is more than simply the relationship between the firm and its capital providers. Corporate governance also implicates how the various constituencies that define the business enterprise serve, and are served by, the corporation. Implicit and explicit relationships between the corporation and its employees, creditors, suppliers, customers, host communities – and relationships

---

[19] An example is M Whincop, *An Economic and Jurisprudential Genealogy of Corporate Law* (2001) 3, claiming that economics is the key to understanding corporate law.
[20] This model is analysed in more detail in Chapter 2.

among these constituencies themselves – fall within the ambit of a relevant definition of corporate governance.[21]

Some writers argue quite strongly that the shareholder primacy model has no compelling moral basis, that shareholders warrant no greater attention or protection than other stakeholders in the corporation, and that the time has come to move away from 'shareholder primacy' towards models that, one way or another, recognise the interests of all stakeholders in the corporation.[22] Others charge that shareholder primacy allows (or, even worse, requires) corporations to ignore or downplay important human rights, environmental, and health and safety concerns.[23] Most shareholders, we are told, are passive, absentee owners, and '[i]f it is not the shareholders' efforts and abilities which direct the economic activities of the corporation, then why should they have the right to have it run purely in their interests?'[24]

Why are these broader concerns not addressed in this book? I assume that one purpose of taking a broader stakeholder approach is to call into question the way we think about the corporation and its purposes as a legal, economic and social institution. For directors, managers, lawyers and other professionals who are involved in the day-to-day business of corporate practice and corporate law, a broader approach demands some significant shifts in attitude and practice. This has been attempted before, in repeated calls for corporate social responsibility or for a communitarian approach to corporate governance.[25] These calls have not been widely accepted in practice, largely, I suspect, because they are seen to depart too

21   M Bradley, C Schipani, A Sundaram, and J Walsh, 'The Purposes and Accountability of the Corporation in Contemporary Society: Corporate Governance at a Crossroads' (1999) 62 *Law and Contemporary Problems* 9, 11.

22   See, for example, P Ireland, 'Company Law and the Myth of Shareholder Ownership' (1999) 62 *Modern Law Review* 32; D Wood, 'Whom Should Business Serve?' (2002) 14 *Australian Journal of Corporate Law* 1; L Stout, 'Bad and Not-So-Bad Arguments for Shareholder Primacy' (2002) 75 *Southern California Law Review* 1189. With Blair, Stout advocates a 'team production' model: M Blair and L Stout, 'A Team Production Theory of Corporate Law' (1999) 86 *Virginia Law Review* 247; M Blair and L Stout, 'Director Accountability and the Mediating Role of the Corporate Board' (2001) 79 *Washington University Law Quarterly* 403. See below n 38 and accompanying text.

23   A clear example of the adverse impact on health and safety concerns is found in the attempt by James Hardie Industries Ltd to isolate its liability for asbestos-related illness from its general operations. See *Report of the Special Commission of Inquiry Into the Medical Research and Compensation Foundation* (September 2004) <http://www.cabinet.nsw.gov.au/hardie/PartA.pdf > at 6 March 2005.

24   M Gilbert, 'Introduction' in M Gilbert (ed), *The Modern Business Enterprise: Selected Readings* (1972) 20.

25   On corporate social responsibility see, for example, D Engel, 'An Approach to Corporate Social Responsibility' (1979) 32 *Stanford Law Review* 1; J Tolmie, 'Corporate Social Responsibility' (1992) 15 *University of New South Wales Law Journal* 268. On communitarian approaches to corporate law, see L Mitchell (ed), *Progressive Corporate Law* (1995); and Symposium, 'New Directions in Corporate Law' (1993) 50 *Washington and Lee Law Review* Issue No 4.

dramatically from the orthodox and prevailing legal and economic view of the corporation. In 1989, for example, an Australian Senate inquiry into the law governing directors' duties considered the possibility of imposing duties towards consumers, employees, or the environment, but concluded that:

> It is appropriate that matters external to the company be dealt with in separate and specific legislation ... This is because companies legislation should deal only with corporate structure and organisation and matters arising as and between the constituents of the body corporate.[26]

This view persists, notwithstanding the more recent inclusion in Australian corporations legislation of provisions to protect the entitlements of employees when a corporation becomes insolvent.[27] The situation is similar in the United Kingdom where Len Sealy has commented that:

> at present our company law lacks the conceptual and remedial tools – and, I think also, its framers lack the will – to reflect our new perception of the company as no longer a shareholders' collective, but an enterprise in which the interests of many stakeholders have to be balanced.[28]

Similarly, in the United States, David Millon has concluded that '[t]he long-standing controversy over the rights of corporate shareholders in relation to nonshareholders involved in or affected by corporate activity is no closer to resolution today than it ever has been'.[29] The shareholder primacy model has proven to be resilient, notwithstanding the importance of broader concerns.[30] I am pessimistic about the prospects for a serious consideration by directors, lawyers, and others of broader perspectives on corporate governance until they can be convinced that a broader approach is consonant with the ideas that underlie the orthodox legal model.

Of course there are those who defend the shareholder primacy model in more positive terms, and on a variety of grounds: for example, that shareholders are the 'owners' of the corporation, that it is the shareholders who appoint the

---

[26] Senate Standing Committee on Legal and Constitutional Affairs, Parliament of Australia, *Company Directors' Duties – Report on the Social and Fiduciary Duties and Obligations of Company Directors* (1989) para 6.55.

[27] *Corporations Act 2001*, Part 5.8A.

[28] L Sealy, 'Perception and Policy in Company Law Reform' in D Feldman and F Miesel (eds), *Corporate and Commercial Law: Modern Developments* (1996) 28. For another, but differently framed assessment of the fate of stakeholding in the UK see S Wheeler, *Corporations and the Third Way* (2002), 29ff.

[29] D Millon, 'The Ambiguous Significance of Corporate Personhood' *Washington & Lee Public Law and Legal Theory Research Paper Series*, Working Paper No 01-6, January 2001, 28.

[30] Theories of 'path dependence' provide one explanation for this. See L Bebchuk and M Roe, 'A Theory of Path Dependence in Corporate Ownership and Governance' (1999) 52 *Stanford Law Review* 127.

directors to act as their agents, that shareholders are the residual claimants and main risk bearers in the corporation,[31] or that a shareholder primacy rule reduces the scope for unwanted managerial discretion.[32] Hansmann and Kraakman have noted that despite some divergence in patterns of share ownership, capital market structures and business culture, the basic law of the corporate form has achieved a high degree of uniformity around the globe.[33] They have predicted further international convergence on the shareholder primacy model of the corporation (indeed, so confident is their prediction that they have proclaimed 'the end of history for corporate law'). In their view, the shareholder primacy model has swept aside other contenders, including the stakeholder model favoured by proponents of corporate social responsibility and ethical capitalism.

I am not convinced that we have witnessed the end of history for corporate law. I am convinced, though, that the way forward means taking the shareholder primacy model seriously. Whatever its shortcomings, that model exercises a powerful grip on the mind-set of corporate managers and officers. And, as we saw earlier in this Chapter, shareholding has become a significant feature of the economic and political climate. Given all this, the challenge is to work *with* the shareholder primacy model. Legally speaking, it is a flexible model and the arguments presented in this book suggest that it can be fine-tuned and used in ways that do not necessarily shut out other sets of interests and concerns. What is required is a way of looking at corporations and shareholders that opens up new possibilities for shareholder involvement. This need not involve fundamental changes to corporate structures or operations. Instead, the idea is to bring out possibilities that already exist in corporate law and corporate organisations. These adaptations might eventually lead to larger changes, but one premise of this book is that while a consideration of broader conceptions of the corporation and corporate governance is a worthwhile exercise, it will occur in small steps. Hence, I take the existing legal model, with its emphasis on the interests of shareholders, as my starting point — not because I wish to defend that model, but because, in pragmatic terms, it is the best place to start. Thus while the purpose of this book is to change the way in which we think about corporations and their governance processes, it does not advocate any fundamental transformations or reforms of basic corporate structures or the corporate legal environment.[34]

Having said that, another concern of this book is that very often the shareholder primacy model does not work, even on its own terms. In legal terms it is an imprecise doctrine, usually expressed as a duty owed by directors to act in the best interests of the corporation, which may mean the corporation as a commercial

---

[31]   See, for example, F Easterbrook and D Fischel, *The Economic Structure of Corporate Law* (1991) 35ff.

[32]   Stout, above n 22, 1199-1201.

[33]   H Hansmann and R Kraakman, 'The End of History for Corporate Law' (2001) 89 *Georgetown Law Journal* 439.

[34]   Though some reforms are discussed throughout the book.

entity or, at other times, the interests of the members as a whole.[35] The upshot of this legal imprecision is that directors have considerable discretionary power. They can choose to adopt short-term strategies to maximise share price instead of looking to the longer-term value of the corporation.[36] This will satisfy the interests of some — perhaps many — shareholders. But there are dangers here. One is that short-term price maximisation comes to be equated with shareholder primacy.[37] Another is that shareholders become marginalised in corporate decision-making processes. From an economic perspective we are told repeatedly that most shareholders are merely passive investors, monitoring corporate performance only to the extent that is necessary for them to decide when to transfer their money from one corporation to some other corporate investment opportunity. Commentators urge that corporate law should recognise this 'reality' and leave more space for corporate managers to get on with the job of profit-maximisation without being overly burdened by the demands of shareholder accountability. One variation of this argument is Blair and Stout's 'team production' theory, according to which the role of the board of directors, operating independently of all contributors to the corporate enterprise, is to allocate the value produced by the team effort amongst the various contributors.[38] An even more extreme argument (which, like stakeholder theory, has yet to find general acceptance) is the 'director primacy' argument which completely 'rejects the notion that shareholders are entitled to either direct or indirect decisionmaking control'.[39] The role of shareholders in public corporations is thus in danger of being reduced to a level that gives inadequate opportunity for their concerns (short-term or not) to be heard and considered. A consequential concern is that this trend makes any consideration of broader approaches to corporate governance even more difficult to contemplate. If those who are supposedly at the centre of doctrinal concerns are given short shrift, what hope is there, eventually, for non-shareholders?

It is one thing to acknowledge that many shareholders are passive investors with little or no interest in corporate issues beyond the current market price of their securities.[40] It is quite another thing to use this as a premise on which

---

[35]   Compare *Greenhalgh v Arderne Cinemas Ltd* [1951] Ch 286, 291 per Evershed MR ('the phrase, "the company as a whole", does not … mean the company as a commercial entity distinct from the corporators') with *Darvall v North Sydney Brick & Tile Co Ltd* (1988) 6 ACLC 154 per Hodgson J ('it is proper to have regard to … the interests of the company as a commercial entity').

[36]   See, eg, L Mitchell, *Corporate Irresponsibility: America's Newest Export* (2001).

[37]   D Millon, 'Why Is Corporate Management Obsessed with Quarterly Earnings and What Should Be Done About It?' (2002) 70 *George Washington Law Review* 890, 900-902.

[38]   Blair and Stout, above n 22.

[39]   S Bainbridge, 'Director Primacy: The Means and Ends of Corporate Governance' (2003) 97 *Northwestern University Law Review* 547, 563. For a law-and-economics based critique of the assumption of passivity, see B Black, 'Shareholder Passivity Reexamined' (1990) 89 *Michigan Law Review* 520.

[40]   In Australia, where compulsory superannuation has brought many people into the share market, the passivity argument may be overstated. Most superannuation schemes now operate as 'accumulation funds' in which the final retirement benefit depends very

to build corporate law rules and corporate governance principles. Evidence of shareholder passivity and lack of shareholder activism should not become the normative and policy foundation for corporate law reform. To adapt a point made by Charkham and Simpson, shareholder passivity may be individually rational, but it is collectively to the detriment of our economic and social structures.[41] This book therefore argues for a new approach to the role of shareholders, one which can serve as the basis for going on to consider the interests of other stakeholders in the corporation.

A New Framework: Corporate Constitutionalism[42]

I have noted already that the contemporary debate about corporate regulation is dominated by references to 'corporate governance'. This is a slippery term. It is found both in discussions about the role of corporations in society (where the reference is to the governance *of* corporations) and in discussions about the roles of, and relations between, directors and shareholders (that is, governance *in* corporations). In the latter case, 'corporate governance' is sometimes used to describe broadly defined goals (for example, corporations should aim to maintain good corporate governance in addition to profitability),[43] and at other times to refer to the means by which certain goals (for example, satisfied shareholders or the efficient use of capital)[44] can be achieved. The term has become so malleable that it is tempting to dismiss it as being devoid of any real content, as a public relations slogan that is invoked by image-conscious corporations seeking to gain or maintain a perceived market advantage.

If, however, we judge it less cynically, the idea of corporate governance does at least remind us that corporations *are* systems of government. In this sense, corporate governance can stand as an organising motif for debates about the role, composition and duties of the board of directors, and the role and rights of shareholders, either individually, in groups or as a whole, and about the ways in which directors and shareholders interact within a corporation. Peeling away the rhetoric, we find that the underlying theme in all of these debates continues to be what Mary Stokes, in her influential essay, described as 'the problem of the

---

much on the success of the share investments made by the fund. This may well be a factor behind the continued media interest in corporate governance in large listed corporations.

[41] J Charkham and A Simpson, *Fair Shares: The Future of Shareholder Power and Responsibility* (1999) 1.

[42] This section draws on parts of S Bottomley 'From Contractualism to Constitutionalism: A Framework for Corporate Governance' (1997) 19 *Sydney Law Review* 277.

[43] For example, Toronto Stock Exchange Committee on Corporate Governance in Canada, *'Where Were the Directors?' Guidelines for Improved Corporate Governance in Canada* (1994).

[44] See, for example, OECD, *Principles of Corporate Governance* (2004) 2.

legitimacy of corporate managerial power'.[45] Viewed in this way, these debates remind us of longer-standing arguments in the political theory literature about ideas such as representation, participation, the separation of powers, majority rule, and the nature of democratic structures.

Whether because of indifference or epistemological resistance, corporate lawyers have not delved into these underlying ideas very deeply, if at all. This contrasts sharply with the investigation of the economic aspects of corporate governance. It is easy to understand that corporations are significant economic actors, and the relevance of economics to the study of corporations and the reform of corporate law has readily been accepted by politicians, regulators and academics. The Australian Government's Corporate Law Economic Reform Program, established in 1997, is a clear manifestation of the political acceptance of an economic framework (even though some economists have criticised it for relying more on economic rhetoric than economic analysis).[46] The economic analysis of corporate law issues has become the staple contribution of the academic research literature in the United States and, to a lesser degree, Australia and the United Kingdom. As Michael Whincop has claimed, '[t]he dominant view of the creation and evolution of corporate law is an economic one'.[47]

By concentrating on economic analyses and paying insufficient attention to political and constitutional theory, corporate lawyers have produced a rather one-dimensional picture of, and occasionally awkward responses to, the problems of corporate governance. Thus the overall purpose of the book is to argue for a reconceptualisation of the corporate legal structure in political terms. Forty years ago Richard Eells made a similar plea:

> [T]he directors of large corporate enterprises are in need of a more substantial doctrine than legal and economic theory has provided as a rationale for the powers they must exercise. Faced as they are with demands for reform of their so-called despotic corporate governments, managers must look to new sources of knowledge about the great collectivities over which they preside. The modern corporation, as a relatively unsurveyed field of social forces, cannot be measured by the old instruments or accounted for alone by the old theories inherited from eighteenth- and nineteenth-century legal and economic theory.[48]

Using a political perspective we can achieve a rich analytical basis for studying and responding to corporate governance issues.

This book does not, however, set out a new 'grand theory of corporate governance'. I do not aim to supply a replacement for economic theories (or any

---

45   M Stokes, 'Company Law and Legal Theory' in W Twining (ed), *Legal Theory and Common Law* (1986) 155.

46   For example M Whincop 'Token economics? One view of the CLERP fundraising reforms' (1997) *Australian Corporate Law Bulletin* 22 [348].

47   Whincop, above n 19, 12.

48   R Eells, *The Government of Corporations* (1962) 11. The economic theory of the corporation has developed considerably since Eells wrote this passage. Nevertheless, his sentiment is still relevant.

other theories) of the corporation. The corporate world is too complex and too variable for any single theory or discipline to be able to supply all of the answers to all of the problems of corporate governance. There are aspects of corporate life for which economic theories are well-suited but, equally, there are other aspects for which we need a different framework, another option on the conceptual menu. Economics can share the analytical stage with other approaches. I describe the framework that is offered in this book as 'corporate constitutionalism'.[49]

The reasons for adopting this label are set out in more detail in Chapters 2 and 3, but can be summarised briefly here. I have chosen the term 'corporate constitutionalism' because of its association with lines of inquiry that draw on political theory and because it directs our attention to questions of institutional structure and process. A corporation is a body politic; it embodies a system of governance. This is not to say that corporations can be equated with parliaments or other institutions of public government. Instead, it means that *in their own way* corporations are political entities. Similarly, constitutions are political; as Stephen Macedo observes, '[c]onstitutional issues are political in the deepest sense of that term'.[50] Amongst other things, constitutions establish structures and processes for institutions. Within corporations, questions of politics and institutional structure are important because, as I argue in Chapter 3, a significant part of corporate life involves processes of decision-making. So, the idea of 'corporate *constitutionalism*' suggests that there are values and ideas in our public political life that can provide useful insights when considering the legal regulation of corporate governance and decision-making. At the same time, the qualifier '*corporate* constitutionalism' indicates that within the corporate context these values and ideas will have different formulations, applications, and consequences than in other political contexts.

The corporate constitutionalist framework that is developed in this book relies on three principles. The first of these is the idea that *accountability* can be enhanced if the role of the board of directors is differentiated from that of the general meeting of shareholders, and also if corporate decision-making processes are characterised by a separation of decision-making powers. The second idea is that corporate decisions should be the product of processes that involve *deliberation*. Thirdly there is the idea that corporate decisions that do not track the interests of members should be readily *contestable*. Taking these three principles together, I argue that corporate constitutionalism provides a normative framework with which we can assess the legitimacy of corporate decision-making.

---

[49]   I am not the first to use this label. To my knowledge it has also been used by Eells, above n 47; M Kahan and E Rock, 'Precommitment and Managerial Incentives: Corporate Constitutionalism: Antitakeover Charter Provisions as Pre-Commitment' (2003) 152 *University of Pennsylvania Law Review* 473. See also A Fraser, *Reinventing Aristocracy: The Constitutional Reformation of Corporate Governance* (1998). Whilst the label is the same, the content of the argument in each case is different.

[50]   S Macedo, *Liberal Virtues: Citizenship, Virtue and Community in Liberal Constitutionalism* (1990) 162.

This normative framework invites us to shift the way in which we think of corporations and corporate relations. There are at least four significant conceptual shifts which become apparent from this constitutional perspective. The first is a shift from purely contractual ways of thinking. The idea of a 'constitution' is intended to supply a counterpoint to legal or economic notions of 'contract' as *the* conceptual foundation of corporate governance. Instead of a contractual separation of corporate ownership from corporate control[51] that is based upon notions of implied consent and bilateral (or even multilateral) agreement, we can think of the corporate constitution as a framework or structure within which decisions are made. Instead of the corporation being regarded as an aggregation of individual actors, the idea of a constitution suggests the possibility that a collective purpose is constituted when a corporation is formed. Contract is a useful way of thinking about interactions between individuals where the aim is maximising individual advantage; constitution is concerned more with 'coordination interactions'. [52] Corporations give rise to both of these interactions, although much more emphasis has been given to the first type, usually to the exclusion of the latter. Accordingly, this book looks at corporate relationships through a constitutional lens to highlight and bring into focus issues and ideas that may otherwise be lost in corporate law scholarship.

Secondly, and consequently, a constitutional perspective invites us to shift our perception of shareholders from their role as investors to that of members. I do not claim that this shift is possible only from a constitutional perspective, just that it is more likely to occur. How we characterise or think of shareholders has strong implications for their role in corporations and for the regulation of that role.[53] When we think of shareholders as investors we give priority to their economic role and to their status as owners of property. From the corporation's point of view the shareholder-as-investor is a supplier of capital or, in the secondary share market, a means of signalling information about the corporation's financial situation to other investors. To think, instead, of shareholders as members requires that we pay more attention to their role as participants in a collective enterprise. The concept of membership has varying connotations. In a weak sense it refers simply to any grouping that is based on some shared identifying characteristic (for example, having brown eyes).[54] In a much stronger sense, membership entails ideas of

---

[51] The separation thesis was popularised by the work of Adolf Berle and Gardiner Means, The *Modern Corporation and Private Property* (revised ed, 1968). It has since become integral to economic analyses of corporate governance, particularly in light of M Jensen and W Meckling, 'Theory of the Firm: Managerial Behaviour, Agency Costs, and Ownership Structure' (1976) 3 *Journal of Financial Economics* 305.

[52] R Hardin, 'Why a Constitution?' in B Grofman and D Wittman (eds), *The Federalist Papers and the New Institutionalism* (1989) 101.

[53] See J Hill, 'Visions and Revisions of the Shareholder' (2000) 48 *The American Journal of Comparative Law* 39.

[54] This description (and example) is taken from Patricia Smith, *Liberalism and Affirmative Obligation* (1998) 81.

participation,[55] identity and identification, responsibility and obligation. As Patricia Smith describes it, '[i]t is the idea of being part of something that is most basic to the idea of membership'.[56] Although corporate law continues to use the term 'member',[57] in practice the implications of 'membership' are frequently under-emphasised or overlooked — in effect, owning shares in a corporation is given the same significance as having brown eyes.

There is a need for balance here. For one thing, 'membership is a deceptively complicated concept'.[58] Further, it is important not to overstate the case for thinking of shareholders as members. The significance of corporate membership will vary between different corporations, but it is safe to say that being a member of a large public corporation is unlikely to have the same significance for someone as, say, being a member of a local community association. And, of course, the role of shareholders as investors *is* important. But while there are many currents that pull us towards the view that shareholders are primarily suppliers of capital (these currents include the popularisation of capital markets, the rise of institutional investors, and the proliferation of financial investment products), there are also indications that the concept of membership still has significance. Recent indications in Australia include the introduction of a statutory form of shareholder derivative action,[59] the 1999-2000 inquiry into shareholder participation in listed public corporations[60] and, more generally, the regular attention which is given by the finance and business press to reporting the proceedings at the annual general meetings of public corporations. Similarly, calls for institutional shareholders to become more active in corporate governance,[61] or for small shareholders to accept their share of responsibility for ensuring good corporate management,[62] rely on the idea that shareholders should act as members,

---

[55] Later in the book I qualify this reference to participation. I argue that corporate constitutionalism does not mean that each and every member must participate in the corporation, and nor does each participating member need to do this in the same way – see Chapter 5 n 36 to n 38 and accompanying text.

[56] Smith, above n 54, 82.

[57] For example, in Australia the *Corporations Act 2001* uses the word 'member' as a generic term to cover corporators in companies with share capital (in which membership is constituted by share ownership) and corporators in companies limited by guarantee (which do not have share capital).

[58] F Baumgartner and B Leech, *Basic Instincts: The Importance of Groups in Politics and in Political Science* (1998) 33.

[59] *Corporations Act 2001* Part 2F.1A, introduced in 1999.

[60] Companies and Securities Advisory Committee, *Shareholder Participation in the Modern Listed Public Company: Final Report* (2000); in the United Kingdom see Company Law Review Steering Group, *Modern Company Law For a Competitive Economy: Final Report* (2001) Chapters 3 and 7.

[61] See generally G Stapledon, *Institutional Shareholders and Corporate Governance* (1996).

[62] See, for example, J Hayes, 'Shootout over which sheriff rides herd on corporate cowboys' *The Weekend Australian* (Sydney) 3-4 August 2002, 35; in the United Kingdom similar calls have been made: Rt Hon Patricia Hewitt (Secretary of State for Trade and Industry), *Speech to Hermes Stewardship and Performance Seminar* (2003)

not simply as self-interested investors. Put simply, there is no necessary contradiction between the pursuit of profits and the idea of shareholders as members.

The third shift emphasised by a corporate constitutional framework is that corporations are seen to have a public dimension in addition to their role as private actors. This idea has been noted by a number of writers and is not exclusive to corporate constitutionalism.[63] The idea is developed in this book by arguing for the possibility that corporations can operate (at least some of the time) as a type of intermediary organisation, occupying a place between individual citizens and the state. In this view, corporations have a role as 'outlets'[64] for views about economic and other issues that extend beyond the self-interest of the individual corporate participants.

The fourth shift to be emphasised stems from the fact that corporations are decision-making organisations, ranging from the many informal decisions that are made on a daily basis by corporate officers and managers, to the fewer formal decisions made on an annual basis at general meetings. The corporate governance literature frequently concerns itself with the effects of corporate decisions, inquiring whether a given decision is efficient or fair. While these are important questions, the answers do not tell us all we need to know about corporate decision-making. The premise of this book is that *how* decisions are made is as important as the outcomes that they achieve. The ideas of accountability, deliberation and contestability are therefore concerned with the processes by which decisions are made. Corporate decisions can be assessed not just by the efficiency or fairness of their results, but also by assessing the quality of *all* of the formal and informal processes that are involved in reaching those decisions. Note that I have stressed 'all' of the processes; as I will argue in Chapter 4, a concern for process is not restricted to the formal counting of votes and adoption of resolutions. Corporate decision-making processes begin well before that point is reached.

Two final points of clarification are needed regarding the idea of 'corporate constitutionalism'. First, the word 'constitutionalism' is not being used in any of the formal or technical senses with which constitutional lawyers are familiar. Nor do I intend this to be a contribution to the literature on theories of constitutionalism, although — as Chapter 2 makes clear — I have mined that literature for ideas. Secondly, the idea of corporate constitutionalism is presented as an evaluative framework rather than an explanatory theory. An explanatory theory of the corporation and of corporate law and regulation would seek to explain the origins and development of the corporate form and of corporate law. It would seek to understand why corporations and corporate law are as they are. It would attempt to predict future developments (for example, that the Anglo-American corporate model will achieve global acceptance), and it might insist on

---

Department of Trade and Industry <http://www.dti.gov.uk/ministers/speeches/hewitt031103.html> at 6 May 2004.

[63] A number of examples are noted in Chapter 2 at n 91.

[64] This term is taken from C Sunstein, 'Beyond the Republican Revival' (1988) 97 *Yale Law Journal* 1539, 1573.

particular developments. This has been the task of the economic approach to corporate phenomena. In contrast, the evaluative framework proposed in this book requires that corporate structures and processes should be assessed according to whether they embody and uphold certain values and principles. This framework does not require that certain outcomes should occur, but it does provide a basis from which people inside and outside a corporation can understand and evaluate what they are doing.

What the Rest of This Book is About

Chapter 2 begins by outlining, and then providing a critique of, contractual approaches to corporate governance and corporate regulation. Contractualism underpins both legal and economic analyses, albeit in different ways. The chapter then presents an argument for adopting an approach that draws on political theory. This involves understanding corporations as 'bodies politic'. The particular species of political theory that is adopted is constitutional theory (defined in broad terms), and the Chapter concludes by outlining what a constitutional theory might tell us about corporations as bodies politic.

Chapter 3 takes up from where Chapter 2 finishes. It adapts the ideas of constitutional theory to map out a corporate constitutional framework. I argue that corporate constitutionalism has an 'external' aspect that is concerned to mediate the state regulation and the private ordering of corporate affairs. Thus, the corporate constitution is multi-faceted, and is not to be found exclusively in a contract-like document to which shareholders are assumed to consent. Corporate constitutionalism also has an 'internal' aspect that is concerned to mediate the private and personal interests of individual members with the corporate and collective interests of the members as a whole. This is where the three key principles, mentioned above, are introduced. Chapter 3 can be read as a more detailed synopsis of the arguments that are elaborated in the remainder of the book.

Taken together, the arguments in Chapters 2 and 3 have two components. First, I argue in favour of adopting an approach to the study of corporate governance that is grounded in political and constitutional thought. Then, secondly (and for the remainder of the book), I argue for a particular type of constitutional approach — one that is republican and deliberative in orientation.[65]

Chapter 4 explores the importance of accountability processes and structures within a corporation. Those processes and structures are based upon the idea of dual decision-making in which decisions made by the board of directors (and by managers who are appointed by the board) are differentiated from decisions made by the general meeting of shareholders. The Chapter then explains how a system of 'separations of powers' (the Chapter explains why this phrase is used in the plural) can be grafted onto this dual system.

---

[65]   This is not, however, an attempt to directly apply republican or deliberative theory to the corporate context. Adaptation is necessary.

In Chapter 5 I examine the idea of deliberation as a pre-requisite to formal decision-making, and how this might be applied in a corporate context. Not all shareholders will deliberate, and those that do will deliberate in different ways. The goal is to devise ways in which even minimal forms of deliberation can be channelled into the formal decision-making processes of the corporation.

Chapter 6 completes the detailed examination of the three main ideas in the book by explaining the importance of contestability in legitimate corporate decision-making. Contestability is not limited to court-based litigation, although that is clearly significant. The Chapter explains the role of contestability mechanisms that are 'internal' to the corporation, such as extraordinary (or special) general meetings.

Lastly, in Chapter 7 I come back to consider how the ideas of accountability, deliberation and contestability work together within a framework of corporate constitutionalism. I look at where this can take us in approaching questions of corporate governance, pulling together some suggestions and ideas raised throughout the book. And, acknowledging that the arguments in the book are premised on the shareholder primacy model, I offer some suggestions as to how corporate constitutionalism can allow us to move beyond the strict parameters of that model.

The Parameters of This Book

I have noted the breadth and diversity of the corporate world and I have commented on the pitfalls of attempting to devise a grand theory for all corporations in all contexts. For these reasons, and in order to keep the argument to a manageable length, there are certain parameters that must be kept in mind throughout the book.

First, the arguments refer generally to corporations that have large and dispersed shareholdings (with, perhaps, one or two major shareholders). These tend to be public corporations (that is, they have the capacity to raise finance from the public) but they can also include large proprietary (or private) corporations.[66] If they are public, they may be listed on a stock exchange, but this is not crucial to the arguments developed in this book. The book does not, however, expressly address the situation of corporations limited by guarantee, closely-held corporations, one-person or wholly-owned corporations, or small to medium sized enterprises (although they are mentioned occasionally). The ideas presented in the book may nevertheless find some resonance with these other corporate forms.

Secondly, the book concentrates on corporations that operate predominantly *within* a national setting, and does not specifically address the issues raised, and the problems posed, by transnational or multinational corporations.

---

[66] In Australia, a proprietary company can have a maximum of fifty shareholders (this limitation does not include employee-shareholders): *Corporations Act 2001* (Cth) s 113(1).

Thirdly, as is apparent already, the book uses Australian corporate law and the Australian corporate environment as its main reference point, although comparisons are made with, and examples are taken from, other jurisdictions.[67] This Australian focus does not imply that the model of corporate constitutionalism is inappropriate elsewhere. Indeed, many aspects of Australian corporate law have their equivalents in Canada, New Zealand, the United Kingdom, and (perhaps to a lesser extent) the United States.[68] However, despite the alleged international ubiquity of the corporate model that is based upon full legal personality, limited liability for shareholders, separation of corporate management from share ownership, and ready transferability of shares, the workability of the arguments made in this book must be assessed by reference to local factors. Thus, the arguments presented in this book draw on the corporate climate and the legislation with which I am most familiar.

---

[67] For this reason, throughout the book the primary reference is to the Australian legislation, the *Corporations Act 2001* (Cth).

[68] There are significant differences in US law regarding the allocation of power between shareholders and directors (eg the power of directors in US corporations to amend the corporation's by-laws: *Revised Model Business Corporations Act* §10.20 (2002). For a challenge to this situation, see L Bebchuk, 'The Case for Increasing Shareholder Power' (2005) 118 *Harvard Law Review* 833.

Chapter 2

From Contract to Constitution

Introduction

Despite the critical attention that has been given to 'corporate governance', and notwithstanding the variety of perspectives used, there is a noticeable uniformity in the underlying conceptualisation of this topic. This Chapter describes and assesses the dominant legal and economic frameworks which continue to structure the way we think about corporate law and corporate governance. It begins by examining the formal legal model that has shaped ideas about corporations and corporate regulation for over a century. This legal model uses the idea of contract to define the nature of relations inside the corporation. The legal-contractual model is then compared with economic models that have exerted considerable influence over the corporate law reform agenda in recent years.

The legal and economic frameworks both rely on a contractual paradigm, and so they have some common points of reference. Importantly, though, there are also significant differences between these two frameworks. As will be discussed, some of these differences involve technical distinctions — for example, lawyers refer to 'the corporation' or 'the company' while economists talk about 'the firm'. These technical distinctions indicate underlying conceptual differences. Legal analysis posits the existence of the corporation as a separate legal entity; economists, on the other hand, generally ignore or downplay the idea of separate legal status. Furthermore, whilst economists and lawyers rely on contract to emphasise the voluntary, consensual, and private nature of corporate relationships, each discipline has its own reasons for doing so. When a lawyer says that the relation between parties in a corporation has effect as a contract, the focus is on the nature of the legal obligations thereby created and, more particularly, on the legal enforceability of those obligations.[1] The lawyer intends to tap into established principles and understandings of contract law (allowing for the peculiarities of this corporate contract, noted later in this Chapter). In contrast, the economist tends to use contract as an analytical method or even as a metaphorical device to describe corporate relations. The economist is not concerned so much with the enforceability of the contract as with emphasising the reciprocal nature of the

---

[1]   See M Eisenberg, 'The Conception that the Corporation is a Nexus of Contracts, and the Dual Nature of the Firm' (1999) 24 *Iowa Journal of Corporate Law* 819, 822.

arrangements that are embodied in the contract.[2] So, despite some similarities in rhetoric, the legal and economic contractual frameworks say different things about corporations and corporate law.

Because of these differences, difficulties can arise when legal and economic analyses intersect, as they do in 'law and economics' scholarship.[3] The difficulty with much law and economics scholarship is that these different uses of the term 'contract' are not always acknowledged; indeed, law and economics writers frequently 'slip back and forth between the two meanings of "contract", exploiting the ambiguity of the term'.[4]

After assessing these two contract-based approaches, the Chapter then considers how a constitutional approach, drawing on political theory, provides a rich conceptual alternative. This requires us, first, to understand the relevance of political theory to the study of corporate governance, and then to consider the relative advantages of constitutional theory over other types of political theory.

Contractualism

The Legal Model of the Corporation

According to corporate law doctrine in jurisdictions such as Australia, a corporation is populated by two groups of people — its directors and officers, and its members or shareholders. Everyone else who is associated with a corporation — its creditors (whether secured or unsecured), its non-managerial employees, its customers and other 'stakeholders' — is regarded as a corporate outsider. In strict terms, therefore, the formal legal model of the corporation is concerned with the exercise of power by, and the relative rights and obligations of, directors/officers and shareholders.

In this model, the only two decision-making components of a corporation are meetings of directors and meetings of members. As a general rule[5] the board of directors is granted the power to manage, or supervise the management of, the corporation. This grant of general managerial power may then be supplemented by more specific grants of power, for example the power to execute negotiable instruments, declare dividends, or call a meeting of the corporation's members.[6]

---

[2]　Ibid.

[3]　As I explain below, there is some diversity in this literature, so it is probably more accurate to talk of 'schools' of law and economics.

[4]　T Joo, 'Contract, Property and the Role of Metaphor in Corporations Law' (2002) 35 *University of California Davis Law Review* 779, 795.

[5]　I say 'as a general rule', because while in some jurisdictions (eg *Canada Business Corporations Act*, RSC 1985, s 102) this division of power is prescribed by statute, in others it is the default position that may be varied by a corporation (eg in Australia the 'replaceable rule' in s 198A *Corporations Act*) although it is rare to find departures from this default position.

[6]　In Australia, see *Corporations Act 2001 ss* 198B, 254U, and 249C respectively.

Notwithstanding this grant of power to the directors, corporations legislation reserves decisions on certain matters exclusively for the members in general meeting. In Australia this includes the adoption, modification or repeal of a corporate constitution, the decision to convert from one type of corporation to another (for example, from public to proprietary), reductions of share capital, and, in the case of a public corporation, the removal of directors.[7] In addition, a corporation may specify in its constitution other matters that are to be decided by the general meeting. This usually includes the appointment of directors, the variation of rights attached to a class of shares, and the removal of directors (in the case of a proprietary company).[8] If a corporation is listed on the Australian Stock Exchange, the Listing Rules of the Exchange also require that certain matters must be approved by the shareholders in general meeting, including any significant change to the corporation's activities, the sale of the corporation's main undertaking, or (in certain instances) a new issue of shares.[9] Finally, there are powers given to the members by principles of fiduciary law, including the power to ratify a breach of duty by the directors.[10]

Corporate law restricts the capacity of members to intervene in the directors' exercise of managerial powers. When a corporation confers general powers of management exclusively on its directors then the members have no power to intervene in the day-to-day exercise of that power or to dictate the manner of its exercise.[11] In the High Court of Australia, Barwick CJ described the legal position this way:

> Directors who are minded to do something which in their honest view is for the benefit of the company are not to be restrained because a majority shareholder or shareholders holding a majority of shares in the company do not want the directors so to act.[12]

In other words, according to the legal model the board of directors is a decision-making organ that has relative autonomy from the general meeting of members.

---

[7] In Australia, see *Corporations Act 2001* ss 136, 162, 256C, 203D, respectively.

[8] In Australia, see the replaceable rules in *Corporations Act 2001* ss 201G, 246B, and 203C.

[9] In Australia, see the Australian Stock Exchange Listing Rules 11.1, 11.2, and 7.1.

[10] *Regal (Hastings) Ltd v Gulliver* [1967] 2 AC 134; *Furs Ltd v Tomkies* (1936) 54 CLR 583.

[11] *Automatic Self-Cleansing Filter Syndicate Co Ltd v Cunninghame* [1906] 2 Ch 34, 44; *John Shaw & Sons (Salford) Ltd v Shaw* [1935] 2 KB 113, 134; *NRMA v Parker* (1986) 4 ACLC 609, 613-614.

[12] *Ashburton Oil NL v Alpha Minerals NL* (1971) 123 CLR 614, 620.

The Contractual Foundation of The Legal Model

A key component of this legal model is that each corporation is regarded as a legal entity, distinct from its members and directors.[13] The legal model posits a set of legal relationships between this corporate legal entity, its directors, and its members. These three sets of legal actors are said to be bound together by a contract that is embodied in the corporation's constitution. This is one of the foundational concepts of Anglo-Australian corporate law. In Australia it is enshrined in s 140(1) of the *Corporations Act 2001* which declares that the provisions in a corporate constitution 'have effect as a contract' between the company and each member, between the company and each director and company secretary, and between a member and each other member.[14] The burden of this contract is that each party agrees to observe and perform the rules in the constitution so far as is applicable to them.

For directors the terms of this contract are supplemented by important fiduciary duties, and each director is required to act in the best interests of 'the company' or (in other formulations) 'the shareholders as a whole'. These duties are not imposed by the corporate contract; instead their basis lies in equitable principles. However, while the statutory corporate contract does not create a director's fiduciary duties, they are exercised within the context of that contract and the relationships it encompasses. According to Bryson J (in the NSW Supreme Court):

> [C]ourts have accepted for the purposes of equitable obligations as for legal obligations the reality of the legal personality of the company and of the structure of rights among shareholders, company and directors created by the legislation and articles of association [now the replaceable rules and corporate constitution] under which they have chosen to conduct their affairs.[15]

The peculiarities of this corporate contract, when compared with general principles of ordinary contract law, have long been noted — but tolerated — by lawyers. In 1924, for example, in the New Zealand Court of Appeal Salmond J (referring to 'the regulations of the company') observed that:

> In the first place, a contract cannot be altered except by the mutual consent of the parties, whereas a regulation can be altered by the legislative authority of the company even as against dissenters. In the second place, a contract is personal and binds only the party who made it and his executors and administrators; whereas a

---

[13]   The authority usually cited for this is the House of Lords decision in *Salomon v Salomon & Co Ltd* [1897] AC 22, although the separate legal status of the company had been recognised prior to this.

[14]   In the United Kingdom see s 14(1) *Companies Act 1985*. No such section exists in the *Canada Business Corporations Act*, RSC 1985.

[15]   *Glavanics v Brunninghausen* (1996) 14 ACLC 345, 355.

regulation binds the owners of the shares for the time being, and the obligation imposed thereby is appurtenant to the shares and passes with them to every person who for the time being is the owner of them.[16]

More recently McHugh and Gummow JJ in the High Court of Australia noted five features of this 'unusual type' of contract.[17] First, the terms of the contract can be altered without the agreement of all of the parties to a contract, since a special resolution requires only a three quarters majority of votes by those members who actually choose to exercise their voting rights.[18] Secondly, 'there is no jurisdiction in a court of Equity to rectify [the terms of the constitution] even if they do not accord with the concurrent intention of all the signatories thereof at the moment of signature'. Thirdly, individual members face considerable obstacles to enforcing the contract against the corporation.[19] Fourthly, their Honours referred to Salmond J's observation (quoted above) that in a corporation with share capital the contract attaches to the shares rather than to the shareholder. Finally, they noted that under present authority a shareholder is precluded 'from suing the company for damages for breach of contract whilst still a member and without seeking recision of the contract whereby the shares were obtained'.[20]

Given that ordinary legal notions of contract are so strained when they are applied in the corporate context we must wonder about the rationale for applying this contractual framework in first place. The historical explanation traces the evolution of modern corporations back to the English unincorporated joint stock companies based on a deed of settlement which were prominent in the eighteenth and early nineteenth centuries. These companies were an amalgamation of partnership and trust concepts, the idea being to escape the restrictions of the *Bubble Act* of 1720.[21] They consisted of large numbers of investors pooling their finances on a joint stock basis. The joint stock was vested in trustees to be managed according to the terms of a deed of settlement which was executed by each member of the company.[22] These deeds of settlement were the forerunners of the later articles of association, and now the corporate constitution. A useful summary of their operation can be found in the judgement of Jordan CJ in *Australian Coal & Shale Employees' Federation v Smith*:

16 *Shalfoon v Cheddar Valley Co-operative Dairy Co Ltd* [1924] NZLR 561, 580.
17 *Bailey v NSW Medical Defence Union Ltd* (1995) 13 ACLC 1698, 1717.
18 *Corporations Act* s 136(2) permits alteration of the constitution by special resolution; s 9 defines 'special resolution'.
19 This observation was made prior to the introduction of the statutory derivative action into the *Corporations Act* (Pt 2F.1A), which is discussed later in this book.
20 Their Honours refer to *Houldsworth v City of Glascow Bank* (1880) 5 App Cas 317 as authority for this point.
21 The *Bubble Act* of 1720 (6 Geo 1, c 18) was an attempt by the English Parliament to regulate the rapid growth in share speculation. The Act prohibited the formation of joint stock companies unless by an Act of Parliament or Royal Charter.
22 For more detail on the history of the modern corporate form, see R Tomasic, S Bottomley and R McQueen, *Corporations Law in Australia* (2nd ed, 2002) Chapter 1.

[T]he Memorandum and Articles comprise what was formerly contained in the deed of settlement of the old unincorporated joint stock companies. Such a deed was executed by all the members of the company, and contained a covenant by the members with a trustee for the company to observe its provisions. This practice was recognised by the English *Companies Act* of 1844 (7 and 8 Vic c 110) which provided by s 7 that no joint stock company should be entitled to receive a certificate of complete registration under that Act unless its deed of settlement contained a covenant on the part of every shareholder to pay up the amount of the instalments on the shares taken by such shareholder and to perform the several engagements in the deed contained on the part of the shareholders.[23]

The 1844 Act that is referred to in this passage was the first English companies statute to introduce incorporation by registration. Indeed, the Act represented the beginning of the modern system of corporate regulation. However the Act still clung to earlier ideas of a joint stock form of association based upon ideas of partnership. Thus, as a prerequisite to registration, the deed of settlement had to be executed by all members.[24] Nevertheless, the advent of incorporation by registration, followed eleven years later by limited liability on incorporation,[25] meant that the number of large joint stock company registrations began to grow. The requirement that each member must execute the deed of settlement became an inconvenience, and thus in 1856 the *Joint Stock Companies Act* introduced a provision that deemed execution to have occurred.[26] This is explained in Jordan CJ's judgement:

> The provision now contained in s 22 of the NSW *Companies Act*, 1936 [a forerunner of *Corporations Act* s 140], that the Memorandum and Articles shall when registered bind the company and the members thereof to the same extent as if they respectively had been signed and sealed by each member and contained covenants on the part of each member to observe all the provisions of the Memorandum and Articles, which has the effect of obviating the necessity for the execution of a deed by the members of the company, first made its appearance in the English *Joint Stock Companies Act* of 1856, ss 9 and 10.[27]

In other words, for most of its history the statutory provision that is now found in s 140 of the *Corporations Act* was not primarily concerned with declaring the contractual status of the corporate constitution. Instead, the earlier provisions were concerned with resolving what was essentially a practical procedural problem: obtaining the execution of the corporation's governing rules by each person in a diverse group of members. Despite this, the focus of subsequent versions of these legislative provisions shifted to declaring the contractual status of intra-company

---

[23]   *Australian Coal & Shale Employees Federation v Smith* (1937) 38 SR (NSW) 48, 54.
[24]   *Companies Act* 1844 ss 7 and 26.
[25]   18 & 19 Vic c 133.
[26]   See W E Patterson and H H Ednie, *Australian Company Law* (2nd ed, 1971) 1444. See also R Gregory, 'The Section 20 Contract' (1981) 44 *Modern Law Review* 526, 528.
[27]   (1937) 38 SR (NSW) 48, 54.

relations, stating that the corporate constitution 'has the effect of a contract under seal' or 'has effect as a contract'.[28] As McHugh and Gummow JJ have noted in the High Court of Australia, the continued inclusion of such sections in corporations statutes has 'evinced the intention, as a matter of form, to preserve the link with the old deed of settlement by carrying over contractual notions to support what, in any event, would later come to be seen as incidents of modern corporate law'.[29]

Modern corporate law thus uses the idea of a contract to define the boundaries of the corporation, to define which legal actors fall within the parameters of the corporation, and who falls outside. Contract is also used to define what types of claims and interests will count for the purposes of intra-corporate governance. For example, in *Andy Kala Pty Ltd v EJ Doherty (Northcote) Pty Ltd*[30] the court had to decide whether a clause in a corporation's articles of association which stipulated a particular method for resolving disputes between members of the corporation thereby created a contractual obligation on a member to accept a determination made under that process. The court held that such a provision was not enforceable as a term of the statutory contract. This conclusion was justified on the grounds that:

> [n]ot every dispute which arises between members of a company, even if it may touch upon their respective obligations as members, is encompassed by [s 140]. ... The "statutory contract" contemplated by such sections as [s 140] arises from and is limited to the nature of the relationships which exist between an entity and its members, or between members, with respect to the entity itself.[31]

Similarly, in *Bailey v New South Wales Medical Defence Union Ltd*, where the plaintiff sought to enforce an indemnity agreement between a member and the corporation, the High Court drew a distinction between rights arising from the statutory contract formed by what is now s 140, and the indemnity agreement which was found in a 'special' contract formed outside the statutory contract.[32]

The use of contract law principles in the corporate context thus does two things: it excludes the interests of those who are deemed to be non-contracting parties,[33] and it excludes what are deemed to be the non-corporate interests of the contracting parties.[34] So, for shareholders, 'the purpose of the [corporate constitution] is to define the position of the shareholder as shareholder, not to bind

---

[28] This 'has effect' formulation was introduced in 1985 (amending what was then s 78 of the *Companies Code 1981*).

[29] *Bailey v NSW Medical Defence Union Ltd* (1995) 13 ACLC 1698, 1717.

[30] (1995) 13 ACLC 1630.

[31] Ibid 1635.

[32] (1995) 13 ACLC 1698.

[33] See, for example, *Forbes v NSW Trotting Club Ltd* [1977] 2 NSWLR 515 (holding that a professional punter who was excluded from admission to race tracks controlled by the company could not enforce provisions in the company's articles of association).

[34] See, for example, the often cited case of *Eley v Positive Government Security Life Assurance Co* (1875) 1 Ex D 20 (holding that a member could not use the articles of association to enforce his rights as the company's solicitor).

him in his capacity as an individual'.[35] By using the device of contract, the corporation is reduced to a limited set of strictly defined relationships.

Economic Models of The Corporation

As I noted in the introduction to this Chapter, economists also rely on contract-based arguments when they study corporations. Economic analysis has had a noticeable (if uneven) influence on corporate law scholarship, policy, and to a lesser extent legislation in Australia since the 1990s.[36] Sometimes this has involved little more than the casual invocation of economic concepts such as efficiency or cost-benefit analyses.[37] On other occasions economics has been used in a much deeper and more thorough analysis of corporate law issues.[38] Most of the time, however, what has been referred to is a 'middle of the road' type of theory that draws upon various strands of contract-based theory developed by 'neo-classical' law and economics scholars in the United States.

Two strands of law and economics scholarship have been prominent in the scholarly analysis of corporations and corporate law.[39] One is agency theory, which is concerned to address the problems that arise when shareholders are not able to perfectly monitor the actions of their 'agents' — the directors and corporate managers who are appointed to exercise power in the shareholders' interests.[40] The other strand is transaction cost economics, which examines why it is that different forms of economic organisation (for example, firms rather than markets) are used to organise productive relations in different settings.[41] Although they have differences in emphasis, these two approaches are complementary.[42] According to

---

[35]   *Bisgood v Henderson's Transvaal Estates Ltd* [1908] 1 Ch 743, 759 per Buckley LJ.

[36]   See the list of indicative Australian work set out in M Whincop, 'Of Fault and Default: Contractarianism as a Theory of Anglo-Australian Law' (1997) 21 *Melbourne University Law Review* 187, 189. The influence in the United States has been much more remarkable, as is evident from even a cursory review of the American corporate law literature.

[37]   The Australian Government's Corporate Law Economic Reform Program, initiated in 1997, is a clear indication of the rhetorical appeal of economics to corporate law reformers. The program has been criticised for its poor use of economics: M Whincop, 'The Political Economy of Corporate Law Reform in Australia' (1999) 27 *Federal Law Review* 77. For an example of a simple use of cost-benefit analysis, see *Registrar-General v Northside Developments Pty Ltd* (1989) 7 ACLC 52, 59 per Kirby P.

[38]   For example M Whincop, *An Economic and Jurisprudential Genealogy of Corporate Law* (2001).

[39]   For a review of these and other economic theories, see O Hart, 'An Economist's Perspective on the Theory of the Firm' (1989) 89 *Columbia Law Review* 1757.

[40]   Agency theory is associated principally with the work of M Jensen and W Meckling, in particular their paper 'Theory of the Firm: Managerial Behaviour, Agency Costs and Ownership Structure' (1976) 3 *Journal of Financial Economics* 305.

[41]   Transaction cost economics is associated principally with the work of Oliver Williamson — see especially *The Mechanics of Governance* (1996) — building on the seminal article by R Coase, 'The Nature of the Firm' (1937) 4 *Economica* 386.

[42]   Williamson, above n 41, 171.

Oliver Williamson, 'both work out of a managerial-discretion setup. They also adopt an efficient-contracting orientation to economic organisation. And both argue that the board of directors in the corporation arises endogenously'.[43] Relying on these commonalities, the following synopsis draws on both of these strands, although I acknowledge along the way that there are some differences in analytical approach.[44]

In the economic world the corporation is analysed as a type of firm. The economic concept of 'the firm' is not synonymous with the legal concept of 'the corporation' or 'the company', despite a tendency in law and economics scholarship to conflate the two. Corporate status is not an essential feature of the firm, which can take the form of an unincorporated association, such as a partnership. According to one definition, 'the firm is simply a set of feasible production plans which buys inputs and sells outputs in well-developed spot markets'.[45] Put another way, a firm is simply a method of organising production, consisting of a series of transactions, or contracts, between investors, managers, employees, creditors and customers. It is also important to bear in mind here that the use of the term 'contract' does not necessarily correspond to the legal idea of contract. Rather, it is intended to draw attention to the adaptive and voluntary nature of the arrangements which are made between the participants.

Agency theory sums up this arrangement in the well-known description of the firm as 'a nexus of contracts', a description that implies that there is no difference between a firm and ordinary market exchanges; a firm, just like a market 'represents a mere series of contracts joining inputs to produce output'.[46] Transaction cost theory does draw a distinction between the market and the firm — one of its key inquiries is why it is that some production processes take place via market exchanges but others adopt a hierarchical firm structure to achieve their output. Thus, transaction cost theory regards the firm as a hierarchical governance structure, rather than a nexus of contracts.[47] Despite this difference, both theories regard the firm as 'a construct of contract', and both 'explain its structural features as cost saving devices of transacting parties'.[48]

The economic framework assumes that, given their wide grant of managerial discretion, there is a real risk that a firm's managers[49] will seek to maximise their own gains in ways that will not necessarily coincide with maximising the firm's profits. Investors in a firm will therefore be concerned to

---

43   Ibid 173.
44   For a discussion of the commonalities and differences see ibid 171-179.
45   R McEwin, 'Public versus Shareholder Control of Directors' (1992) 10 *Companies & Securities Law Journal* 182, 185.
46   W Bratton, 'The "Nexus of Contracts" Corporation: A Critical Appraisal' (1989) 74 *Cornell Law Review* 407, 420.
47   Williamson, above n 41, 173.
48   Bratton, above n 46, 422.
49   This is another difference between legal and economic analysis: the economist's 'manager' is not necessarily restricted to the legal category 'director'.

ensure that the managers — their 'agents'[50] — will run the firm in a way that maximises profits rather than managerial self-interest. The problem for investors then lies in monitoring managers' behaviour effectively. Monitoring requires time, knowledge, money and coordination between the investors. For their part, the managers will be concerned to retain their positions, and therefore they will seek to assure investors that their interests are not at risk from managerial misconduct. Therefore, contracts between managers and investors will try, amongst other things, to minimise these 'agency costs'[51] (or, in the language of transaction-cost economics, they will try to reduce managerial opportunism).

The process of negotiating these contracts is imperfect. Investors will be limited in the amount of time and knowledge they can devote to negotiations (in transaction-cost terms, investors have 'bounded rationality').[52] Moreover, in firms with widespread ownership the opportunities for collective or coordinated negotiation amongst investors will be very small. In summary, the prospects of effective monitoring are low, and the transaction costs of negotiating contracts to deal with the problem are high.

In the case of corporations, economic analysis argues that there are two mechanisms that can reduce these transaction costs and act as an efficient substitute for investor monitoring of management behaviour. The first mechanism is the free operation of efficient, competitive market forces. The three markets that are most commonly referred to are: the market for corporate securities (whereby information about a corporation, including the terms which bind the managers, is said to be built into the price of the corporation's securities); the market for corporate control (whereby under-performing and inefficient corporations will be taken over by those who place a higher value on the corporation's assets); and the market for corporate managers (which controls the risk of negligence or the abuse of managerial power). The operation of these competitive markets supplies information about corporations to investors, and constrains the misuse of private economic power.[53]

The second mechanism is provided by a system of corporate law. According to Easterbrook and Fischel:

> [C]orporate law is a set of terms available off-the-rack so that participants in corporate ventures can save the costs of contracting. ... Corporate codes and existing judicial decisions supply these terms 'for free' to every corporation,

---

50   Yet another difference between corporate lawyers and economists is that in the context of intra-corporate relations, the law does not classify directors strictly as agents of shareholders. The fiduciary position of directors is sui generis: 'In some respects they resemble agents, in others they do not' *Regal (Hastings) Ltd v Gulliver* [1942] 1 All ER 378, 387.

51   Jensen and Meckling, above n 40.

52   O Williamson, 'Transaction Cost Economics', reprinted in R Romano (ed), *Foundations of Corporate Law* (1993) 13.

53   See M Stokes, 'Company Law and Legal Theory' in W Twining (ed), *Legal Theory and Common Law* (1986) 157.

enabling the venturers to concentrate on matters that are specific to their undertaking. ... Corporate law - and in particular the fiduciary principle enforced by the courts - fills in the blanks and oversights with the terms that people would have bargained for had they anticipated the problems and been able to contract costlessly in advance. On this view corporate law supplements but never displaces actual bargains...[54]

This passage emphasises the private and voluntary nature of corporate relationships within the economic model. Corporations are not regarded as though they are 'creatures of the state in any important or fundamental sense'.[55] A consequence of this private, consensual view is that corporate law rules ought to be regarded only as default options, allowing tailor-made contracts to be adopted within individual corporations.[56] Corporate actors should have the freedom to opt out of statutory or judicially created rules and to construct their own contractual arrangements. Some law and economics writers take a less dogmatic view, allowing that corporate law should prescribe some mandatory rules and impose some duties and responsibilities in order to correct potential problems that arise from the principal-agent relationship.[57]

A Critique of Contractualism

The legal and economic models just described offer the promise of 'illuminating the internal operation of the firm',[58] but they fail to deliver completely on that promise. The shortcomings in each approach can be traced, in different ways, to their contractual origins. Below, I list four limitations or problems for corporate law and corporate theory that result from this preoccupation with the contractual paradigm. I emphasise the word 'limitations'; I am not arguing that we should abandon contractual approaches. When we look at corporations and corporate law through a contractual lens we are able to see some things quite clearly (for example, the different roles played by various participants in the corporate enterprise, and

---

[54] F Easterbrook and D Fischel, *The Economic Structure of Corporate Law* (1991) 34. For an argument that fiduciary obligations should not be regarded as hypothetical contract terms see D DeMott, 'Beyond Metaphor: An Analysis of Fiduciary Obligation' [1988] *Duke Law Journal* 879.

[55] R Clark, 'Contracts, Elites, and Traditions in the Making of Corporate Law' (1989) 89 *Columbia Law Review* 1703, 1706.

[56] There are different versions of this argument. Coffee, for example, argues that default terms can be excluded but only after careful judicial scrutiny of the new replacement terms: J Coffee, 'The Mandatory/Enabling Balance in Corporate Law: An Essay on the Judicial Role' (1989) 89 *Columbia Law Review* 1618.

[57] For example, C Riley, 'Contracting Out of Company Law: Section 459 of the Companies Act 1985 and the Role of the Courts' (1992) *Modern Law Review* 782.

[58] V Brudney 'Corporate Governance, Agency Costs, and the Rhetoric of Contract' (1985) 85 *Columbia Law Review* 1403.

the need to assess the variable impact of market forces and legal rules on them).[59] Through the same lens, however, some issues become distorted (for example, the argument that market forces are a presumptively preferable form of regulation to mandatory rules),[60] and we risk losing sight completely of other concerns (for example, the identification of a corporate or collective interest, or the possibility of other-regarding behaviour by shareholders).

The first limitation is that the contract paradigm has a tendency to reduce complex relationships between many people to agreements between pairs of individual legal or economic actors. The resulting image of the corporation is that of an arena in which members and managers meet each other one to one as private and individual actors in the pursuit of private and individual goals. This is quite obvious with the economic contractual models, which rely on the philosophy of methodological individualism, emphasising that only the actions of individuals are relevant in explaining social and economic phenomena: '[m]ethodological individualism holds that only individuals are responsible, and that corporate action or corporate responsibility is no more than the sum of its individual parts'.[61] Indeed, the very idea of the corporation is dismissed as an abstraction or, at best, treated as 'a matter of convenience rather than reality'.[62] In this view, corporations only involve the actions of individual actors and the only relevant function of that activity is to maximise the returns to individual investors. The corporation is reduced to a multiplicity of dyadic agreements; it is a 'nexus of contracts'.[63] Corporations are thus analysed on the same dimension as sole traders; they are regarded simply as different ways of organising production.

The legal model promises some relief from this one-dimensional image by bringing the corporation into the picture as a separate contracting party. Nevertheless, the result is a set of individualised contracts, summarised in s 140 of the *Corporations Act*, between the corporation as an entity and 'each' director and 'each' member. Brennan and Buchanan's reminder that '2 remains the magic number for the economic analyst' also holds for the legal framework.[64] Furthermore, the role and nature of the corporation as one of these contracting parties remains unclear. We are presented with a disjointed collection of rules in which the concept of the corporation is sometimes reduced to a mere legal device (the corporation categorised as a legal person for liability purposes), but at other times is described by reference to the decisions of majority voters at a general

---

[59] Brudney concedes this: ibid 1404.

[60] M Eisenberg, 'Bad Arguments in Corporate Law' (1990) *Georgetown Law Journal* 1551.

[61] B Fisse and J Braithwaite, *Corporations, Crime and Accountability* (1993) 18. See also S Lukes, *Essays in Social Theory* (1977) chapter 9.

[62] Easterbrook and Fischel, above n 54, 12. Whincop described the idea as 'a pragmatic compromise': above n 37, 45-47.

[63] Later in this Chapter I discuss another strand of contract theory that seeks to escape this limitation by referring to 'relational contracts'. See below n 74 and accompanying text.

[64] G Brennan and J Buchanan, *The Reason of Rules: Constitutional Political Economy* (1985) 28.

meeting, or 'the interests of the members as a whole', or as an entity with interests that transcend the immediate concerns of its present members and directors.

It is, of course, true that the majority of corporations are designed to further private rights and interests,[65] but these need not be considered solely in individualistic terms. None of these models provides an image of the corporation as an organisation. Yet, as William Bratton has reminded us, 'the "organisation" remains central to our experience of corporation'.[66] The organisational life of a corporation is not just the sum of the actions of individual corporate insiders.[67] What individuals do as members or directors of a corporation involves a complex interplay of power relations, hierarchies, loyalties, and systems of control which may vary over time and from one decision-making context to another. As Ewick emphasises:

> Although organisations are not synonymous with individuals (or their interests and goals), neither are they entirely distinct from the individuals who comprise them. .... The relationship is dialectic. Individuals can no more be separated or detached from their organisational affiliations than the organisation can be abstracted from its membership.[68]

Some may object that the idea of 'organisational affiliations' is hardly an apt description of the relationship between the typical investor and the modern public corporation. Surely, it will be said, shareholders are more concerned with market price than corporate identity. In other words, if shareholders choose to behave like short-term maximisers of personal wealth, isn't it appropriate to analyse them in contractual terms? The answer that is developed throughout this book is that while this is certainly true of some shareholders it is not true of all, and it should not be accepted as the basis of an all-encompassing model for corporate governance. Contract-based frameworks on their own cannot cope adequately with the complexity, variety and shifting nature of relations between individuals and corporate organisation, nor with the great variety of organisational structures that are produced as a result.

The second limitation of contract-based models is that they display a general orientation towards economic analyses of corporate governance issues to the exclusion of other perspectives. This is not surprising: contracts are concerned chiefly with bringing about an effective exchange between parties. They are the

---

[65] There is an argument that this is not the sole legitimate purpose of corporations, and that they should also have regard to public or social interests. For an elaboration, see J Parkinson, *Corporate Power and Responsibility* (1993).

[66] W Bratton, 'The Economic Structure of the Post-Contractual Corporation' (1992) 87 *Northwestern University Law Review* 180, 209.

[67] P Selznick, *The Moral Commonwealth: Social Theory and the Promise of Community* (1992) 242. For a revealing sociological study that makes this point, see R Jackall, *Moral Mazes: The World of Corporate Managers* (1988).

[68] P Ewick, '"In the Belly of the Beast": Rethinking Rights, Persons and Organisations' (1988) 13 *Law and Social Inquiry* 175, 179 and 181.

paradigmatic arrangement for economic analysis. Viewed from this perspective, the corporation is assessed simply on economic means to achieve economic ends. As I indicated in Chapter 1, one important perspective that is ignored by this preoccupation with economic analysis is political theory.

The label 'political theory' is used here in its broadest sense. The difference between 'economic' and 'political' perspectives is explained succinctly by Kukathas and Pettit:

> When two or more people seek to make an agreement which affects their interests differently, so that each would most prefer a different arrangement from the other, the agreement may be pursued in either of two ways: one we describe as economic, the other as political. The economic way is for each to calculate what best suits his own interests and then to try to get this: say, to bargain with the other or others, seeking to win the largest benefit possible at the least concession from themselves. The political way is for the parties to put aside their own particular interests and to debate about the arrangement that best answers to such considerations – usually considerations in some sense to do with the common good – as all can equally countenance as relevant. The economic approach is institutionalized in the process of market negotiation, the political – at least ideally – in the forum of discussion where the parties are blocked, if only by the sanction of social disapproval, from arguing by reference to special as distinct from common concerns.[69]

One consequence of focusing on the economic instead of the political is that shareholders are regarded (and come to see themselves) as investors rather than as members. That is (and despite the persistence of the term 'member' in the *Corporations Act*) we look more to the role of shareholders in supplying capital than to their role as rights-bearing and duty-owing participants in an enterprise.

The third limitation follows on from this. The contractual frameworks are oriented towards end results. In philosophical terms, they tend to be teleological rather than deontological. This orientation is permitted by liberal attitudes about consent and voluntariness that are embodied in the standard contractual paradigm. Classical liberal theory argues that, as far as possible, individuals should be free from interference and constraint imposed by others. Interference with that freedom can be justified, however, if the individual gives their consent. In the corporate context, potentially freedom-interfering actions, such as the exercise of power by directors (or by a majority block of shareholders) or the allocation and removal of corporate rights and benefits, are legitimated by the voluntary and informed consent of each shareholder which is presumed to be embodied in the corporate contract. It is this 'primal act of consent that legitimate[s] the subsequent exercise of authority by the office holders'.[70] The result is that provided corporate actions and decisions comply with the terms of the contract, they can be judged primarily in terms of whether they achieve some desired goal rather than by reference to their impact on the rights or interests of the persons involved.

---

[69] C Kukathas and P Pettit, *Rawls — A Theory of Justice and Its Critics* (1990) 32-33.

[70] S Wolin, 'Collective Identity and Constitutional Power' in G Bryner and D Thompson (eds), *The Constitution and the Regulation of Society* (1988) 97.

The fourth and final limitation is that under a contractual paradigm we tend to treat corporations and the things they do as essentially private phenomena. The origins of contract law lie in facilitation of private economic exchanges, and even though contract analysis has been applied to the exercise of public power, contract-based analyses of corporations and corporate law have an overwhelmingly private orientation. Corporate law is generally regarded as a body of rules that facilitates private, voluntary, individual agreements. Consequently, legislators, judges and corporate regulators bear the burden of justifying why there should be any external regulation of corporate activity, and why market forces should not be given free reign. In the same vein, any apparent intrusion of public law-like concepts into the world of corporate law, such as natural justice, procedural fairness, or equality of opportunity, is also judged with suspicion.[71] Of course to say that corporate law is completely private is an overstatement. Despite the claims of some economists, the market has not been entirely successful in controlling the conduct of corporate managers.[72] For all of its alleged (and sometimes demonstrable) deficiencies, the state's involvement in corporate life has not withered away, and it cannot be dismissed simply as an historical anachronism.[73]

To sum up: the application of contract-based approaches to the study of corporate governance is limited because their approach is essentially individualistic, economic, teleological, and private. Again, in listing these limitations, I am not suggesting that contract has no role in analysing corporate governance and corporate regulation. My criticism is directed at the tendency for these ideas to be used to the exclusion of other approaches, or to be regarded as the 'default setting' for corporate law analysis. Furthermore, I suggest that the contractual paradigm offers little scope for moving beyond these limitations. What is needed is a complementary framework that draws upon a different paradigm. Before moving to explore the detail of that paradigm, it is worthwhile considering one attempt by contract scholars to broaden their analysis.

A Response: Corporations as Relational Contracts?

There is another strand of contractual theory that has developed in response to some of the limitations of the classical legal and economic contract models. Unlike classical contract theory, relational contract theory recognises that many contracts involve complex and often long-term relations between parties, rather than discrete transactions.[74]

---

71   See L Griggs and R Snell, 'Natural Justice - An Alternative Ground for Intervention in Corporate Decision-making?' (1994) 10 *Queensland University of Technology Law Journal* 22.

72   W Bratton, 'Public Values and Corporate Fiduciary Law' (1992) 44 *Rutgers Law Review* 675, 682.

73   A similar point is made in K Greenfield, 'From Rights to Regulation in Corporate Law' in F Macmillan Patfield (ed), *Perspectives on Company Law: 2* (1997) 1, 21.

74   Relational contract theory is most commonly associated with the work of Ian Macneil. For example, 'Contracts: Adjustment of Long-Term Economic Relations Under

Although discrete transactions (such as a simple sale/purchase contract) and relational contracts all involve economic exchanges, relational contracts are also said to involve 'significant elements of non-economic personal satisfaction'.[75] The complexity and the relational nature of these exchanges makes it difficult for the parties to specify all the terms of their agreement in advance. In addition, these relationships are characterised by uncertainty about the future conditions under which the agreement will be performed, coupled with the difficulty of defining in advance the sorts of adjustments that the parties should make to meet those future contingencies.[76] Relational contract theory thus recognises the importance of flexible and generalised obligations in contracts, such as the requirement that one party must use their 'best endeavours' to meet the expectations of the other party. Similarly, the parties might agree to certain processes and structures that will allow for future adjustments and negotiations between the parties. Relational theory acknowledges that obligations, like the relationship itself, can evolve. Relational theory also recognises the existence of multiparty contracts which can create a collective identity amongst the participants, moving away from the two-party model favoured by classical contract theory.[77]

Relational contract theory has been suggested as a more appropriate framework for understanding relations between corporations, directors and shareholders than the classical contract ideas which underpin agency theory.[78] Certainly there is much about the association between a shareholder and a public corporation that fits the relational theorist's description of complexity, uncertainty and difficulty in specifying detailed terms. The imposition of fiduciary obligations of good faith on directors can be read as a flexible response to these problems, offering the possibility of future adjustments to contractual obligations. In the same way, '[m]echanisms such as the general meeting and other governance processes to which the shareholders have access enable members to contribute to the final form of alterations'.[79] Relational theory also offers the conceptual advantage over classical contract approaches by emphasising the importance of the relationship between the corporate parties, rather than focusing on the intended product of that relationship.[80]

Classical, Neoclassical and Relational Contract Law' (1977-78) 78 *Northwestern University Law Review* 854. Many, but not all, relational contract theorists adopt arguments that are congruent with aspects of law and economics scholarship: see A Schwartz, 'Relational Contracts in the Courts: An Analysis of Incomplete Agreements and Judicial Strategies' (1992) 21 *Journal of Legal Studies* 271, 275-276.

[75] I Macneil, 'The Many Futures of Contracts (1974) 47 *Southern California Law Review* 691, 723.

[76] C Goetz and R Scott, 'Principles of Relational Contracts' (1981) 67 *Virginia Law Review* 1089, 1090-1091.

[77] Macneil, above n 75, 748 and 792-793.

[78] Bratton, above n 46. Also M Whincop, 'A Relational and Doctrinal Critique of Shareholders' Special Contracts' (1997) 19 *Sydney Law Review* 314.

[79] Whincop, above n 78, 331.

[80] Ibid 328.

Clearly, relational contract theory goes beyond some of the limitations of classical contract thought, and it does have some attractions for analysing the complexity and uncertainty of intra-corporate relations. It has a conceptual advantage over classical contract approaches by seeming to emphasise the importance of the relationship between the corporate parties, rather than focusing on the intended product of that relationship.[81] Nevertheless, as is explained in the remainder of this Chapter, rather than opting for a more open-textured contractual model, this book argues for a constitutional perspective. One reason for this is that it is not at all clear that the type of relations which tend to be the focus for relational theorists — so-called 'primary relations', such as marriage or employment[82] — are a useful analogue for the relations between corporation members or between members and the corporation. More importantly, there is a concern that even in relational theory the underlying idea of 'contract' continues to exert a pull on the direction that is taken in the analysis of corporate issues. Despite the fact that it allows for the necessity of interaction between the parties after the initial exchange of promises, relationalism is still concerned fundamentally with *exchange* interactions between contracting parties, rather than *coordination* interactions between members.[83] Put bluntly, while relational contract theory may escape some of the limitations of classical contract theory, its focus is still essentially economic, individualistic and private. The attraction of pursuing a constitutional/political perspective is that it opens up directions of analysis that tend to be closed off even by a broad contractual perspective, such as the sometimes mixed private and public dimensions of corporate operations.

Political Theory and Constitutionalism

> A different vision of the company might draw upon the democratic ideal which inspires the relation of the citizen to the state. The democratic ideal asserts that those who are substantially affected by the decisions made by political and social institutions in our society should be involved in the making of those decisions.[84]

In this Part I begin to develop 'a different vision of the company' under the banner of corporate constitutionalism. I begin by explaining the relevance of political theory to corporations. Then I consider briefly two other political approaches before going on to explain my preference for a framework based on the idea of constitutionalism.

---

[81]   Ibid.

[82]   For example, Macneil, above n 75, 720ff and 795-796.

[83]   See Russell Hardin, 'Why a Constitution?' in B Grofman and D Wittman (eds), *The Federalist Papers and the New Institutionalism* (1989) 101.

[84]   Stokes, above n 53, 180.

Corporations and Political Theory

As I argued in Chapter 1, taking a constitutionalist perspective means introducing political considerations into the analysis of corporate institutions.[85] It is necessary to explain in more detail why political theory is a useful perspective from which to assess corporate issues, and what it is that the perspective of constitutionalism can offer us that the contract-based models cannot.

Political theory has a broad and indefinite domain. For the purposes of constructing a constitutional framework for corporations, I will work from Philip Pettit's definition:

> Political theory is a normative discipline, designed to let us evaluate rather than explain; in this it resembles moral or ethical theory. What distinguishes it is that it is designed to facilitate in particular the evaluation of government ... . We are to identify the purposes of government - more strictly, the proper purposes of government - so that we can decide on which arrangements it is best for a government to foster in a society: which basic constitution it is best to establish and which procedures or outcomes it is best to prescribe in the day-to-day operation of the society.[86]

Pettit identifies three main approaches to political theorising. The contract approach asks what sort of societal institutions people would choose if they were put in a suitable position of choice.[87] Secondly, the value-centred approach asks what goods or rights institutions should realise so as to support recognised political values. Thirdly, the institution-centred approach examines the institutional feasibility of different values.[88] In pursuing these different aims, political theories draw ideas from diverse disciplines including law, philosophy, political science and economics. To summarise its application to corporations, and with apologies to Kukathas and Pettit, political theory invites us to consider questions such as: What is the purpose of a corporation? How should corporations be organised? What claims do corporations have over their members?[89]

The intuitively simple justification for resorting to a political theory to evaluate corporations is that corporations are political entities. There are two complementary ways in which this is true. The first, while important, is of less concern in this book. Corporations, particularly the stock market leaders, are prominent and powerful actors in public life. Chapter 1 noted that corporations are major employers and taxpayers; their actions, collectively and individually have considerable impact on our social and economic structures and the environment.

---

[85] For an earlier argument about corporations and constitutionalism, see R Eells, *The Government of Corporations* (1962).

[86] Philip Pettit, *The Common Mind: An Essay on Psychology, Society and Politics* (1993) 284 (references omitted).

[87] See, for example, J Rawls, *A Theory of Justice* (1971).

[88] Pettit, above n 86, 222 and 284.

[89] See Kukathas and Pettit, above n 69, 1.

Corporations frequently act, in effect, as regulatory agencies, implementing government policies and enforcing regulatory mandates.[90] As political institutions corporations therefore have significance as public as well as private actors.

This is hardly a new or startling observation, even though it does seem to go largely unacknowledged in legal analysis. For many years a variety of commentators, writing from a variety of perspectives, have made the same point.[91] Maitland described the corporation and the state as two species within a single genus of more or less permanently organised groups of individual actors; they are group units to which we attribute actions, intentions, praise and blame.[92] More recently, the critical legal scholar Roberto Unger has made the similar observation that modern society looks more like 'a constellation of governments, rather than an association of individuals held together by a single government'.[93]

Unger's observation takes us to the second sense in which corporations can be said to be political entities, and this point is the primary focus of this book. Corporations are political not simply because they are players in societal power relations, but also because they themselves are arenas in which power and authority, rights and obligations, duties and expectations, benefits and disadvantages, are allocated and exercised, either actively or passively, collectively or individually, in relationships that can be characterised by conflict, control, competition, or co-operation. In short, each corporation is a body politic, a governance system. This is as true, albeit in different ways, for the closely-held corporation as it is for the largest public corporation. Again, this is not a novel observation. Writers as diverse as Thomas Hobbes, C Wright Mills, and Adolf Berle Jnr have made the same point.[94] Nor is this an incidental or trivial feature of corporations. While we might describe some corporations as being more political than others — perhaps because they are 'racked by disputation over their structure

---

[90] J Freeman, 'The Private Role in Public Governance' (2000) 75 *New York University Law Review* 543, 547.

[91] For example, P Blumberg, 'The Politicalization of the Corporation' [1971] *The Business Lawyer* 1551; R Stevenson Jr 'The Corporation as a Political Institution' (1979) 8 *Hofstra Law Review* 39.

[92] F W Maitland, 'Introduction' to Otto von Gierke, *Political Theories of the Middle Age* (1938) ix.

[93] R M Unger, *Law in Modern Society - Toward a Criticism of Social Theory* (1976) 193.

[94] This is noted by E Latham, 'The Body Politic of the Corporation' in E Mason (ed), *The Corporation in Modern Society* (1960) 218, 219. See also Eells, above n 85, 10; A Fraser, *Reinventing Aristocracy: The Constitutional Reformation of Corporate Governance* (1998); J Pound, 'The Rise of the Political Model of Corporate Governance and Corporate Control' (1993) 68 *New York University Law Review* 1003. Sometimes the point is expressed by describing corporations as private governments - eg A S Miller, 'Private Governments and the Constitution' in A Hacker (ed), *The Corporation Takeover* (1965) 117.

and governance' — all corporations are political as much as they are economic entities.[95]

Thinking of corporations as political entities does *not* mean treating them as analogues of parliamentary systems of public government. Despite superficial similarities — the election of a group of policy-makers by a diverse group of voters, with day-to-day implementation of policies being delegated to an unelected bureaucracy — corporations differ from the institutions of public government in many significant ways. For example, unlike a parliament, a board of directors is not a representative body, at least not in the sense that each director represents a specific constituency. Directors must act for the entire corporation.[96] Moreover, directors need not be drawn from the ranks of the shareholders who elect them. There are other obvious differences: there is no institutionalised 'opposition party' to challenge the views of the elected directors; voting rights in a corporation attach to shares not to the shareowner, so there is no fundamental concept of 'one person, one vote'; and shareholders have very limited rights of access to corporate information. [97] None of this, however, undermines the value of regarding corporations as 'bodies politic' that can be analysed in ways that have echoes in our approach to institutions of public government. As Pound observes: '[t]he political approach to corporate governance accords with ... values about how major institutions in our society should be governed, emphasising due process, substantive debate, and the use of formal voting referenda'.[98]

A political theory of corporate governance does not necessarily entail the proposition that directors and managers owe duties to non-shareholder stakeholders or other constituencies (although it is open to that proposition). Nor does it compel the application of notions of representative or participatory democracy to corporations. It means simply that existing corporate governance structures and patterns can be evaluated according to political, as much as economic, criteria. Rather than focusing exclusively on corporate outcomes we can look at corporate processes and ask what values ought to be protected and enhanced.[99]

The choice between an overtly political theory of corporate governance and the more widely used economic analysis of corporate law has been explored by several scholars. Lynne Dallas, for example, advocates a 'power model' of the firm,

---

[95]   Stevenson, above n 91, 40. The quoted words were used to describe NRMA Ltd in *NRMA Ltd v Snodgrass* (2001) 19 ACLC 1675 by Mason P.

[96]   The appointment of nominee directors may be an exception to this. While English authority insists that such directors must only consider the interests of the company as a whole, Australian decisions have permitted greater scope to consider the interests of the director's appointers. Compare *Scottish Co-operative Wholesale Society Ltd v Meyer* [1959] AC 324 with *Levin v Clark* [1962] NSWR 686 and *Re Broadcasting Station 2GB Pty Ltd* [1964-5] NSWR 1648.

[97]   There is no equivalent of 'freedom of information' legislation for company members.

[98]   Pound, above n 94, 1009. This echoes Frug's point that public law and corporate law are two versions of the same story: G Frug, 'The Ideology of Bureaucracy in American Law' (1984) 97 *Harvard Law Review* 1276.

[99]   See Selznick, above n 67, 351.

which stands in opposition to the 'efficiency model' (the latter being located in the economic-contractualist framework described earlier in this chapter).[100] The power model draws upon organisational and management theory. It 'focuses upon the political nature of decision-making in the large corporation', and sees the firm as 'an organic institution with its own internal structure and processes that impact on the control of the firm'.[101] Importantly, Dallas argues that managers are not simply agents of shareholders; management is a strategic player in the power coalitions within the firm. Mel Eisenberg, on the other hand, favours what he calls the Economic Model over the Political Model of the large publicly held corporation.[102] As he depicts it, the latter model posits the corporation as 'essentially a political institution' whose legitimacy 'depends upon the extent to which it is governed by principles appropriate to a democratic state'.[103] Those principles, according to Eisenberg, require a system of representative government which allows participation in decision-making by the various constituencies in the corporation. Eisenberg questions the relevance of this model to large corporations. In his assessment, the Economic Model better reflects both 'accepted conceptions of institutional competence and legitimacy' and the functional characteristics of the large public corporation.[104]

The argument which I present in this book differs from these positions in two ways. First, unlike Dallas and Eisenberg, I do not think that it is useful to advocate one model or framework to the exclusion of all others. Whilst I argue for a broadly political framework, I do so with the intention that it should be considered as an additional option to, rather than a substitute for, economic analysis. Because corporations can be categorised as political as much as economic institutions, they can be subject to political as much as economic analysis. Corporations can be 'many things at one and the same time' and, as Gareth Morgan reminds us, there can be no privileged or ultimate analytical framework for studying the complexity of corporate organisations.[105] Different theoretical frameworks will reveal different things about corporations and their internal organisation. When analysing a corporate governance situation or issue (be it a share restructuring, a takeover defence, or the validity of a resolution) the first step is to discern the character of the situation by referring to different frameworks and noting what aspects of the situation are highlighted by each framework. The next step is to make a critical and deliberate evaluation of these different interpretations of the situation, asking whether all interpretations are equally useful, whether they

---

[100] L Dallas, 'Two Models of Corporate Governance: Beyond Berle and Means' (1988) 22 *University of Michigan Journal of Law Reform* 19.

[101] Ibid 25-26.

[102] M Eisenberg, 'Corporate Legitimacy, Conduct, and Governance - Two Models of the Corporation' (1983) 17 *Creighton Law Review* 1.

[103] Ibid 2.

[104] Ibid 17.

[105] G Morgan, *Images of Organisation* (1986) 321.

are reconcilable, and where each leads us.[106] In particular, this two-step process requires us to make a comparative evaluation of economic criteria such as efficiency against constitutionalist criteria such as participation.

Secondly, in studying corporations and their regulation, political theory must be adapted, not simply adopted. Eisenberg apparently sees all political theory in terms of public (ie state) politics, leading him to dismiss it as inappropriate for the study of corporations. [107] In his view, the proposition that 'all political institutions should be governed by political principles, and that any institution that makes decisions of major importance to society is a political institution', [108] trivialises the critical differences that exist between the state and the corporation. As I have noted already, these differences are important, but acknowledging them does not then require us to abandon the job of tackling more complex questions about the ways in which, and extent to which, political theory should influence corporations. What is needed is a corporate species of political theory. This is what I mean by referring to *corporate* constitutionalism.

It is relatively easy to demonstrate the relevance of a political approach to the study of corporations and corporate law. The more difficult step is to decide upon a particular approach within the broad domain of political theory. In what follows I consider three possible approaches which apply politics to corporations, although in different ways: concession theory, social contract theory, and constitutional theory. These approaches do not, of course, exhaust the field. I have selected the first two because they are already recognised in the corporate governance literature; the case for the third option is made throughout this book.

Concession Theory[109]

The concession theory of corporations can be classified as a political theory in the sense that it seeks to tie each corporation into a system of public regulation. Concession theory entails two related claims. Each claim has a weak and a strong version.[110] The first claim (I call it 'the status claim') is that the creation of a body corporate and the legal incidents that are usually associated with incorporation (such as separate legal agency, perpetual succession, and limited liability of members) is a concession that is granted by the state. Another way of putting this is to describe the state grant of corporate status as a privilege, thereby underlining the

---

[106] This two step analysis is taken from Morgan, above n 105, 322. It must also be stressed that there cannot be (nor should there be) any meta-rule for determining when to use any particular framework.

[107] This is a common argument – see, for example, R Austin, 'Commentary on Hill' in R Grantham and C Rickett (eds), *Corporate Personality in the 20th Century* (1998) 211.

[108] Eisenberg, above n 102, 4.

[109] The following discussion is taken from S Bottomley, 'The Birds, the Beasts, and the Bat: Developing a Constitutionalist Theory of Corporate Regulation' (1999) 27 *Federal Law Review* 243.

[110] William Bratton also distinguishes weak and strong versions, although he draws the categories in a slightly different way – see 'The New Economic Theory of the Firm: Critical Perspectives from History' (1989) 41 *Stanford Law Review* 1471, 1475.

state's claim to control the process of incorporation and its subsequent use. An illustration of this view and its consequences is found in the New Zealand Court of Appeal's judgement in *Nicholson v Permakraft Ltd* where Cooke J stated that:

> limited liability is a privilege. It is a privilege healthy as tending to the expansion of opportunities and commerce, but it is open to abuse. Irresponsible structural engineering – involving the creating, dissolving or transforming of incorporated companies to the prejudice of creditors – is a mischief to which the courts should be alive.[111]

The status claim has two variants. The weak version limits itself to the proposition that a corporation owes its *legal* existence and powers to the grant of corporate status from the state. The weak version therefore seeks to avoid the metaphysical question 'what is a corporation?' by confining itself to the legal aspects of corporate status. The strong version is that the corporation is an artificial entity which owes its very existence to the state, thereby inviting a much wider debate about the legitimacy of state-based corporate regulation.

The second claim ('the regulatory claim') can be read as a *quid pro quo* for the grant of corporate status. As a consequence of being created by the state, concession theory argues that there is a presumption in favour of state regulation of a corporation's post-incorporation activity.[112] This presumption purports to give the state control over both the extent of the corporation's legal capacity and the exercise of that capacity.[113] This is the weak version of the regulatory claim. The claim is occasionally put in stronger terms, requiring not just compliance with public regulations but also creating a positive duty to act in the public interest or in a socially responsible manner.[114] The idea that a corporation should act in the public interest was first developed at a time when charters of incorporation were granted primarily to those enterprises which could demonstrate the pursuit of some sort of public purpose or utility (eg development of trade by overseas trading corporations such as the Hudson's Bay Company, or the construction of

---

[111] (1985) 3 ACLC 453, 459. Other examples can be found in the High Court of Australia's decision in *Northside Developments Pty Ltd v Registrar-General* (1990) 8 ACLC 611, 626 (per Brennan J) and in *Salomon v Salomon & Co Ltd* [1897] AC 22, 29 and 51. Concession theory was also influential in early United States corporate jurisprudence – see *Trustees of Dartmouth College v Woodward* (1819) 17 US 518, 636 per Chief Justice Marshall.

[112] Roberta Romano argues that there is no necessary link between these two claims. Having created a new legal actor, the state 'could conceivable imbue it with inviolable rights'. See R Romano, 'Metapolitics and Corporate Law Reform' (1984) 36 *Stanford Law Review* 923, 933.

[113] A S Dewing, *The Financial Policy of Corporations* (5th ed 1953) vol 1, 12.

[114] Noted in Parkinson, above n 65, 26. Parkinson disputes this claim, arguing that the social responsibilities of corporations stem from a political theory about the legitimacy of private power, and not from any theory about the state's role in the creation of corporations. See Chapter 3 n 15 and accompanying text.

railways).[115] It seems to be generally accepted in modern corporate law scholarship that the strong regulatory claim was an early casualty of the introduction of general incorporation statutes. However, remnants of the idea have survived in the form of arguments about the need for corporate social responsibility, and in the theory that corporations should be regarded essentially as social enterprises.[116]

While the origins of concession theory can be dated back to Roman times, it became prominent in discussions about corporate regulation in the early nineteenth century in both England and the United States.[117] There is, for example, Blackstone's statement in 1765 that '[w]ith us, in England, the king's consent is absolutely necessary to the erection of any corporation, either impliedly or expressly given'.[118] Over time the theory appears to have served two different purposes: with the rise of the nation state the theory served to reinforce the power of the state against the potential claims of other groupings of power, including business organisations.[119] Then, with the growing reliance on the corporate form in economic activity in the early nineteenth century, came the realisation that these incorporated concentrations of private power might use the legal incidents and consequences of corporate status to cause harm to individuals who deal with the corporation (including its own members). Thus the theory served to justify the regulation of corporate activity in the interests of individual actors in their dealings with corporations.[120]

Most of the criticisms of concession theory have come from adherents of contract-based theories of the corporation (especially neoclassical economic theory).[121] The debate is cast in stark terms: concession theory is aligned with arguments in favour of public regulation, even with organic/holistic visions of the community,[122] while neoclassical economic theory advocates the private and individual ordering of private affairs.

Contract-based criticisms of concession theory combine a number of claims, all of which seek to minimise the role of the state in the creation and

---

[115] Ibid, 28-29. See also C A Cooke, *Corporation, Trust and Company* (1950) 102. The alternative to incorporation was to organise an unincorporated association along joint-stock lines. For discussion of a similar situation in the United States, see J Hurst, *The Legitimacy of the Business Corporation in the Law of the United States 1780-1970* (1970) 33-47.

[116] See, eg, Parkinson, above n 65, 22-23, and Greenfield, above n 73.

[117] As noted in the text above, it has continued to be cited in judicial opinions throughout the twentieth century.

[118] Cited in Dewing, above n 113, 11. See also Cooke, above n 115, 78.

[119] J Dewey, 'The Historic Background of Corporate Legal Personality' (1926) 35 *Yale Law Journal* 655, 666-667.

[120] See Bratton, above n 110, 1486-1489 for a description of how corporate law doctrine continued to respond to individualist concerns in the absence of concession theory.

[121] This is a generalisation — not all critics would identify themselves as contract-based theorists. See for example, Parkinson, above n 64. It has been suggested that advocates of the neoclassical economics have resurrected concession theory simply as 'a foil for the new economic theory': Bratton, above n 46, 433-434.

[122] Romano, above n 112, 933-934.

regulation of corporations. One claim is empirical: concession theory does not fit the facts of modern corporate life. Concession theory may have made sense at a time when corporate status could only be obtained by the grant of a special charter or by a special Act of Parliament, but the advent of general incorporation laws in the late nineteenth century, widespread usage of which was sanctioned by the House of Lords in *Salomon's Case*,[123] and the availability of standardised corporate structures, means that concession theory has long since lost its relevance. As Bratton puts it, '[o]nce equal and substantially free access to the corporate form became the norm, the notion of 'concession' no longer described the practice of incorporation'.[124] Most commentators, whether contractualist or not, agree that on this ground the concession theory of corporate regulation no longer has any theoretical use.[125] A second set of claims takes a stance in favour of private ordering. A good example is Butler and Ribstein's argument that:

> because corporations are not wards of the state, and because the capital markets that discipline corporate contracts do not require more legal intervention than other markets, it follows that there is no justification for subjecting corporate arrangements to a higher level of regulation than other contracts.[126]

Hessen takes a similar approach, arguing that the three features most commonly associated with the corporate form — separate entity status, perpetual succession, and limited liability — can each be achieved through ordinary contract or trust arrangements and therefore that the state has no special role to play in the creation or continued regulation of corporations.[127] In other words, the state grant of these attributes is simply a cost-saving exercise for the incorporators, sparing them the effort of having to secure these advantages by private negotiation. Hessen's argument is not convincing; as John Parkinson points out, in all practical terms these state granted attributes are 'beyond the reach of private agreement'.[128]

These criticisms set up a false dichotomy: the corporation is to be categorised either as a 'ward of the state' or (the favoured position) as the product of a freely-constructed private contractual agreements. In this way, neo-classical contractarian critics tie the fate of concession theory to the fate of state regulation of corporations.[129] The theory of corporate constitutionalism developed in this book

---

[123] *Salomon v Salomon & Co Ltd* [1897] AC 22.
[124] Bratton, above n 46, 435 (footnote omitted). See also M Horwitz, '*Santa Clara* Revisited: The Development of Corporate History' (1985) 88 *West Virginia Law Review* 173, 181-183.
[125] In addition to Bratton, above n 46, and Horwitz, ibid, see Parkinson, above n 65, 25-32.
[126] H N Butler and L E Ribstein, *The Corporation and the Constitution* (1995) 2.
[127] R Hessen, *In Defense of the Corporation* (1979) Chapter 2. See also G M Anderson and R D Tollison, 'The Myth of the Corporation as a Creation of the State' (1983) 3 *International Review of Law and Economics* 107.
[128] Parkinson, above n 65, 32.
[129] A point also noted by M Whincop and M Keyes, 'Corporation, Contract, Community: An Analysis of Governance in the Privatisation of Public Enterprise and the Publicisation of Private Corporate Law' (1997) 25 *Federal Law Review* 51, 67.

tries to separate these two ideas. It accepts that the state does have a valid role to play in regulating corporations. It also acknowledges that concession theory places too much emphasis on the state's responsibility for control of corporations, leading to inappropriate command-control styles of corporate regulation and giving insufficient weight to the importance of private interests and concerns in forming and running corporations.

Social Contract Theory

Given the attraction of contract-based frameworks for legal and economic analyses of corporate law, it seems obvious to ask whether we should use a similar framework when analysing corporations as political institutions. Contract-based approaches to political theory have a long heritage, often being based on the idea of a social contract between the citizen and the state. Courts have occasionally described the corporate constitution as a social contract, although the meaning of the term in this context has not been explained.[130]

Tom Campbell's general description of the idea of a social contract is helpful:

> A social contract ... is an agreement between potential citizens (or between such persons and a potential ruler or rulers) about the terms on which they are to enter into either social or political relationships (or both). Social contract theory posits a situation – called a 'state of nature' — in which persons who have no existing political (and perhaps social) rights or obligations reach (usually unanimous) agreement about the basis on which to establish a social and/or political system in which they do have recognised rights and obligations, including the obligation to conform to the agreement reached, respect the rights of other citizens and obey the appointed ruler(s). The social contract is used both to explain the general obligation of citizens to obey the law (and the possible limits of that obligation), and to provide a way of determining the proper content of the rights and obligations which bind members of a civil and political society. It serves, therefore, both to establish the grounds of social, political and legal obligation, and to justify a particular set of positive social and political norms.[131]

A social contract that is voluntarily agreed to by all citizens is said to form the basis of the social and political obligations which those citizens owe to each other and to the state. At the same time, it legitimates intrusions into individual freedom and restrictions on personal liberty.[132] As Campbell explains, political theorists such as Hobbes, Locke, Rousseau, and Rawls have formulated the details of the

---

[130] For example, the judgements of Isaacs J in *Ardlethan Options Ltd v Easdown* (1915) 20 CLR 285, 294; *Dutton v Gordon* (1917) 23 CLR 362, 395; *Wood v W & G Wood Pty Ltd* (1929) 43 CLR 77, 87.

[131] T Campbell, *Justice* (2nd ed, 2001) 92-93.

[132] K Scheppele and J Waldron, 'Contractarian Methods in Political and Legal Evaluation' (1991) 3 *Yale Journal of Law and the Humanities* 195, 200-201.

social contract in different ways.[133] This is not the place for a detailed description of these various arguments, but it is useful to highlight three elements of social contract theory.

First, the *purpose* of the agreement which is embodied in the social contract is to define, protect and advance the interests and needs of individual citizens. This, like other forms of contract-based argument, seeks to legitimate political structures and processes on the grounds of individual consent. Social contract is a theory about how individuals live in society; it is not a theory about society itself.

The second element concerns the *nature* of the agreement. How do citizens express their consent to be ruled? Social contract theorists have provided three answers to this question. The weakest answer is that the social contract must be the result of actual agreement between citizens who have actually addressed their minds to the issues. There is an obvious empirical problem with this argument — there is little, if any, evidence that people in modern society have gone through this process. A slightly stronger answer suggests that consent is given implicitly by individual citizens, for example, by voting in an election or simply by continuing to live within the political group. The problems with this argument lie in identifying the actions which will constitute consent, and in determining the extent of obligation which can be supported by implied consent.[134] The third answer is that these agreements are hypothetical. This argument suggests that:

> [t]o resolve a normative disagreement on some political or legal issue, it may be helpful to ask what the people involved in the dispute would have agreed to do about the issue had they considered the possibility of disagreement before reaching the point at which the actual disagreement took place.[135]

This idea of a hypothetical contract, which is similar to the neoclassical economists' model of the rational economic actor, establishes a benchmark against which actual political arrangements can be assessed and their legitimacy determined.

The third element of social contract theory concerns the *terms* of the agreement: on what basis do citizens transfer power to the rulers? Broadly speaking, two alternatives have been argued. One position, originally put by Hobbes, is that an agreement to obey a ruler entails a full surrender of power and sovereignty to the ruler. The other position, less autocratic and more widely accepted, is identified with Locke who argued that the people 'lend' power to the

---

133   See also D Held, *Models of Democracy* (1987).

134   See J Hampton, 'Contract and Consent' in R Goodin and P Pettit (eds), *A Companion to Contemporary Political Philosophy* (1993) 379, 381. An alternative argument is that consent can be implied from the fact that each individual is free to exit the contract if they choose – see R Hills Jr, 'The Constitutional Rights of Private Governments' (2003) 78 *New York University Law Review* 144.

135   Scheppele and Waldron, above n 132, 196. John Rawls' theory of justice is perhaps the best known modern example of the hypothetical social contract approach: J Rawls, *A Theory of Justice* (1971).

ruler on the condition that it can later be withdrawn if the people so wish. In this 'agency' form of social contract theory, the people retain ultimate sovereignty.[136]

Social contract theory has limitations and disadvantages for developing a political approach to modern corporate governance. To the extent that social contract theory is built upon the ideal of implied individual agreements and agency-based grants of power then the criticisms about the limitations of the economic contractual models which I made earlier in this Chapter are relevant.[137] This emphasis on individual rights and their protection seems to offer little scope for parties to the contract to 'put aside their own particular interests' and to enter into debates about 'the common good'.[138] A more particular problem arises because the social contract is based on the premise that each and every person must give their consent before there can be a legitimate exercise of power over them. This is at odds with the idea of decisions made by a majority vote, in which the non-consent of persons in the minority is disregarded.[139] Corporate law presumes that majority rule is the means by which decisions are made within a company.[140] A political theory which cannot accommodate this method of decision-making is therefore of limited use in the corporate context.

Constitutional Theory[141]

The type of political inquiry that I argue has most to offer corporate law derives from constitutional theory. The term 'constitutional theory' is slightly misleading — there are many specific theories that can be grouped under this heading. Here I will introduce some of the key ideas in constitutional theory in broad terms. In the next Chapter I will 'corporatise' the concept by setting out a theory of corporate constitutionalism.

There is considerable diversity in the way in which terms such as 'constitution' and 'constitutionalism' are defined and used. For present purposes, two broad approaches can be contrasted: the first approach categorises

---

[136] Hampton, above n 134, 380. The preceding summation of the Hobbesian and Lockean approaches is taken from Hampton's review.

[137] See also Hardin, above n 83, criticising social contract theory and the idea of agreement as the basis for constitutional order.

[138] See Kukathas and Pettit, above n 69.

[139] Scheppele and Waldron, above n 132, 198 and 221, also pointing out that although the contract may leave certain issues to be resolved by majority vote, the theory still requires unanimous agreement in advance on what issues can be settled in this manner.

[140] It is worth remembering that majority rule in the corporate context can mean either a majority of voting shareholders or a majority of voting shares. That is, a minority of members who own a majority of the voting shares can control decisions at company meetings.

[141] The following discussion develops some of the ideas in S Bottomley, 'From Contractualism to Constitutionalism: A Framework for Corporate Governance' (1997) 19 *Sydney Law Review* 277, 293ff.

constitutions as agreements, the second regards them as frameworks for reaching agreement.[142]

In the first approach a constitution is regarded as an agreement according to which certain substantive goals and interests are to be achieved and served. These goals and interests pre-date the formulation of the constitution. In the corporate context one such goal might be the efficient use of the corporation's capital. Thus the purpose of a constitution is simply to permit the fulfilment of those pre-determined goals and interests. It is easy to see how classical contract-based perspectives fit within this approach.[143]

One particular example of this approach is found in the economic theory of constitutions.[144] This strand of economics is concerned principally with the situation of the rational individual who is faced with a choice about participating in a collective decision. Constitutional economics argues that the individual's course of action will depend upon the rules which govern collective decisions in that setting – for example, does the decision require a bare majority, a special majority, or unanimity? The role of a constitution is to specify these rules, and the purpose of studying constitutions is to decide what the optimal rules will be. Two concerns of this theory are the need to agree upon rules which will reduce decision-making costs within a collective, and the necessity of imposing constraints on collective action in order to protect individual interests. Thus, while this theory takes collective decision-making seriously, its perspective is that of the individual. The constitution is regarded as a framework within which each individual consents to specific rules governing collective decision-making. To put it another way, constitutional economics is concerned with how decisions are constituted, not with how the group that makes those decisions is constituted. It also eschews any conception of concepts such as 'the common good' or 'the public interest'.

In the second approach a constitution is regarded as a framework within which the members of the constituted organisation can identify or formulate preferences and make decisions. This approach is also based on pre-determined ideas, but in this case they are not primarily substantive goals and interests. Instead, they are questions of structure and procedure, or what some commentators have

---

[142] This analysis is prompted by, but not necessarily consistent with, S L Elkin, 'Constitutionalism: Old and New' in S L Elkin and K E Soltan (eds), *A New Constitutionalism: Designing Political Institutions for a Good Society* (1993) 20, and R Bellamy and D Castiglione, 'Constitutionalism and Democracy - Political Theory and the American Constitution' (1997) 27 *British Journal of Political Science* 595.

[143] W J Stankiewicz, *Aspects of Political Theory: Classical Concepts in an Age of Relativism* (1976) 12-14.

[144] See, for example, J Buchanan and G Tullock, *The Calculus of Consent: Logical Foundations of Constitutional Democracy* (1965), and G Brennan and J Buchanan, *The Reason of Rules: Constitutional Political Economy* (1985). For an application to corporate decision-making, see M Whincop, 'The Role of the Shareholder in Corporate Governance: A Theoretical Approach' (2001) 25 *Melbourne University Law Review* 418.

referred to as 'matters of institutional design'.[145] These questions have been central to the liberal democratic approach that has influenced much of modern constitutional thought in countries such as Australia.

Liberal democratic approaches to constitutionalism have been concerned primarily with three issues.[146] These approaches begin from the proposition that the systems of direct or self-government are not feasible in modern large-scale societies. At the same time, there is a concern to preserve, as much as is possible, the idea that individuals can participate in the processes of societal decision-making. Hence, what is required is a system of representative government by which a smaller number of elected individuals can exercise state functions and make decisions that are binding on the entire community.[147] Representative government, however, is no guarantee against arbitrary rule; there is always the possibility that those who are elected to govern may use their power to ignore the mandate of representation and serve only the interests of the majority faction in society ('the tyranny of the majority') or of a smaller elite. Thus, like constitutional economics, the liberal democratic version of constitutional theory is concerned to restrain the public exercise of power and on the creation of structures to maintain those restraints in the interests of individual citizens. In liberal theory, constitutionalism defines and tries to maintain a formal separation between 'the private' and 'the public'. One way to reduce the possibility of this abuse of power is to break up concentrations of government power and to impose a system of checks and balances on the exercise of that power. These goals are usually summarised in the idea of the separation of powers.[148] In particular, the power to make rules (legislative power) should be separated from the power to enforce those rules (executive power), and both should be independent of the power of the judiciary in deciding disputes about the validity and application of the rules. This separation of powers is reinforced by the recognition of constitutionally reinforced rights and liberties. Where these safeguards fail there may then be calls for avenues of political participation that go beyond mere electoral processes.

The liberal democratic concept of constitutionalism has a strong association with legal thought. Within legal discourse the idea of constitutionalism is allied with, and often treated as a synonym for, the rule of law. Whatever the degree of linkage between these two ideas, the point is the same: constitutionalism

---

[145] Bellamy and Castiglione, above n 142, 602. The importance of structure and process in corporate law is emphasised by D Branson, 'The Death of Contractarianism and the Vindication of Structure and Authority in Corporate Governance and Corporate Law' in L E Mitchell (ed), *Progressive Corporate Law* (1995) 92.

[146] Here I am rolling together the diverse theories of Hobbes, Locke, Madison, Bentham, and J S Mill. Not all had something to say about the three points made in the text.

[147] Of course, different theorists have different explanations for why and how this system of representation should operate, and about the nature of the relationship between the representatives and those whom they represent. These arguments include competing attitudes about issues such as majority rule and the allocation of voting rights.

[148] The origins of this idea are commonly attributed to Montesquieu's *The Spirit of Laws*, published in 1748.

is usually defined in terms of procedures and structures. As an example, constitutionalism is said to refer to:

> specific constitutional devices and procedures, such as the separation of powers between the legislature, the executive and the judiciary, the independence of the judiciary, due process or fair hearings for those charged with criminal offences, and respect for individual rights, which are partly constitutive of a liberal democratic system of government.[149]

The distinction between 'the constitution as agreement' and 'the constitution as framework' is not clear-cut. Many constitutions — including corporate constitutions — contain elements of both. The purpose of highlighting this distinction, however, is to direct the analysis away from an exclusive focus on a rules-based idea of constitutions, which is sometimes found in economic or legal analyses. All too often, as Schochet notes, 'constitutionalism supports a rule formalism that maintains the status quo, leaves no room for political discretion, is incapable of sanctioning resolute responses to emergencies and radically new situations, and is indifferent to political substances'.[150]

As noted earlier, there are different versions of constitutional theory. The approach that is developed in this book draws on strands of republican and deliberative theories,[151] and its primary purpose is to focus attention on the processes and structures of corporate decision-making. For the purposes of this book, taking a constitutionalist perspective means recognising that a constitution creates and defines the key governance structures and processes of a political institution. Although a constitution does not necessarily direct the ends to which those structures and processes will be used, there are some constraints. This is because a constitution rests upon a set of principles or values which, though not necessarily written explicitly into the constitution, nevertheless condition the exercise of power and authority within the constituted entity.[152]

In this way a constitution helps to define the institution itself. That is, while a constitution recognises and reinforces the place of individual actors (or *constituents*) within the group, at the same time it *constitutes* them as a group or a community. Different types of institutions will be constituted in different ways; there is no single archetype of a constitutional organisation. As Schochet notes, 'no one set of political arrangements is uniquely required by constitutionalism'.[153] This

---

[149] C Ten, 'Constitutionalism and the Rule of Law' in Goodin and Pettit, above n 134, 394.

[150] G Schochet, 'Introduction: Constitutionalism, Liberalism, and the Study of Politics' in J R Pennock and J W Chapman (eds), *Nomos XX: Constitutionalism* (1979) 8.

[151] There is generally no accepted demarcation between liberal, deliberative, and republican theories, and I am not concerned to locate this book within any particular category. However, I do want to distinguish a constitutional approach from a contractual approach and for that reason I lean more heavily on republican and deliberative approaches.

[152] See M Perry, 'What is "the Constitution"? (and Other Fundamental Questions)' in L Alexander (ed), *Constitutionalism: Philosophical Foundations* (1998).

[153] Schochet, above n 150, 11.

applies not only to comparisons between corporations and states, but also between different types of corporations. Because of this, different applications of political theory, different conceptions of democratic organisation and process, and different political standards (eg levels of voter participation) will be required for different types of institution.

Constitutional theory thus has the capacity to direct our attention to what it is that pulls individuals together in a group, rather than just what separates them. It allows us to contemplate the relations between the group and the individuals who comprise the group. In other words, a constitution has an integrating role. Sheldon Wolin puts it this way:

> A constitution not only constitutes a structure of power and authority, it constitutes a people in a certain way. It proposes a distinctive identity and envisions a form of politicalness for individuals in their new collective capacity.[154]

He also argues that:

> [A] constitution is an experiment in the forging of a collective identity. The identity of the collectivity, who it is and what it stands for politically, is made known through the constitutionally sanctioned actions of public officials and the response, or lack thereof, of the collectivity to those actions. Thus, a constitution has a circular nature: it is constituted by the collectivity ... and the actions performed under it, in turn, constitute the collectivity.[155]

A constitutional framework allows us to take into account the shifting complexity of the relationship between individual members and the group as a whole. It allows us to recognise that this relationship involves a continuous process of negotiating and redefining power relations according to accepted procedures, rather than applying pre-determined conceptions of what those relationships should be.

Of course, these can be difficult decisions. Determining what is in the group interest and what counts as a legitimate individual interest, and then mediating between the two can be problematical. In large part this is because there is not always a neat dichotomy between these interests.[156] The relationship between the group and the individual emerges from a continuous process of negotiating and defining power relations. Not only does a constitutionalist framework assist in recognising the complexity of the relationship between the individual and the group, it also assists in understanding the role of the individual as a 'citizen' or a 'member'. That is, both the public and the private aspects of a person's existence in a society are recognised. This recognition of citizenship has two aspects — recognition of the rights and of the responsibilities of citizenship.

---

[154]   Wolin, above n 70, 94.
[155]   Ibid 98.
[156]   See text accompanying n 68.

Conclusion

In this Chapter I have charted a route that takes us away from the idea of contract as the sole organising framework for analysing corporations and takes us towards the idea of a constitution. The argument is that there are qualitative differences between contracts and constitutions. Of course, in the corporate context the difference between contract and constitution is not always stark. It is true that corporate constitutions have more 'contract-like' features than do the constitutions of nation states. Nevertheless, important differences persist, even in the corporate context. As I have argued in this Chapter, contracts are concerned with bringing about an exchange between individual parties; constitutions, on the other hand, are concerned with the co-ordination of relations between constituents.

To conclude, the idea of 'constitutionalism' which is employed here has rhetorical, methodological, and normative uses. It is rhetorical in that I use it to import political theory into the discussion of corporate governance. It is methodological in that it presumes that 'in order to discuss individuals one must look first at their communities and their communal relationships'.[157] It is normative in that it provides a benchmark against which to evaluate the structures and processes of particular governance systems. The next step is to apply these constitutional ideas to the corporation, to develop the idea of *corporate constitutionalism*. That is the task of the next Chapter.

---

[157] S Avineri and A De-Shalit (eds), *Communitarianism and Individualism* (1992) 2. This contrasts with methodological individualism, discussed earlier – above n 61.

Chapter 3

Corporate Constitutionalism

Introduction

In the previous Chapter I juxtaposed two different ways of thinking about corporate governance. One — the dominant approach for legal purposes — is based on contract, and it tends to favour the use of economic criteria in evaluating corporate governance issues. The other is based on the idea of a constitution, and it draws primarily on a political understanding of corporate affairs. This Chapter presents the framework of corporate constitutionalism in more detail, building on the ideas presented in the final sections of the previous Chapter. As I have already noted,[1] corporations *are* political institutions, but they are political institutions in different ways from the institutions of public governance. This means that constitutionalist ideas must be *adapted* to the corporate context, not simply adopted by it.

The constitutionalist ideas discussed in the previous Chapter have been developed with reference to the constitutions of nation states. Corporate constitutions differ from the constitutions of nation states in a number of ways. For example, persons establishing a corporation have fewer options about the content of their particular corporate constitution, because constraints and mandatory terms are imposed by external laws and regulatory systems. This has implications for how we identify the corporate constitution, as I explain later in this Chapter. Another difference is that corporate constitutions are more amenable to later alteration and modification than are state constitutions. While this has the advantage of flexibility, it also has the potential for manipulation and abuse of power. In this Chapter I outline some key principles of corporate constitutionalism that are intended to protect against these potential problems. The final difference to note here (although this does not exhaust the list) is that in a public corporation disagreement and dissent is often dealt with by shareholders choosing to sell their shares and leave the corporation, rather than remaining to argue the issue. In other words, the use of the 'exit' option frequently has greater prominence in the corporate context than does the 'voice' option.[2] This does not mean, however, that

---

[1]   See Chapter 2 at text accompanying n 94.
[2]   The ideas of voice and exit are taken from Albert O Hirschman, *Exit, Voice, and Loyalty: Responses to Decline in Firms, Organisations and States* (1970).

the option of voicing dissent should be ignored; the principle of 'contestability' that I outline later addresses this question.

Acknowledging these differences, the adaptation of constitutionalist thought to the corporate context is nevertheless not as novel as it may first seem. History and everyday usage suggest that corporate law has already accommodated some constitutional language and ideas. Historically, as Harold Berman has shown, it was early corporate law which played an important role in the development of the constitutional structures of the church in Europe during the late eleventh and twelfth centuries. Berman points out that:

> it was the church as a corporate legal entity that conferred jurisdiction upon individual ecclesiastical officers (pope, bishops, abbot), and it was the law of corporations that determined the nature and limits of the jurisdiction thus conferred.[3]

Today the term 'constitution' is used commonly in the everyday language of corporate governance to describe the rules and regulations that govern internal management of a company. In Australia this usage is reinforced by the *Corporations Act*,[4] and it has more than just descriptive significance. Eisenberg has emphasised the link between corporate and the ideas of constitutional law, observing that:

> Corporate law is constitutional law; that is, its dominant function is to regulate the manner in which the corporate institution is constituted, to define the relative rights and duties of those participating in the institution, and to delimit the powers of the institution vis-à-vis the external world.[5]

Eisenberg's observation emphasises that constitutionalism, generally defined, seeks to mediate the public and the private aspects of social and political life. Adapted to the corporate setting, a constitutionalist framework plays a similar role.

Working from Eisenberg's observation, I argue that the corporation is an institution in which public and private interests and values meet. From this perspective, the idea of 'corporate constitutionalism' has a double meaning. First, corporate constitutionalism has an internal aspect, dealing with certain relations inside a corporation.[6] In other words, a corporation is a constitutional arrangement in which individual choices are expressed and group decisions are made. Secondly, and simultaneously, corporations operate within a wider constitutional setting in

---

[3]   H Berman, *Law and Revolution: The Formation of the Western Legal Tradition* (1983) 215.

[4]   *Corporations Act 2001* s 136 (providing, inter alia, that a company may adopt a constitution in substitution for, or in addition to, the replaceable rules found in the Act).

[5]   M Eisenberg, 'The Legal Roles of Shareholders and Management in Modern Corporate Decisionmaking' (1969) 57 *California Law Review* 1, 4.

[6]   See D Millon, 'Theories of the Corporation' (1990) *Duke Law Journal* 201, 201-202 for a discussion of external and internal perspectives. See also W Bratton, 'Public Values and Corporate Fiduciary Law' (1992) 44 *Rutgers Law Review* 675, 690-691.

which the state has responsibilities and powers in relation to individual citizens, groups, and organisations. This external aspect of corporate constitutionalism deals with the relationship between the corporation, on the one hand, and the state and society on the other.

This Chapter examines these two aspects in more detail. First, it looks at the external aspect of corporate constitutionalism, explaining how the corporate constitution contains private and public elements. This also involves an examination of the form and content of the corporate constitution. The Chapter then examines the internal aspect, looking at the role played by the corporate constitution in constituting relations between members and directors in a corporation. This leads to a summary discussion of the key constitutional ideas that underpin these relations; these ideas are then elaborated in subsequent Chapters.

By the end of the present Chapter it will be obvious that the idea of corporate constitutionalism draws on many strands. In particular, it has elements of liberal constitutionalism (a regard for individual rights and interests), communitarianism (the idea that, in addition to individual members, the group has significance), and republicanism (stressing, in particular, the idea of governance according to the common good).

The External Aspect of Corporate Constitutions

A corporate constitutionalist framework entails a claim about the political and legal status of the corporation and where the rules that govern corporate behaviour should come from.[7] This also has implications for how we understand the form of a corporate constitution. Under this sub-heading I examine the claim about political and legal status; under the next sub-heading I look at the form of the corporate constitution.

As we saw in Chapter 2, arguments about corporate regulation tend to be grouped on either side of a public/private dichotomy. Concession theory, for example, points to the fact that corporations depend on a state grant of corporate status, and argues that this justifies a system of public regulation of corporate activity. In contrast, many versions of economic theory argue that corporations are essentially private arrangements that should therefore be subject to minimal public regulation. The limitations of these either/or approaches have already been noted. What is needed in their place is recognition that corporations and corporate regulation embody a complex interplay between the public regulation and the private ordering of corporate affairs. As Bratton puts it, '[c]orporate law is not an entirely 'private' proposition, even though it tends to lie on the private side of the broader continuum of public and private law'.[8] Corporations are organisations in

---

[7]   From a different angle, economic contractualists recognise the same point. Their arguments about the contractual nature of intra-corporate relations are tied to wider arguments about the legal status of companies as private economic actors.

[8]   Bratton, above n 6, 696.

56 *The Constitutional Corporation*

which private actors exercise powers that are both privately generated and state-sanctioned. Richard Eells describes it this way:

> The governmental system of a corporation derives essentially from the *permissive* action of states, by legislation, through administrative rulings, and in judicial interpretation of charters and general corporation law.[9]

One idea behind corporate constitutionalism is to develop a framework within which we can understand the interplay between state and corporate contributions to the governance of, and governance within, corporations.

Consider, first, state inputs and the role of state regulation. From a corporate constitutionalist perspective there are justifiable constraints and costs which the state, via the legal system, imposes on corporate activity. The justification for this proposition is derived from recent republican theorising about the role of the state.

According to republican political theory the state has a unique role in protecting and furthering public values. Public values are derived ultimately from individual conceptions of 'the public interest' or 'the common good'. As Seidenfeld explains it:

> Each individual has some subjective notion of the common good — a notion that embodies public values shared with others in the community. Civic republicanism requires that the government base its actions on these public values rather than on the private desires that citizens bring into political discourse.[10]

Determining what the common good is on a given issue requires that government and legislators make impartial judgements and not give undue weight to particular private or factional interests.[11] Moreover, the state has a role in deterring or constraining behaviour that is inimical to these public norms or values. Provided that these state actions are not arbitrary, they need not be automatically regarded as an affront to individual freedom.[12] This is not to say that state regulation is an unqualified good — governments, laws, and the agencies that administer those laws can be oppressive and unfair, and so we require legal processes and structures that will constrain arbitrary and unwarranted state action. But the republican message is that state regulation should, *and can*, be beneficial for society as a whole.

---

[9] R Eells, *The Government of Corporations* (1962) 67 (emphasis in original). Eells highlights the permissive nature of this action because of the capacity which corporations have to amend the constitution after incorporation.

[10] M Seidenfeld, 'A Civic Republican Justification for the Bureaucratic State' (1992) 105 *Harvard Law Review* 1512, 1536-1537. See also C Sunstein, 'Beyond the Republican Revival' (1988) 97 *Yale Law Journal* 1539, 1574.

[11] M Sellers, *Republican Legal Theory: The History, Constitution and Purposes of Law in a Free State* (2003) 32. Of course the process of determining the public good will frequently be a complex and difficult process.

[12] P Pettit, *Republicanism: A Theory of Freedom and Government* (1997) 148-150.

A particular concern of the state should be the potential threats to liberty that can arise when private organisations accumulate and exercise power. As was noted in Chapter 1, the actions of corporations frequently have significant public and private consequences. Corporations become powerful intermediate organisations between citizens and the state. It is the role of government and the courts to 'play a role in limiting the power of such organisations without denying the importance of their continued existence'.[13] The republican message is that we can think favourably about a system of government that gives the law and the state a considerable range of responsibilities regarding corporate regulation, and that operates to challenge unaccountable accumulations of power and authority.[14]

Implicit in this argument is the idea that corporations are not entirely private associations. As John Parkinson describes it, they are also social enterprises:

> [C]ompanies are able to make choices which have important social consequences: they make private decisions which have public results. It is possession of this kind of power that gives rise to a distinct need for justification, and which forms the basis for the claim that companies must be required to act in the public interest.[15]

Parkinson goes on to argue that the 'practical significance [of this claim] is to hold that the state is entitled to prescribe the terms on which corporate power may be possessed and exercised'.[16] To be clear: the state's role as a corporate regulator arises not from the state grant of corporate powers and attributes (as concession theory argues), but from the potential for the accumulation of private power created by those powers and attributes. As Parkinson explains, 'it is not the legal qualities of limited liability or separate personality in themselves that justify intervention [by the state], but the concentration of power in private hands that has come about partly as a result of their existence'.[17]

Joining this idea with the republican perspective on state regulation, we can say that along with facilitating the realisation of private interests, a system of corporate law should be concerned to enhance public values such as the avoidance of oppressive or unfair behaviour, the use of objective, rather than purely subjective, standards in the evaluation of corporate behaviour, and the importance of accountability in the exercise of power within and by corporations. Values such as these are already prominent in contemporary corporate law jurisprudence. For example, a concern about oppressive or unfair conduct is enshrined in legislation

---

[13] Sunstein, above n 10, 1574.

[14] Pettit, above n 12, 150.

[15] J Parkinson, *Corporate Power and Responsibility: Issues in the Theory of Company Law* (1993) 10.

[16] Ibid 23.

[17] Ibid 30. This argument is therefore distinct from the concession theory, outlined in Chapter 2, which argues that the state's right to regulate companies is a necessary quid pro quo for the grant of corporate status.

such as s 232 of the Australian *Corporations Act*,[18] as well as in judicial opinion (a prominent example being the High Court of Australia's decision in *Gambotto v WCP Ltd*).[19] There is a discernible trend towards the use of objective standards in recent judicial pronouncements on the law of directors' fiduciary duties, both in general law and in statute.[20] The requirement of accountability in financial and managerial decision-making is a mainstay of the regulatory system of modern corporate law.[21]

Turning now from state regulation to private governance, we begin with the claim made in Chapter 2 that corporations are polities in their own right. While corporate constitutionalism entails a claim that the status of corporations as legal actors is dependent on state action, this does not mean that the state is the sole source of corporate governance rules. That is, the second aspect of this governance and regulatory framework is supplied by the private ordering of the members and directors.[22] A corporation is not simply a microcosm of society at large; corporate relationships are also structured by their own sets of values.[23] Presumably this is what Eells has in mind when, as noted before, he emphasises 'the *permissive* action of states'.[24] Eells highlights the permissive nature of this action because of the capacity which members have to engage in private constitutional ordering by amending terms of their constitution after incorporation. If corporations are thought of as polities, then it becomes easy to see why the corporators should have some space to determine and pursue their conception of the corporation's best interests.

It is important to be clear about the relationship between state regulation and private ordering in this framework. Unlike the command-control model of regulation, the state does not occupy centre-stage in this regulatory scheme; instead, to use Clifford Shearing's description, the state's role is 'decentred'.[25] Nor should

---

[18]   The UK equivalent is s 459 *Companies Act 1989* which refers to unfairly prejudicial conduct. Of course, sections such as these have generated considerable debate about their appropriate scope, meaning, and application.

[19]   (1995) 13 ACLC 342.

[20]   See eg *Permanent Building Society (in liq) v Wheeler* (1994) 12 ACLC 674 (proper purpose to be objectively determined) and *R v Byrnes; R v Hopwood* (1995) 13 ACLC 1488 (the test of impropriety in what are now ss 182 and 183 of the *Corporations Act* is objective).

[21]   Taken together these ideals have parallels with Philip Pettit's idea of freedom as non-domination ie freedom as the absence of arbitrary and unchecked interference with the choices of another person — see above n 12. John Coffee also emphasises the role of the courts in recognising mandatory minimum standards such as a duty of good faith and protection against unconscionable provisions: J Coffee, 'The Mandatory/Enabling Balance in Corporate Law: An Essay on the Judicial Role' (1989) *Columbia Law Review* 1617, 1623.

[22]   C Shearing, 'A Constitutive Concept of Regulation' in P Grabosky and J Braithwaite (eds), *Business Regulation and Australia's Future* (1993) 73.

[23]   Bratton, above n 6, 695.

[24]   Above n 9.

[25]   Above n 22, 73.

state regulation be regarded as superior to, or having automatic precedence over, private ordering. To quote Shearing again: 'the state's claim to the apex of a regulatory hierarchy with private regulators performing no more than delegated roles is unfounded'.[26] Similar comments apply to private ordering: this framework differs from contractarian theories in that private ordering is seen neither as a substitute for state regulation, nor as an inherently preferable alternative. State regulation and private ordering are both necessary but neither of them alone is sufficient.

The Form and Content of Corporate Constitutions

Another way of describing the dual function of a corporate constitution is to consider the form and content of the constitution itself. What does a corporate constitution consist of? Where do we look when we want to identify a corporation's decision-making structures and processes? These are important questions because, as I argued under the previous heading, a corporate constitution has internal and external aspects: it sets out the allocation of power within a corporation, and it constitutes that corporation as an economic, social, and political entity. If we define the corporate constitution too narrowly (or too broadly) we are likely to generate distorted understandings of intra-corporate power relations, and of the nature of the corporation itself.

According to general constitutional theory, there is no single model for determining what is and what is not a constitution.[27] As I argued in the previous Chapter, two key features of a constitution are that it constitutes a political system and it defines how decision-making power is allocated within that polity (or how this allocation will be decided). A constitution is concerned with questions of structure and process:[28] it can specify what processes must be followed in order for decisions to be made legitimately. A constitution can also specify what rights, duties, powers and functions are reserved for, or allocated to, the members and officers of the polity. With this broad definition in mind, we can identify — in a general and indicative way — some of the particular elements that can comprise a corporate constitution.

Corporate lawyers commonly describe a corporation's 'internal rules' as its 'constitution' (referring to what used to be known as the articles of

---

26 Ibid.
27 W F Murphy, 'Constitutions, Constitutionalism, and Democracy' in D Greenberg et al (eds), *Constitutionalism and Democracy: Transitions in the Contemporary World* (1993) 3.
28 See D Branson, 'The Death of Contractarianism and the Vindication of Structure and Authority in Corporate Governance and Corporate Law' in L Mitchell (ed), *Progressive Corporate Law* (1995) 99, arguing that modern corporate law has abandoned a concern with detailed rules in favour of relying on structure and process.

association).[29] This usage is reflected in s 136 of the Australian *Corporations Act*, which allows a company to adopt a constitution to govern the corporation's internal management in addition to, or as a substitute for, the 'replaceable rules' that are set out in the statute. This usage usually reflects a narrow view, in which the term 'constitution' stands as a synonym for 'agreement' or 'contract'.[30] The idea of a corporate constitution that I develop here is broader than this.

The limitations of this contractual usage of the term 'constitution' are illustrated by the case of *Wilcox v Kogarah Golf Club Ltd.*[31] The articles of association of an incorporated club gave the board of directors the power to make rules and by-laws dealing with the rights and obligations of members, including matters such as membership fees and the suspension or expulsion of members. A dispute arose in which the plaintiff complained that his rights under the by-laws had been breached. The question before Young J was whether the by-laws could be enforced by a member, relying on the 'statutory contract' created by what is now s 140 of the *Corporations Act*.[32] His Honour held that this was not possible; the by-laws were merely a 'a consensual compact' between the members and it was a feature of this compact that members should not be able to legally enforce its terms except in limited situations. The by-laws were not enforceable as part of the statutory contract created by the statute.[33] Young J stated that:

> merely because a committee has power under a constitution which is registered with the State to make By-laws does not make those By-laws part of the constitution of the company or give them the same status as the constitution of the company.[34]

Young J drew a categorical distinction between the corporation's memorandum and articles of association, regarded as a mutually enforceable contractual agreement, and the by-laws, regarded as having a lesser status. This decision was dictated by the terms of what is now s 140, but even within a contract-based framework it is a difficult distinction to justify.[35] Young J acknowledged as much when he conceded that the court would enforce the by-laws in cases where a member was expelled, where there was interference with the capacity of a salaried officer to earn income, or if there was a disturbance in the company which could only be solved by court intervention. From a constitutionalist perspective it is

---

[29]   In the UK, for example, see P Davies, *Gower and Davies' Principles of Modern Company Law* (7th ed, 2003) 55. In Australia the requirement for a memorandum and articles of association was replaced by a single constitution in 1998.
[30]   See R Hardin, 'Why a Constitution?' in B Grofman and D Wittman (eds), *The Federalist Papers and the New Institutionalism* (1989), arguing that constitutions are categorically distinct from the ideas of agreement and contract.
[31]   (1996) 14 ACLC 421.
[32]   The idea of the statutory contract is explained in Chapter 2 n 13 and accompanying text.
[33]   Above n 31. The judgement does not explain what a 'consensual compact' is.
[34]   Ibid, 425.
[35]   Not least because in this case the Articles of Association made express reference to the by-laws.

difficult to see why in cases such as this where the by-laws deal with fundamental aspects of membership, those by-laws should not be treated as part of a constitution which binds the members.

To be useful, a conception of the corporate constitution should be capable of extending beyond the formal statutory document. As I noted earlier, a constitution defines the place of members in an organisation — it constitutes them as members. More specifically, one function of a corporate constitution is to define who the members are and which interests of members are to count. We find similar concerns in the long-established body of case law that puts the interests of non-members, and the non-membership interests of members, outside the bounds of the corporate constitution.[36] This case law has drawn sharp lines between the statutory constitutional documents and so-called special contracts. It has also shown that defining what counts as a membership interest and what does not can sometimes be difficult and will vary from one corporation to another.[37] The argument here is that the courts should not be too quick to remove from consideration documents that play a key part in defining the members, their interests, or corporate decision-making processes. As the *Kogarah Golf Club Ltd* case indicates, there can be other sources that create or significantly affect the structure of authority relationships in a corporation that are not dealt with explicitly by its formal constitution, or which are dealt with only by implication. The formal internal rules alone, whilst important, will not reveal everything about 'the real ground rules for the scope and nature of corporate powers'.[38] Hence, a corporate constitution must be understood to include, or must be read in the context of, sources outside these internal rules.

This wider construction could, in certain cases, include shareholder agreements. Shareholder agreements are contractual arrangements between individual shareholders that bind the parties on matters such as the exercise of voting rights, buy-out of shares in the event of a dispute, and restrictions on the transfer of shares. Such agreements are typically found in small proprietary companies,[39] and in joint-venture companies. They often (though not necessarily) bind all shareholders in the company. Subject to a later comment, shareholder agreements could be regarded as part of the corporate constitution where they purport to affect or define the processes of decision-making in a corporation.[40] A

---

[36]   *Eley v Positive Government Security Life Assurance Company* (1876) 1 Ex D 88; *Hickman v Kent or Romney Marsh Sheep-Breeders' Association* [1915] 1 Ch 881.
[37]   See the High Court of Australia's decision in *Bailey v NSW Medical Defence Union Ltd* (1995) 13 ACLC 1689 holding that a clause in the constitution of a mutual insurance company that provided for the indemnification of members for liability arising from their medical practices did not confer an entitlement on them as members; criticised in M Whincop, 'A Relational and Doctrinal Critique of Shareholders' Special Contracts' (1997) 19 *Sydney Law Review* 314.
[38]   Eells, above n 9, 59.
[39]   Thus falling outside the parameters of this book.
[40]   Davies suggests that for this reason the UK *Companies Act 1985* s 35A(3)(b) includes shareholder agreements in the meaning of the constitution of a company for the purposes of sections dealing with outsiders and corporate contracts: above n 29, 66.

good example of why can be seen in *Hopkins v Foyster*[41] where a shareholders agreement was made between the corporation, its major shareholder, and 'each other person who becomes a shareholder of the Company'. The agreement dealt with the composition of the board of directors. Without deciding whether the agreement was binding, the court nevertheless granted an interim injunction to restrain the majority shareholders from exercising their voting rights at a general meeting on the grounds that the contractual rights of minority shareholders under the agreement might be infringed. Thus, in the court's view, the agreement was of sufficient weight to override the exercise of rights in the formal corporate constitution.

A further source of constitutional rules is found in the general corporations legislation. This includes, but extends beyond, those provisions that apply to a corporation as default constitutional terms.[42] To the extent that provisions in the legislation require, facilitate or constrain certain decision-making structures and processes within corporations, then those sections can be read as a part of a corporate constitution. This includes, for example, sections dealing with the rights of members to requisition or convene a special general meeting; sections that prescribe processes for the removal of directors; sections that prescribe methods for modifying the formal constitution; and sections that provide statutory rights of action for members (eg actions for oppressive conduct or derivative actions).[43] Necessarily it also includes binding judicial interpretations of those sections, as well as supplementary or complementary common law doctrines.[44] In this way a corporate constitution permits public values in corporate law (such as accountability and fairness) to be brought to bear on the power and authority structures of each corporation. In the same way, the 'text' of the corporate constitution also includes the fiduciary duties and the duty of care and diligence owed by directors to members.[45] The corporate constitution need not be restricted to the text of formal documents. As I noted in the conclusion to Chapter 2,

[41]   (2002) 20 ACLC 396.
[42]   In Australia, these are the 'replaceable rules' (found throughout the legislation) that apply to a corporation by virtue of *Corporations Act 2001* s 135 unless modified or replaced. In the United Kingdom a similar result is achieved through the model articles of association set out in Table A of the *Companies (Tables A to F) Regulations 1985*, applied by virtue of *Companies Act 1985* s 8(2).
[43]   In Australia these sections are: *Corporations Act 2001* ss 249D-249F (members' right to call meetings); ss 203C-203E (removal of directors); s 136 (modification of constitution); ss 232-235 (action for oppression); ss 236-242 (derivative action).
[44]   Stock exchange listing rules that impose similar requirements about company decisions should also be added to this picture.
[45]   The same argument applies to the proper purpose and absence of oppression requirements specified by the High Court in relation to alterations to the corporate constitution that involves an expropriation of shares: *Gambotto v WCP Ltd* (1995) 13 ACLC 342.

corporate constitutions have contract-like features, one of which is that, in appropriate circumstances, terms can be implied into the constitution.[46]

It is important to add that in order to properly understand the operation of a corporate constitution (in the expanded sense just described), account must also be taken of unwritten conventions, understandings and practices that lie outside the constitution but which commonly affect and guide the conduct of corporate directors, officers and members.[47] Constitutional lawyers have long recognised this point in relation to state constitutions.[48] Well-recognised and established conventions and practices can assist in the interpretation and affect the application of more formally expressed rules without being justiciable in themselves. The same is true for corporate constitutions.

One example of an accepted corporate 'convention' or practice is found in the appointment of directors to the boards of public corporations. Typically, a corporate constitution provides that the power to appoint directors lies with the members in general meeting. Even where the board has power to appoint a director in order to fill a casual vacancy, the usual requirement is that this appointment must be subsequently confirmed at a general meeting. All this suggests a level of shareholder control over board appointments that, in practice, is not often found. It is widely accepted that the power to make casual appointments, combined with the operation of the proxy system of voting, frequently gives the incumbent directors de facto control over the composition of the board;[49] it is not common for a general meeting to refuse to confirm a board appointment. This is reinforced by various corporate codes of conduct which urge the creation of board nomination committees and the need for careful succession planning by directors.[50]

There is a limit to the extent to which things such as shareholder agreements or implied terms can be given constitutional significance. It should

---

[46] H Ford, R Austin, I Ramsay, *Ford's Principles of Corporations Law* (12th ed, 2005) 189, citing *Stanham v National Trust of Australia* (NSW) (1989) 15 ACLR 87; 7 ACLC 628.

[47] Practices that are widely accepted in the corporate community are sometimes converted into formal requirements. For example, it is common practice in Australian listed corporations for the auditor to attend the AGM: S Bottomley, The Role of Shareholders' Meetings in Improving Corporate Governance (Research Report, Centre for Commercial Law, Australian National University, 2003) 32. In 2004 this was made a statutory obligation: s 250RA of the *Corporations Act* requires that auditors attend the annual general meetings of listed public companies.

[48] See, for example, S A de Smith and R Brazier, *Constitutional and Administrative Law* (7th ed, 1994) 27-41.

[49] See, for example, *Re Marra Developments Ltd* (1976) 1 ACLR 470.

[50] See, for example, the UK's *Combined Code on Corporate Governance* (2003) Principle A.4.1 <http://www.fsa.gov.uk/pubs/ukla/lr_comcode2003.pdf> at 5 Jan 2006; Australian Stock Exchange Corporate Governance Council, *Principles of Good Corporate Governance and Best Practice Recommendations* (2003), Recommendation 2.4.

always be kept in mind that 'a careful prospective shareholder'[51] may wish to know, before acquiring shares in a corporation, what rights and potential liabilities she may be exposed to, and how those rights and liabilities may be affected by the corporation's governance structures. Existing members 'should not become bound to do something unrelated by their membership of a company as a consequence of a provision one would not expect to find in the constitution of the company in question'.[52]

With this caution in mind, we arrive at a concept of a corporate constitution that can have many dimensions. It can be partly written, with elements that include the corporation's own formal internal rules and relevant sections of the legislation, and partly unwritten, including common law doctrines. This reflects the idea of a multi-dimensional constitution that is well recognised in the wider constitutionalist literature. With this in mind, Eells' definition of the corporate constitution is apt:

> [the corporate constitution is] that body of fundamental principles, whether codified or uncodified, written or unwritten, which in practice determines the authority and power relationships within the core area of administrative co-ordination and in the wider area of its contractual and noncontractual relationships with groups of interests that make contributions to and assert claims upon the corporation.[53]

It will be apparent from this description that there are aspects of the corporate constitution which cannot be determined or changed directly by the members of the corporation. To the extent that corporations legislation requires certain procedures or structures then its provisions prevail over those in the internal rules of a corporation. Moreover, those parts of the corporate constitution that are found in statute or in judicially created standards can be altered without the consent or involvement of the members. This is a necessary feature of a corporate constitutionalist model. The corporate constitution is more than an agreement or contract between constituents of the corporation. It embodies an allocation of powers and responsibilities between the state and the corporation and, within the corporation, between the corporators. Constitutional debate in the corporate context therefore takes place at two levels. One is societal. Since aspects of the corporations legislation form part of the corporate constitution then it is important that there be informed public debate about reforms to that legislation. The second level is intra-corporate, involving, for example, debates about amendments to the formal internal rules.

---

[51]   *Bratton Seymour Service Co Ltd v Oxborough* [1992] BCLC 693, 699 per Sir Christopher Slade.

[52]   *Bailey v NSW Medical Defence Union Ltd* (1995) 13 ACLC 1698, 1718 (McHugh and Gummow JJ).

[53]   Eells, above n 9, 85.

Balancing State and Corporate Inputs

Having established the idea that the corporate constitution is based on both state and corporate inputs, the next task is to consider the ways in which each might contribute to the overall constitutional framework. A range of possible approaches might be considered. For example: should the state supply broad standards, leaving it to the corporations to formulate more specific or detailed rules? Should the state deal only with extra-corporate affairs or only with non-member concerns, leaving internal member-related matters to be decided by each corporation? Should the state mandate certain structures and processes and, if so, to what extent?

The model outlined in this Chapter suggests that at a minimum there should be certain mandatory standards set by the state. I have suggested that these would include the avoidance of oppressive or unfair conduct and the need for financial and decision-making accountability. Enforcement of such standards would, in extreme cases, justify judicial intervention in a corporation's constitutional affairs. In Australia an example of this power is found in s 233(1)(c) of the *Corporations Act* which permits a court to make an order regulating the conduct of a corporation's affairs.[54] The corporate constitutionalist model also suggests that there will be a mix of empowering rules, facilitative rules, and guidelines. Corporators should be able to add their own constitutional rules and to vary optional rules supplied by the state, provided that this is done by expressly including provisions in the corporate constitution. The requirement of express alterations is not just for efficiency reasons, as Coffee argues,[55] but also for reasons of transparency. Such a requirement allows all corporators to see and assess the extent to which they might be compromising or advancing corporate values.

Beyond these broad observations, it is not feasible to prescribe a single, neat constitutional blueprint for all corporations in advance. The nature of the state's role will depend on factors such as the size and type of corporation (compare, for example, widely-held public companies, closely-held proprietary companies, and government-owned companies), the extent to which particular aspects of corporate law are statute-based or formed by common law, and whether those laws are expressed as rules or standards. For some types of corporate law issues, and for some types of companies, we may find that a standards-oriented approach is more appropriate. With closely-held companies, for example, where face-to-face negotiation is more likely, it might be thought preferable to rely on

---

[54] In *Hannes v MJH Pty Ltd* (1992) 10 ACLC 400 the NSW Court of Appeal held that the Court's power to alter the articles of association is limited — a Court's order should not alter the balance of power in the company radically (at 418).

[55] Coffee, above n 21, 1680-1681, argues that a requirement for express alteration of default rules is efficient because it creates an incentive for careful and precise formulation of the terms of corporate rules.

standards rather than detailed prescription.[56] It is clear the question of the state's regulatory role is complex, requiring attention (at minimum) to issues of organisational theory, law, and political theory.

So much for what I have called the 'external aspect' of the corporate constitution — the aspect that locates each corporation in its wider political, economic and social context. This discussion forms the backdrop for the other part of the picture which occupies the remainder of this book — the role of the corporate constitution in internal corporate relations.

The Internal Aspect of Corporate Constitutions

I suggested earlier that a corporation can be described as a constitutional arrangement in which individual interests are expressed and group decisions are made. As Bratton describes it, corporations 'advance each participant's self-interest, but they also demand individual sacrifices to effectuate collective goals'.[57] The formation of a corporation brings together the individual and private concerns and interests of shareholders and directors,[58] and gives those concerns and interests a collective (or a corporate) dimension. Thus, each participant in a corporation is part of a set of corporate interests while, at the same time, retaining interests that are individual or personal. To illustrate this point by analogy, as a member of my community I have a dual status as a voter (one of my public roles) and as a parent (one of my private roles). Similarly, a shareholder can be regarded both as a member of a company (their corporate role) and also an investor in the securities market (one of their personal or individual roles). Much time is spent in the corporate law literature defending or promoting the latter dimension of corporate share ownership. The point being emphasised here is that each shareholder also has a role (potential or actual) in the corporate dimension of each company in which they hold shares.

The legal model of the corporation already recognises these two dimensions of corporate life — the corporate and the individual — although not without some confusion. For example, the basic fiduciary duty of a director stresses the importance of protecting the interests of 'the company as a whole', which is sometimes taken to mean 'the interests of the shareholders as a whole' or 'the interests of the corporators as a general body'.[59] Likewise, the *Corporations Act* gives the courts wide powers to intervene when the conduct of a corporation's affairs is contrary to the interests of the members as a whole.[60] At the same time,

---

[56] Coffee, ibid 1677, disagrees, suggesting that the close relations between corporators in this type of company may impede effective negotiation, thereby justifying the need for mandatory rules.

[57] Above n 6, 690.

[58] As a reminder, and as foreshadowed in Chapter 1, I am using the standard legal model of the limited liability public company with share capital as the basis for my argument.

[59] *Greenhalgh v Arderne Cinemas Ltd* [1951] Ch 286.

[60] *Corporations Act 2001* s 232(d).

corporate law recognises that an individual member may take action to protect their personal rights against intrusions by the majority of members.[61] A key function of a corporate constitution is to establish structures and processes for mediating these two dimensions of corporate life. In other words, corporate constitutionalism can do for shareholders in corporations what a wider theory of constitutionalism does for citizens in society at large.

The rest of this book is concerned principally with a more detailed examination of how these two internal dimensions — the individual and the collective — interact.[62] This examination is conducted under three headings, each of which refers to a key constitutional value or principle that ought to be reflected in every corporate constitution.

Three Principles of Corporate Constitutionalism

The three principles identified here are accountability, deliberation, and contestability. In the remainder of this Chapter I give a brief outline of each of these principles, and explain why I have highlighted them. They are each subjected to a more detailed analysis in the three subsequent chapters.

These three principles — jointly and severally — are concerned with decision-making in corporations. Each of these three aspects of corporate constitutionalism stems from the idea that decision-making is a central part of corporate life. Indeed, some organisational theorists claim that 'decision-making is *the* organisational activity'.[63] Decisions — and here I refer to decisions that have strategic importance for the corporation — must be made about the deployment of assets, raising of corporate finance, management, employment, production, marketing, business expansion or contraction and so on. Of course decisions such as these are rarely isolated events; a decision is usually the outcome of many other actions and decisions that occur throughout the corporate organisation.[64] Actual decision-making processes are likely to vary from one company to another, and within a large corporation there will be many decision-making sites. The fact remains, however, that a large part of corporate life is devoted to the processes of decision-making.[65] Those processes are political in nature.[66] They require the

---

[61] See, for example, *Residues Treatment & Trading Co Ltd v Southern Resources Ltd* (1988) 6 ACLC 1160, and *Gambotto v WCP Ltd* (1995) 13 ACLC 342.

[62] The term 'collective' in this context does not imply that there will necessarily be consensus on all issues. In many instances it will simply mean that there has been a joint decision.

[63] A Pettigrew, *The Politics of Organisational Decision-Making* (1973) 5, citing Chester Barnard, *The Functions of the Executive* (1938) and Herbert Simon, *Administrative Behaviour* (1957).

[64] G Parry, 'The Idea of Political Participation' in G Parry (ed), *Participation in Politics* (1972) 1, 6.

[65] G Lowe, 'Corporations as Objects of Regulation' (1987) 5 *Law in Context* 35.

[66] Pettigrew, above n 63, chapter 2.

exercise of power and authority, they will involve strategies and tactics, they will have implications for resource allocation and control, and they will be affected by problems of hierarchy and specialization.

I have noted already that the law on corporate governance is concerned primarily with the decisions that are made by directors in corporate board rooms and, to a lesser extent, by shareholders in general meetings.[67] A large part of modern corporate law is devoted to rules, doctrines and standards dealing with different aspects of these decision-making forums. There are, for example, rules governing the production of information that is relevant to prospective decisions (eg annual financial reporting requirements); rules relating to the convening and conduct of meetings; and rules prescribing standards for decision-making (eg the duty of directors to exercise care and diligence and the business judgement rule).[68]

Implicit in these rules, doctrines and standards is the idea that shareholders do have a role to play in corporate decision-making. It may be a role that is exercised only intermittently, and it is a role that is heavily circumscribed by legal principles, but nevertheless it has remained as one of the cornerstones of corporate law in jurisdictions such as Australia and the United Kingdom. A corporation is not presumed to be a directors' autocracy. While it is true that some corporations may in practice become autocracies — perhaps through the appointment of a governing director, or as a result of being wholly-owned by one shareholder — the point remains that this is not the model that is assumed by corporate law or by the corporate governance literature. So this analysis proceeds on the basis that corporations are decision-making institutions, and that shareholders play an important, if underrated, role in those processes.

Why choose these three particular principles? Acknowledging that different versions of constitutional theory will likely generate different principles,[69] I suggest that a model of inclusive or responsive decision-making should seek to emphasise three things: (1) the importance of access to information so that decisions are properly informed; (2) the need to provide opportunities for involvement in decision-making so that the information can be properly assessed and debated by those who will be affected by the decision; and (3) the availability of mechanisms to challenge and review decisions after they have been made.[70] The principles of accountability, deliberation and contestability represent the corporate versions of this list. In a corporate setting the law limits shareholder access to corporate information. This is because of the need to protect sensitive information:

---

[67] Of course, in the case of a company that is insolvent (or is nearly insolvent) the focus shifts to decisions made by creditors and by administrators or liquidators.
[68] Eg *Corporations Act 2001* s 180.
[69] See R West, 'Progressive and Conservative Constitutionalism' (1990) 88 *Michigan Law Review* 641.
[70] In one of those serendipitous moments that characterises much research, the formulation of this list was crystallised for me by a chance reading of Principle 10 of the United Nations Conference on Environment and Development, *Rio Declaration on Environment and Development* (1992) <http://www.un.org/documents/ga/conf151/aconf15126-1annex1.htm> at 27 May 2004.

shareholders do not owe duties of loyalty to the corporation. Under Australian corporate law, a member must obtain the consent of the directors or the general meeting, or a court order, to inspect the books of their corporation.[71] In the absence of a general right to receive information, shareholders must be assured that those who do have the information are using it responsibly and effectively. So, in the corporate context, the principle of accountability substitutes for the idea of access to information. Similarly, as I have already noted, legal and practical considerations mean that there are few opportunities for participation in corporate decision-making. As I hope to show, deliberation provides a useful standard by which to assess involvement in corporate decisions. The third principle — contestability — meets the requirement of having review mechanisms.

The ideas of accountability, deliberation and contestability draw our attention to the structures and processes of corporate decision-making. These principles should not necessarily be read as descriptions of what actually occurs within every corporation. Nor will they necessarily be found stated expressly in corporate constitutional texts. This is an evaluative exercise; these principles provide benchmarks against which actual corporate practice and its legal regulation can be assessed. At the same time, these principles are not new or foreign to corporate law and corporate governance. Examples of each can be found in current corporate law doctrine, although their importance is often under-emphasized and under-estimated by corporate lawyers and corporate personnel.

Accountability

The first principle — accountability — is familiar to corporate directors, shareholders, and regulators. Much of our present corporations legislation and regulatory regime is concerned with establishing and enforcing mechanisms of accountability. Corporate lawyers have long been alert to the problems of promoting and ensuring accountability. We see this, for example, in debates about how corporate managers can best be monitored (should this be left to the marketplace or is some degree of public regulation required?), about the effectiveness of mandatory disclosure requirements,[72] and about how to ensure auditor independence.[73]

---

[71] *Corporations Act 2001* ss 247A and 247D. The capacity of the directors or the general meeting to grant this authority requires that the corporation's constitution contain a clause to that effect (s 247D).

[72] For example, J Coffee, 'Market Failure and the Economic Case for a Mandatory Disclosure System' (1984) 70 *Virginia Law Review* 717; I Ramsay, 'Models of Corporate Regulation: The Mandatory/Enabling Debate' in C Rickett and R Grantham (eds), *Corporate Personality in The 20th Century* (1998).

[73] For example, I Ramsay, *Independence of Australian Company Auditors: Review of Current Australian Requirements and Proposals for Reform*, Department of Treasury, Canberra (2001); Joint Standing Committee on Public Accounts and Audit, Parliament of Australia, *Review of Independent Auditing by Registered Company Auditors*, Report 391 (2002).

These familiar manifestations of the accountability question can disguise the variety of dimensions and meanings that may be attached to the term 'accountability'. To 'be accountable' can mean simply providing accurate information about financial and operational performance at regular intervals or, going one step further, it can mean providing an explanation of, or a justification for, actions that have been taken. An even stronger sense of accountability requires that persons be held responsible for their actions. Along with these different modes of accountability, consideration must also be given to the timeframe for accountability (for example, should it be ex ante or ex post, or both?), the different arenas within which accountability is exercised (for example, board meetings, audit committees, general meetings, and the marketplace), and the different instruments of accountability (for example, deliberation at a general meeting, or independent audits).[74]

A system of corporate accountability must include requirements that force office-holders and decision-makers to give an account of their use of office and power and to comply with relevant rules and standards. But it must also provide a framework that can protect against the improper exercise of power in the first place, with the aim of diffusing corporate decision-making power while at the same time rendering it accountable through a plurality of checks and balances. I argue that this can be achieved through a division and a separation of decision-making power in corporations.

First, there is a formal division of decision-making authority between the board of directors and the general meeting of members. Corporate decision-making has a dual structure. Economic theory tells us that the purpose of this division between decision and risk-bearing functions is to reduce the transaction and opportunity costs for shareholders.[75] Managerial theory tells us that the division allows the appointment of directors with skill and expertise to run the corporation for the benefit of the shareholders.[76] This is all true, but there is a further reason for this division of power. As I suggested earlier, the key function of a corporation is to work for the common good of all of its members. Republican theory argues that defining what the common good is on a given issue at a given time requires that decision-makers should stand aside from their private interests and make impartial judgements. It is possible that shareholders could do this — possible, but not certain. So, we require a separate body of decision-makers, selected by the shareholders and responsible to them, to make these judgements. Thus, it is the fundamental duty of directors to make non-sectional decisions, to act for the benefit of the shareholders as a whole. The directors must do this accountably, and so an important function of the corporate constitution is to constitute these two separate decision-making sites, to confer specific decision-making powers on each

---

[74] The idea that there are different arenas and instruments of accountability is suggested by John Uhr, *Deliberative Democracy in Australia* (1998) 158.

[75] See, for example, E Fama and M Jensen, 'Separation of Ownership and Control' (1983) 26 *Journal of Law and Economics* 301.

[76] See the discussion in W Bratton, 'The "Nexus of Contracts" Corporation: A Critical Appraisal' (1989) 74 *Cornell Law Review* 407, 413-414.

of them, to regulate the exercise of those powers, and to guard against encroachment by one upon the other. As will be seen in Chapter 4, the significance of this dual structure is not diminished by the fact that decisions by members in general meetings are much less frequent and concern a narrower range of topics than those made by the board of directors. If for no other reason, this dual structure is crucial to achieving accountability because of the power of the general meeting over the election and dismissal of directors.

Secondly, there should be a separation of powers within the corporation. Constitutional and public lawyers talk about the classical separation of legislative, executive and judicial powers. In the corporate constitutional context I use the idea of separation of powers in a broader and looser sense.[77] Corporate decision-making is not restricted to the formal division between the board and the general meeting, so a separation argument is not limited to the formal aspects of decision-making power, and it has a broad definition of the types of power with which we should be concerned. Thus, as will be seen in Chapter 4, in a corporate context the separation of powers (or, to be precise, the separations of powers) means paying attention to the role of independent non-executive directors, independent chairpersons, external and internal auditors, institutional shareholders and other related elements of corporate organisations. There is nothing new in highlighting the role of these corporate players — indeed this is the bread and butter of the corporate governance literature. However there *is* something new, for corporate lawyers at least, about conceptualising these issues in terms of a separation of powers.

Accountability by itself does not supply a sufficient rationale for the division and separation of decision-making power in the corporation. It is only one part of the corporate constitutionalist picture. For one thing, if accountability was all that was required, the need to hold actual meetings might be called into question. Furthermore, flaws in one aspect of the accountability framework (such as poor audit practices) must be capable of being dealt with or remedied by other means, such as processes of deliberation at company meetings, or through contestation by members.

Deliberation

The principle of deliberation seeks to ensure that, as far as possible, the processes of corporate decision-making are open and genuine, that they are based on consideration of all relevant arguments (as opposed to a mere aggregation of votes), and that they are capable of producing decisions that represent a collective judgement about the issue at hand. Corporate decision-making will be legitimate insofar as it is a consequence of deliberative processes that meet these criteria.

I will postpone a detailed explanation of this definition of deliberation until Chapter 5, but some brief points can be made here (all of which are elaborated in the later Chapter). First, in assessing the quality of corporate decision-making,

---

[77]   This approach follows the argument in J Braithwaite, 'On Speaking Softly and Carrying Big Sticks: Neglected Dimensions of a Republican Separation of Powers' (1997) 47 *University of Toronto Law Journal* 305.

the principle of deliberation directs our attention to *how* a decision is made, not simply to the content of the decision itself or whether it is supported by the requisite number of votes. Deliberation reminds us that the process of reaching a decision is as important as the decision itself. In particular, it tells us to take meetings seriously. Secondly, the idea of deliberation does not mean that every decision must be unanimous. Deliberation is consistent with majority voting but — importantly — it is inconsistent with majority domination of decision-making processes. Thirdly, in a corporate context, deliberative processes do not necessarily require full and direct participation by all persons who are affected by the decision, nor do they presume any particular mode of participation. Board meetings and general meetings are the main deliberative forums of a corporation, but they are not the only forums. In Chapter 5 we will see that the nature of share ownership in the modern public listed corporation requires a wider application of the deliberative principle to ensure the quality of decision-making processes. As I will argue, this might include the use of internet chat-sites, the business media, and mechanisms to represent particular interests at general meetings.

Corporate law already embodies the principle of deliberative decision-making in a number of ways, even though this is often overlooked or not realised. As I have noted already, corporations legislation typically contains detailed procedural requirements for the calling and conduct of meetings, including notice requirements[78] as well as voting, quorum, proxy and minutes requirements.[79] A clear instance of the deliberative principle is found in s 250S of the *Corporations Act 2001*, which requires the chair of a public company annual general meeting to allow a reasonable opportunity for the members as a whole to ask questions about or make comments on the management of the company. All of these requirements are premised on the idea that the general meeting is a forum in which issues will be raised and arguments will be heard, following which decisions will be made. Further evidence of the deliberative principle can be found in case law concerning the duties of care and diligence owed by company directors. Since the 1990s a succession of decisions in the Australian courts[80] has stressed the obligation of each director in a company to participate actively in the board's decision-making processes.

Despite these legal resonances, there is still room for debate about the importance of deliberation in the corporate decision-making context. In Chapter 5 I chart a course between two possible extremes in this debate. At one extreme, critics of deliberation might argue that the size and diversity of most public company share registers means that for practical purposes general meetings can be little more than ritualised affairs, and that deliberative decision-making in such a context is an impossible ideal. Moreover, it might be argued that an emphasis on

---

[78] In Australia see *Corporations Act 2001* ss 249H – L.
[79] For general meetings, see s 249T [quorum]; ss 250E – M [voting]; ss 249X – 250D [proxies]; s 251A – B [minutes]. For directors' meetings, see s 248F [quorum]; s. 248G [voting].
[80] For example, *Statewide Tobacco Services Ltd v Morley* (1990) 8 ACLC 827; *Daniels v Anderson* (1995) 13 ACLC 614.

deliberation at meetings has the potential to impede timely, efficient and effective decision-making. At the other extreme, some advocates of deliberation might argue that we cannot choose to be only a little deliberative. The argument might be made that proper deliberation requires the full and equal participation of all shareholders (at least) on all significant corporate decisions. The task in a corporate setting, as I argue in Chapter 5, is to avoid each of these extremes. We should not promote efficient decision-making at the expense of deliberation, but neither should we promote deliberation at the expense of effective decision-making.

The final point to emphasise about deliberation — for the moment — is that deliberative processes by themselves are not enough. For example, a board that meets its deliberative obligations must also meet the requirement to be accountable (as discussed above) and there must be possibilities for contestability.

Contestability

The third principle of corporate constitutionalism is contestability. [81] In the corporate context, contestability refers to the permanent possibility that members (or directors) [82] of a corporation can effectively contest decisions that conflict with the corporation's interests as they are perceived by those persons.

I examine the detail of this idea in Chapter 6. For the moment, the importance of contestability in a corporate context can be illustrated in the following way. Imagine a system of corporate law in which directors and managers were free to make decisions without fear of challenge or liability. Imagine, in particular, that company members had no effective recourse to challenge the improper exercise of power by directors or managers. Such a system would be likely to encourage some level of self-interested decision-making by directors and managers, and that possibility alone would be likely to create mistrust and suspicion in the minds of the members. It would not matter whether the actual decisions being made in a corporation were proper or improper; the fact that they were beyond challenge would make them all suspect. One response to this might be to argue that the quality of the decisions could be judged by the results for the corporation and its members. The various markets for corporate control, for corporate managers, and for the company's products and services could assess the quality of decisions and supply the necessary corrective influence. One problem with this argument is that members could not have any ex ante confidence in directors' decisions — they would always have to wait for ex post results. Another

---

[81]   I have adapted this idea from Philip Pettit's work, principally his book on *Republicanism*, above n 12, together with more recent work, cited in Chapter 6 of this book.

[82]   Although my focus is on contestation by members, in some instances a director may want to contest a decision made by directors and members. In *Talbot v NRMA Ltd* (2000) 18 ACLC 600 the Supreme Court of New South Wales stated that before taking such a step, a director must believe that the litigation will be in the company's best interests and that he or she would be in breach of his or her own duties by not taking the action.

problem with the ex post argument is that it slides easily into the belief that the ends will always justify the means and that a beneficial outcome is good, regardless of how it has been achieved. If, instead, a corporate law system has clear mechanisms for contestability then there is scope for ex ante confidence. Members can assume that directors make their decisions against the threat of challenge where, for example, those decisions are contaminated by improper self-interest. A contestatory system directs attention to the procedures by which decisions are made as much as to the substance of those decisions.

Another response to the hypothetical posed above might be to say that the decisions would be legitimated by the ideas of consent and majority-rule. Members, it might be argued, are presumed to have consented to the distribution of decision-making power in their company. This consent is implied from the act of voluntarily purchasing shares and thereby accepting the terms of the corporate contract. A key term of that contract is the idea of majority decision-making. The problem with this argument is that when these two ideas — implied consent and majority rule — are brought together, they can create and disguise problems such as lack of accountability, oppressive or self-serving behaviour by directors or majority shareholders, and a slide from majority decision-making to majority domination of decision-making processes. Contestability works differently as a legitimating mechanism, because every decision is made against the *factual* possibility that it might be contested by the members and thereby be subject to review.

Corporate law is already familiar with mechanisms of contestability. These include the action for oppressive or unfair conduct (in Australia found in *Corporations Act 2001* Part 2F.1), the statutory derivative action (found in Part 2F.1A of the Act), actions to protect class rights (Part 2F.2), and the injunction remedy (s 1324). In Chapter 6 I will examine in more detail the value of some of these actions as contestability mechanisms.

Three further, interrelated, points can be noted briefly about the principle of contestability. First, it does not require that there actually be contestation of each and every corporate decision or action. What is important is that the *possibility* of contestation should be realised, and be realistic.[83] The second point is related to this: contestability does not mean condoning any and all claims by dissenting or disgruntled members. Contestability is not the same thing as giving each member a potential power of veto over each decision. Being in the minority on an issue does not of itself activate the principle of contestability. Similarly, contestability mechanisms must be able to weed out frivolous or vexatious challenges. The criterion for determining what interests should be counted as relevant or non-frivolous will necessarily be couched in general terms, such as 'the interests of the members as a whole', but at their base they are — to adapt Pettit's description — the interests that those who are part of a system of government within a corporation may reasonably expect that system to track.[84] Thirdly, contestability relies on the

---

[83]   Pettit, above n 12, 185.

[84]   P Pettit, 'Republican Freedom and Contestatory Democratization' in I Shapiro and C Hacker-Cordón (eds) *Democracy's Value* (1999) 163, 176.

capacity and willingness of members to challenge decisions that do not meet this criterion, rather than selling their shares and leaving the corporation. That is, contestability promotes the exercise of 'voice' over the option of 'exit'.[85] Again, the point is not to rule out exit as an appropriate response in a given situation; instead, the aim is to resuscitate the use of voice as a response.

Contestability will work effectively if there are adequate mechanisms for accountability, ensuring the provision of information and explanations, and ensuring, by a separation of powers, that the powers of members are not eroded. Contestability can also be enhanced, and its possible overuse curbed, by proper deliberative procedures.

Conclusion

This Chapter has outlined the framework of corporate constitutionalism. It is worth repeating that I have used the term 'framework' deliberately, in preference to 'theory'. Unlike a theory of the corporation, corporate constitutionalism does not try to predict the outcomes of corporate decision-making, nor does it mandate particular outcomes. Instead, it requires that corporations should have in place structures and processes that embody certain values and principles, and that decisions should be assessed by reference to the operation of those structures and processes.

I have explained in this Chapter that the corporate constitutional framework has an external aspect, serving to connect the public regulation of corporations with the private ordering of corporate affairs. The focal point of that connection is the corporate constitution which, as this Chapter has explained, is comprised of state and corporate inputs, both written and unwritten. The other aspect of corporate constitutionalism is internal. Here we are concerned with interaction between the individual and the collective dimensions of corporate life, mediating the personal and private concerns of individual members with the collective and corporate concerns of the company as a whole.

The internal aspect of the corporate constitution was then elaborated by introducing three key principles of corporate constitutionalism — deliberation, accountability, and contestability. Although I will describe and assess them one at a time in the following chapters, they are, and must be, interdependent, as I will explain in Chapter 7.[86]

Another point that has been emphasised in this Chapter is that aspects of these three principles can easily be read into the existing formal legal model of the company (eg the separation of function between the board and the general meeting). Other aspects (such as the idea of deliberation) require us to make a more conscious reappraisal of that model. But I have argued that there is nothing in this framework that is completely foreign to the basic legal structures within which

---

85   Hirschman, above n 2.
86   Pettit suggests, however, that contestability underlies other 'democratic desiderata', including deliberation, and the division and separation of powers – see above n 84, 185.

corporate entities operate everyday. As I noted in Chapter 1, the purpose of a corporate constitutional framework is to reconceptualise existing rules and practices, rather than to argue for a radical reformation of the corporate form.

Finally, as this Chapter has made clear, corporate constitutionalism is concerned primarily with issues of structure and process, rather than with substantive legal doctrines. In the next three Chapters I examine in closer detail the implications of each of the three principles of corporate constitutionalism for the structures and processes of corporate governance. Chapter 4 deals with accountability, emphasising structural questions, particularly the importance of divisions between the board and the general meeting, and separations of power within the corporate structure (eg the need for independent directors and external auditors). In Chapter 5 the analysis of deliberation focuses on the processes and conduct of company general meetings and board meetings. Chapter 6 argues for the importance of ensuring mechanisms of contestability by analysing the role of the statutory derivative action and the action for oppression or unfairness.

Chapter 4

Corporate Accountability

Introduction

Shareholders and directors are familiar with the idea of accountability. A large part of our system of corporate law rules and doctrines is concerned with mechanisms for achieving financial and fiduciary accountability. When those rules fail, each new wave of corporate collapses seems to herald a re-examination of these corporate accountability systems. Of course, the corporate world does not have a monopoly on the concept of accountability. Accountability seems to be regarded as an unqualified good by anyone who has an interest in processes of governance, whether private or public. But the ubiquity of the concept, and the often casual way in which it is invoked, suggests that it might also be problematical, too vague to be useful in assessing or controlling corporate behaviour. As one commentator has warned:

> [accountability] has been viewed as both an end and a means; it has been defined in terms of procedures, results, disclosure of information, recourse, and compliance with regulations; and it is often indistinguishable from such concepts as evaluation, efficiency, effectiveness, control and responsibility.[1]

Certainly there is a risk that because it is used in so many different contexts, proponents of accountability will talk past each other, relying on different assumptions about what the concept means and what structures and processes are to be counted as delivering accountable behaviour. As a result, the idea of accountability may be devalued. This Chapter begins, therefore, with a brief description of the dimensions of accountability that are relevant to the corporate context. The purpose of this discussion is to set the parameters for the remainder of the Chapter, which is concerned with examining the structures that are necessary to achieve accountability in a corporate constitutional framework.

---

[1]   R Kramer, *Voluntary Agencies in the Welfare State* (1981) at 290. For a more recent critique see R Mulgan, '"Accountability": An Ever-Expanding Concept?' (2000) 78 *Public Administration* 555.

The Many Dimensions of Accountability

There are several questions that must be answered when we insist that corporate behaviour should be accountable. What conduct will satisfy the requirement for accountable behaviour in (or by) a corporation? Who should be accountable? To whom should they be accountable? When should accountability be provided? Addressing each of these questions reveals even more dimensions of the concept.

There are different criteria for deciding whether a particular corporation, or group of decision-makers within a corporation, is being accountable. A corporation may be said to be accountable if it provides accurate information about its activities when it is required to do so. This type of accountability has been described as 'accounting for' or 'accountability as verification',[2] and it is the focus of the financial reporting and disclosure provisions that are a familiar feature in modern corporate law statutes. To paraphrase John Uhr, accountability through disclosure has the aim of allowing members and others to compare what corporations and their managers say they are doing with investigations of what corporations and their managers are actually doing.[3] This is summed up in Brandeis' well-known aphorism that '[s]unlight is ... the best of disinfectants; electric light the most efficient policeman'.[4]

A stronger form of accountability requires that in addition to providing information, the corporation or corporate decision-maker should be able to explain or justify its actions. This is accountability in the sense of 'accounting to', or 'explanatory accountability'.[5] An opportunity for this form of accountability can be found in those provisions of the Australian *Corporations Act* that require company members to be given a reasonable opportunity to question the directors and the auditor about company management or the audit process.[6] We can make a further distinction between weak and strong forms of explanatory accountability, depending on whether the explanation is primarily reactive and defensive (providing explanations only when asked and only about what has been asked) or proactive and responsive (offering information and anticipating the concerns of the accountability audience).[7] Corporate laws may influence the options here. For example, under the rules governing the continuous disclosure of information, a

---

[2]   J Uhr, 'Redesigning accountability: From muddles to maps' (1993) 65 *Australian Quarterly* 1.

[3]   J Uhr, 'Accountability, Scrutiny and Oversight' (Background paper prepared for The Commonwealth Secretariat Canberra Workshop, May 2001) 4.

[4]   L Brandeis, *Other People's Money and How the Bankers Use It* (first published 1914, 1995 ed) 89.

[5]   Uhr, above n 3.

[6]   See ss 250PA, 250S and 250T.

[7]   Uhr, above n 3, 8.

listed company in Australia must disclose price sensitive information to the Australian Stock Exchange immediately the company becomes aware of it.[8]

Finally, an even stronger form of accountability requires that the corporation or the decision-maker should also be held responsible for its activities, thus providing accountability in the sense of 'being held to account'; we can call this 'accountability as responsibility'. This version of accountability is found in one of the cornerstones of corporate law—the requirement that directors, as fiduciaries, owe duties to the company for which they can be held personally liable.[9]

Along with these different types of accountability there are choices about who should be held accountable or who should provide the accountability (and in a large corporation this is not necessarily the same thing).[10] In large corporations we typically concentrate on the primary accountability requirements that are imposed on the individuals who direct and manage the corporation. But the range of potential 'accountors' is greater than this. Mark Bovens provides a typology of four candidates for accountability which, in theory, can apply in large organisations.[11] First, individuals in the organisation may be accountable to the extent that their actions contributed to the organisation's conduct; secondly, there is the possibility of corporate accountability, where the organisation is held to account as if it were an autonomous actor; thirdly, a system of hierarchical accountability makes the people at the top of the organisation's management hierarchy accountable for the conduct of the entire organisation; and fourthly, Bovens posits the idea of collective accountability, where everyone in the organisation is personally accountable in equal measure for the conduct of the organisation.

To whom should these accountors (whoever they are) be accountable? The standard corporate model in countries such as Australia, the United Kingdom and the United States dictates that while the company is solvent the shareholders are the primary accountability audience. Once more, however, in most corporations the range of potential 'accountees' is more diverse than this. It certainly includes the shareholders (recognising that this usually includes large or institutional shareholders along with a diversified group of other shareholders), but, stepping outside the parameters of corporate law, it can be expanded to include secured creditors, regulatory agencies (whether public, quasi-public, [12] or non-government)[13] and consumers.

---

[8] *Corporations Act 2001* s 674, ASX Listing Rule 3.1

[9] Mulgan argues that being called to account is the 'core sense' of accountability and that we should limit our use of the term to this – see above, n 1.

[10] An extreme example is the 'vice-president responsible for going to jail' described in J Braithwaite, *Corporate Crime in the Pharmaceutical Industry* (1984) 308.

[11] M Bovens, *The Quest for Responsibility – Accountability and Citizenship in Complex Organisations* (1998)

[12] For example, stock-exchanges.

[13] An Australian example is the Australian Banking Industry Ombudsman.

Another question concerns the timeliness of the accountability. There are three obvious possibilities. Ex ante accountability is provided before significant policy or resource decisions are made; process accountability occurs while policies are being implemented and resources are being used; and ex post accountability operates after the event. [14] As Goldring and Thynne point out, different accountability timeframes will apply depending upon who the accountability audience is, and on the method by which that accountability is conveyed. For example, the financial accountability of a company to most of its shareholders is usually ex post, however accountability to significant major shareholders may also be ex ante.

This discussion does not exhaust the ways in which the concept of accountability can be dissected. Other dimensions can be added to this picture — for example, we can distinguish between horizontal accountability (accountability between groups, individuals or agents who are roughly equal in power and authority, such as the accountability of individual directors to the board as a whole) and vertical accountability (accountability between groups, individuals or agents who stand in principal and subordinate relationships with each other). [15] As a further example, we can place different forms or modes of accountability along a scale that ranges from 'internal' accountability to 'external' corporate accountability. Examples of internal accountability include the managerial accountability of senior executives to the board of directors, or the accountability of a board sub-committee to the whole board. The prime example of external accountability is found in the various obligations imposed on corporations to report to public regulators, but we can add other examples, including court cases in which the actions of directors are examined.

Questions of Structure and Process

Clearly, the idea of accountability is capable of being used and applied in different ways. I do not intend to enter the debate about the 'proper' meaning or usage of the concept. [16] Instead, this brief survey is a reminder that in thinking about accountability we ought to be concerned with accountability processes and structures as much as we are with the content or subject matter of the accountability obligations. Much of the debate about corporate accountability has been concerned with the latter — for example, whether the focus of the law should be confined to financial and fiduciary reporting, or whether the obligations should be widened to the 'triple bottom line' of financial, environmental and social concerns. It is only relatively recently that the corporate governance literature has begun to concentrate on process and structure issues (for example, questions of auditor independence, the composition of corporate boards, or the need for board

---

[14] J Goldring and I Thynne, *Accountability and Control – Government Officials and the Exercise of Power* (1987) 226.

[15] Uhr, above n 3, 14-15.

[16] See, eg, Mulgan, above n 1.

sub-committees). The remainder of this Chapter examines these issues. It is concerned with examining the corporate structures and processes in which, and by which, accountability can be achieved (regardless of whether accountability has a single or a triple bottom line). More particularly, the Chapter examines how a constitutional framework can help us to identify and assess these structures and processes.

The concern, then, is to establish and maintain structures and processes that can guard against unauthorised, overreaching or inadequate exercises of authority and power in a corporate decision-making system. In a nutshell, I argue that the construction of an effective corporate accountability structure must involve both the division and the separation of corporate decision-making powers. These two concepts are, of course, familiar features of the federal systems of liberal constitutional government in countries such as Australia, Canada and the United States.[17] The arguments developed in this Chapter differ considerably from public constitutional doctrines, although the underlying concerns are similar. That is, by seeking to ensure the possibility that decision makers will be held accountable, the aim is to control or constrain the exercise of power within political systems.[18]

The remainder of this Chapter is concerned with how divisions and separations of power can be achieved in the corporate context. It is worth repeating here what was said in Chapter 2 — this is not an argument that corporations are analogous to public constitutional governmental systems. Corporations *are* constitutional systems, and so there are some core constitutional concepts that can usefully be deployed in corporate analysis. But they are constitutional systems of a unique kind, so those concepts must be amended to meet the demands of corporate government. In the remainder of this Chapter I discuss, firstly, the division of decision-making power between the board of directors and the general meeting of shareholders and then, secondly, the need for multiple separations of power within a company's decision-making processes. The structures and processes that will be referred to are already well known to those who are familiar with the corporate governance literature, although their significance as accountability mechanisms is not always recognised. Through a constitutional framework we can reassess these structures in terms of their significance for ensuring structural accountability in the corporation.

Dual Decision-making

As I noted in an earlier Chapter, the corporate law systems of Australia, the United Kingdom and similar jurisdictions recognise only two formal decision-making sites in a corporation while it is solvent — the board of directors and meetings of

---

[17] See, for example, M J C Vile, *Constitutionalism and the Separation of Powers* (1967) 7.
[18] Mulgan, above n 1, 563.

shareholders.[19] Depending on the jurisdiction, the law either prescribes or presumes that the directors will exercise the general power of company management, including the power to appoint the officers who will carry out the board's directions.[20] At the same time, through a combination of legislation, individual corporate constitutions and stock exchange listing rules, decisions on certain matters are reserved exclusively for the members in general meeting. These matters include the election and removal of directors, appointment and removal of the corporation's external auditor, amendments to the corporation's own constitution, and certain changes to the corporate share structure (eg reductions of share capital). Further powers are given to the members by common law principles — most significantly, the power to ratify a breach of fiduciary duty by directors.[21] Members' decisions are constrained by a variety of constitutional conditions, including notice requirements and special majority voting requirements.

Since the 1906 case of *Automatic Self-Cleansing Filter Syndicate Co Ltd v Cunninghame*,[22] courts in the United Kingdom and Australia have accepted that where the board of directors is given exclusive powers to manage the corporation then neither individual members nor the general meeting may intervene in or dictate the exercise of that power.[23] It follows from this that the board of directors is not simply the servant or agent of the general meeting. The board exercises an original grant of power. This point was made clear in the 1935 case of *John Shaw & Sons (Salford) Ltd v Shaw*. In a blunt summation of the legal position, Greer LJ stated that:

> [I]f powers of management are vested in the directors, they and they alone can exercise those powers. The only way in which the general body of shareholders can control the exercise of the powers vested ... in the directors is by altering their [constitution], or ... by refusing to re-elect the directors of whose actions they disapprove. They cannot themselves usurp the powers which by the [corporation's

---

[19] In Australia, for example, see *Corporations Act 2001* Pt 2G.1 directors' meetings, and Pt 2G.2 meetings of members of companies. See the discussion in Chapter 2 above, n 5 to 12 and accompanying text.

[20] In some jurisdictions (eg Canada: *Canada Business Corporations Act*, RSC 1985, s 102; United States: the *Revised Model Business Corporations Act* s 8.01 (2002); *Delaware General Corporation Law* s 141) this division of power is prescribed by statute. In Australia it is the default position that may be varied by a corporation (see the 'replaceable rule' in s 198A *Corporations Act 2001*).

[21] *Hogg v Cramphorn Ltd* [1967] Ch 254; *Bamford v Bamford* [1968] 2 All ER 655; *Winthrop Investments Ltd v Winns Ltd* [1975] 2 NSWLR 666.

[22] [1906] 2 Ch 34.

[23] There is authority that the general meeting has a reserve power to act when the board is unable or unwilling to exercise its powers. However the scope of this reserve power is unclear and has been interpreted narrowly in Australian courts — see *Massey v Wales* (2003) 21 ACLC 1978. Courts are similarly cautious about the unanimous consent rule whereby a unanimous decision of all of the members is treated as a decision of the corporation regardless of any division of powers in the corporate constitution — HAJ Ford, RP Austin, IM Ramsay, *Ford's Principles of Corporations Law* (12th ed, 2005) 301-305.

constitution is] vested in the directors any more than the directors can usurp the powers vested ... in the general body of shareholders.[24]

Conversely, the board of directors cannot easily interfere with decision-making processes in the general meeting. This is apparent in a number of court decisions dealing with the exercise by directors of their power to issue shares. Typically this power is granted so that directors may raise capital for the corporation. Where, however, directors have sought to issue shares to alter voting patterns in a corporation the courts have held this to be an improper exercise of the power. Take, for example, the statement of Buckley LJ in *Hogg v Cramphorn Ltd*:

> A majority of shareholders in general meeting is entitled to pursue what course it chooses within the company's powers, however wrong-headed it may appear to others, provided the majority do not unfairly oppress other members of the company.[25]

In *Residues Treatment & Trading Co Ltd v Southern Resources Ltd* this freedom from interference in voting rights through the improper actions of directors was expressed as a personal right of each shareholder. King CJ in the Supreme Court of South Australia argued that:

> A member's voting rights and the rights of participation which they provide in the decision-making of the company are a fundamental attribute of membership and are rights which the member should be able to protect by legal action against improper diminution.[26]

The formal division of corporate decision-making power into a dual structure is a key part of the corporate constitutional framework.[27] Implicitly, this structure recognises that there are two types of corporate decision. One type is reserved for the members in general meeting. These are resolutions that concern the ground rules and matters of basic corporate structure. Examples include decisions to amend the corporate constitution, to remove the directors, or to alter the corporation's share capital structure. The second type of decision is made by (or under the delegation of) the directors. These decisions clearly have great

---

[24] [1935] 2 KB 113, 134 (references to the articles of association have been replaced with references to the corporate constitution).

[25] [1967] Ch 254 at 268; see also *Howard Smith Ltd v Ampol Petroleum Ltd* [1974] AC 821.

[26] (1988) 6 ACLC 1160 at 1165.

[27] What follows is prompted by Bruce Ackerman's theory of 'dualist democracy' - B Ackerman, 'Constitutional Politics/Constitutional Law' (1989) 99 *Yale Law Journal* 453 [hereafter, 'Constitutional Politics'], and 'The Storrs Lectures: Discovering the Constitution' (1984) 93 *Yale Law Journal* 1013 [hereafter, 'Storrs Lectures']. This is a selective adaptation, not an application, of Ackerman's ideas. As far as I can tell, Ackerman did not intend his argument to be used in the corporate context.

significance for the daily operation of the corporation, but they cannot alter its fundamental structures.

In this dual system, decisions made by the members in a general meeting are not everyday events. In fact, in most corporations they are quite rare, occurring, at best, on an annual basis[28] and only under special conditions. For example, there are notice requirements governing the provision of information, and rules requiring time to consider this information. There are voting rules and requirements that stipulate — in some cases — the need for special majorities. Nevertheless, despite their infrequency, these decisions are fundamental to the affairs of the corporation. And despite the routine way in which these decisions are often made, general meetings have a formal significance that is not possessed by directors' meetings. A general meeting is a gathering of members and directors; it is a meeting *of* the corporation. In accountability terms, this division of power gives the members of the corporation the right and the authority to call the directors to account and to demand answers. As Mulgan emphasises, 'those calling for an account are asserting rights of superior authority over those who are accountable, including the rights to demand answers and to impose sanctions'.[29]

Decision-making by directors occurs much more frequently. As noted above, the directors exercise general managerial power. The directors can then delegate aspects of this power to senior managers in the corporation. Indeed, if we group decisions of the board together with those made by managers exercising power delegated by the directors, we see that these decisions are part of the daily life of the company. Borrowing Bruce Ackerman's phrase, this can be regarded as the 'normal politics' for corporate decision-making.[30] That is, normal corporate decision-making is, with the authority of the members, largely the business of directors and managers.[31] However, despite their closer connection to daily corporate operations, board meetings are not usually described as meetings *of* the company. Directors' meetings are not constrained by as many procedural requirements as meetings of shareholders. The corporate constitution may specify rules about notice, procedures at board meetings and voting, but '[o]rdinarily, less formality is required for a directors' meeting than a meeting of members of a corporation'.[32]

Two points should be emphasised before proceeding further. The first concerns the status of the corporate constitution in this model. On one view, the

---

[28]   In Australia only public companies are required to hold an annual general meeting (*Corporations Act* s 250N). No similar requirement is imposed on proprietary (ie private) companies.

[29]   Above n 1, 555.

[30]   Ackerman, 'Constitutional Politics', above n 27, 461.

[31]   This sentence paraphrases F Schauer, 'Deliberating about Deliberation' (1992) 90 *Michigan Law Review* 1187, 1188.

[32]   *Wilson v Manna Hill Mining Company Pty Ltd* [2004] FCA 912 [15]. One restraint is found in s 195 *Corporations Act 2001* which restricts a director of a public company who has a material personal interest in a matter being considered by the board from participating in the board's consideration of and voting on the matter.

corporate constitution embodies the terms of an agreement between the members and directors about a division of power in the corporation. This is symptomatic of the contractual approach and is typified in Cozens-Hardy LJ's judgement in *Automatic Self-Cleansing Filter Syndicate Co Ltd v Cunninghame*:

> [T]he shareholders have by their express contract mutually stipulated that their common affairs should be managed by certain directors to be appointed by the shareholders in the manner described by other articles, such directors being liable to be removed only by special resolution. If you once get a stipulation of that kind in a contract made between the parties, what right is there to interfere with the contract, apart, of course, from any misconduct on the part of the directors?[33]

It is a different thing to say that the corporate constitution, being comprised of privately and publicly determined elements,[34] confers powers on each of those two bodies. This second formulation puts the corporate constitution above the status of a contractual agreement between individual corporators. An example of this approach can be found in the Privy Council's reasoning in *Howard Smith Ltd v Ampol Petroleum Ltd*:

> Just as it is established that directors, within their management powers, may take decisions against the wishes of the majority of shareholders, and indeed that the majority of shareholders cannot control them in the exercise of these powers while they remain in office ... , so it must be unconstitutional for directors to use their fiduciary powers over the shares in the company purely for the purpose of destroying an existing majority, or creating a new majority which did not previously exist. To do so is to interfere with that element of the company's constitution which is separate from and set against their powers.[35]

In this approach, the constitution sits apart from the day-to-day concerns and interests of the corporate personnel. It constrains conduct by imposing structures and processes that are not susceptible to easy variation.

The second point to emphasise is that this characterisation of the different corporate decision-making sites and processes does not depend on the substantive content of the particular decisions that are made. The dual decision-making model acknowledges that in many corporations there are matters that most members will not understand, will not want to become involved in, or will not have the resources to pursue, even though their interests are ultimately affected. Decisions to enter into complex funding agreements, or to hire or fire senior managerial staff are examples. These are matters that are usually left to the directors and/or managers to decide. Describing the general meeting as the site for fundamental decision-making does not deny the obvious fact that directors make many significant decisions

---

[33] [1906] 2 Ch 34, 44.

[34] See Chapter 3 n 27 to n 53 and accompanying text.

[35] [1974] AC 821 at 837. Ross Grantham makes a similar point, but attributes the Court's approach to an organic model of the company — see 'The Unanimous Consent Rule in Company Law' (1993) 52 *Cambridge Law Journal* 245, 268-269.

which affect the ordinary operations of the corporation, or that general meetings
often make seemingly mundane decisions. The importance of the dual model is
demonstrated in debates about the matters that should be decided by the members.
For example, should members be able to pass advisory (or non-binding) resolutions
on matters of corporate management that are outside the power of the general
meeting? This is possible in some countries.[36] However, a suggestion that such
resolutions be permitted in Australian corporate law was dismissed in 2000, on the
grounds that 'the boundaries ... between the role of directors and that of the
shareholders in general meeting should not become confused'.[37] The key difference
between board decisions and general meeting decisions is that the board is
answerable to the shareholders for its exercise of decision-making power.
Although, as we have seen, shareholders cannot dictate to the board or seek to be
part of the board's decision-making processes, this does not diminish the
constitutional significance of the board's accountability to the shareholders.
Notwithstanding the rule of member non-intervention, directors cannot assume that
by being elected to office they have a mandate to do as they wish.[38] Shareholders in
general meeting, by contrast, are not prima facie required to explain their decisions
(subject to what I say in Chapter 6 about contestability). In this sense their
decisions are constitutionally superior to those of the directors.

There are two important implications of this dual decision-making system.
First, the system operates as a signalling device to corporate insiders and outsiders
about which issues, and therefore which interests and values, are regarded as
fundamental to the corporation.[39] Those issues that are allocated to the general
meeting may be presumed to be those which are regarded as having fundamental
importance for the corporation. To the extent that a corporation is able to tailor-
make its own constitutional provisions, then different corporations can send
different signals. The second implication takes us to the issue of structural
accountability: the dual process, with the attendant constitutional constraints,
provides a structure that is intended to secure designated rights or interests from
easy or expedient interference by controlling interests in a corporation. Thus
decisions are made by directors on the basis of ultimate accountability to the
general meeting (particularly via the power of shareholders to remove directors, or
to ratify breaches of duty), while those made at the general meeting are open to
scrutiny and deliberation by all members.

---

[36]   For example, the *Canada Business Corporations Act*, RSC 1985, s 137, and the New
       Zealand *Companies Act 1993* s 109.
[37]   Companies and Securities Advisory Committee, *Shareholder Participation in the
       Modern Listed Public Company*, Final Report (2000) [3.55]. The *Corporations Act
       2001* has since been amended to require that the adoption of the remuneration report at
       a listed company's AGM be decided by an advisory resolution (s 250R(2) and (3)).
[38]   Richard Buxbaum describes the shareholders as the 'the upstream neighbour' of the
       board: 'Corporate Governance and Corporate Monitoring: The Whys and Hows' (1996)
       6 *Australian Journal of Corporate Law* 309, 313.
[39]   Ackerman, 'Storrs Lectures', above n 27, 1039.

Criticisms of the Dual Model

There are three broad objections that might be raised about relying on this dual model. One is that it emphasises the role of directors and members at the expense of other important constituencies. Secondly, it might be said that the model gives too much significance to the role of the board at the expense of the members. The third objection reverses the second, arguing that the dual model gives undue prominence to the role of the members. I consider each of these arguments in turn.

The first objection was discussed in Chapter 1 of this book. Stakeholder and communitarian theorists (amongst others) have objected that the dual model defines the set of relevant corporate interests too narrowly. As was noted in Chapter 1, there is an argument that, given their general passivity, members have the least right to insist that their interests be recognised against the interests of other stakeholders. [40] Stakeholder theorists argue that existing corporate legal structures should be reformed so as to cater for a wider range of non-shareholder constituencies, principally employees, but also creditors, customers, suppliers, and local communities. As I pointed out in Chapter 1, it is not the purpose of a corporate constitutional framework to rule out these concerns. Instead, the aim is to develop a model which permits those concerns to be heard and expressed within the still-dominant assumptions of shareholder centrism. As I hope will become apparent, particularly in Chapter 5, once the constitutional parameters of the shareholder-centred model have been evaluated, corporate constitutionalism could well be used as the basis for considering the claims of non-shareholder interests in the corporate governance process.

The second objection reminds us of the contract-based agency argument that was discussed in Chapter 2. It argues that the dual model fractures the agency relationship between managers and owners of the corporation. Agency theory regards all decision-making processes within a company as having the same weight and significance. According to this theory, while the shareholders could potentially make all decisions, it is more rational and efficient for them to appoint others to make the decisions for them. For an agency theorist, the only issue of interest that follows from this is how to monitor and control the managers in exercising that power. Thus, rather than a division of power, the agency model looks more to a rational division of labour:

> The corporate form of firm organization has obvious advantages for shareholders (suppliers of capital) and managers. Shareholders can participate in the gains from entrepreneurial ventures even though they lack management skills; managers can pursue profitable business opportunities even though they lack large personal wealth. *Both parties benefit from this division of labour.*[41]

---

[40] See Chapter 1 n 20 to n 23 and accompanying text.
[41] D Fischel, 'The Corporate Governance Movement' (1982) 35 *Vanderbilt Law Review* 1259, 1262 (emphasis added).

In the final analysis, the principal/agent analysis treats any decisions made by the agent as if they were decisions of the principal. In contrast, the dual model highlights the point that director and member decisions are the product of categorically different processes.

The third objection to the dual decision-making model takes essentially the opposite stance to the agency theorists, arguing that the model gives undue recognition to the members when what really counts is decision-making by directors and managers. This objection is based on the idea that if the directors are properly elected and are given full managerial power, then they have plenary decision-making authority in the corporation. Of course members retain formal decision-making power over certain matters specified in the corporate constitution, including the power to elect and remove directors. But this power, if it has to be exercised at all, should be exercised with circumspection. The result is a governance system based on the idea of 'director primacy' rather than 'shareholder primacy'.[42] I will deal with this argument in a little more detail here, because it has not been canvassed previously in this book.

This objection finds expression in both economic and political theory. In the economic literature it is found in the managerialist conception of the corporation. Prompted by the classic study of Berle and Means in 1932,[43] which highlighted the separation between ownership and control functions in large corporations, '[t]he managerialist picture puts corporate management at the strategic center of the large firm'.[44] Managers obtain their power because the wide dispersal of shareholdings effectively cedes control to them.[45]

There is a similar argument in political theory, described as democratic or competitive elitism.[46] With its origins in the works of writers such as Joseph Schumpeter and Max Weber, it offers a procedural, rather than a substantive theory of democracy. As Schumpeter defines it, 'the democratic method is that institutional arrangement for arriving at political decisions in which individuals acquire the power to decide by means of a competitive struggle for the people's vote'.[47] Schumpeter's reference to an 'institutional arrangement' indicates that democracy is defined by reference to the procedure by which voters choose their political leaders. That procedure involves an electoral system in which there is a

---

[42]   L Stout, 'The Shareholder as Ulysses: Some Empirical Evidence On Why Investors in Public Corporations Tolerate Board Governance' (2003) 152 *University of Pennsylvania Law Review* 667, 669, referring to S Bainbridge, 'Director Primacy: The Means and Ends of Corporate Governance' (2003) 97 *Northwestern University Law Review* 547.

[43]   Adolph A Berle and Gardiner C Means, *The Modern Corporation and Private Property* (1932).

[44]   William Bratton, 'The "Nexus of Contracts" Corporation: A Critical Appraisal' (1989) 74 *Cornell Law Review* 407, 413.

[45]   See J Parkinson, *Corporate Power and Responsibility* (1993) 56-72.

[46]   The label 'democratic elitism' is taken from Philip Green (ed), *Democracy* (1993), while David Held, *Models of Democracy* (1987) uses the term 'competitive elitism'.

[47]   J Schumpeter, *Capitalism, Socialism and Democracy* (1987 ed) 269.

'competitive struggle' for leadership.[48] The only function of the electorate in this process is to exercise its free vote to 'produce a government',[49] (this function also includes the power to evict that government). This is the limit of the electorate's control over the leadership. Using Schumpeter's description again:

> Voters do not decide issues. ... In all normal cases the initiative lies with the candidate who makes a bid for the office of member of parliament and such local leadership as that may imply. Voters confine themselves to accepting this bid in preference to others or refusing to accept it.[50]

It follows from this that, having elected their leaders, voters must refrain from acting as 'back seat drivers',[51] interfering in the processes of government. Schumpeter urges that voters 'must respect the division of labour between themselves and the politicians they elect'.[52] Weber makes the same point in more blunt terms:

> In a democracy the people choose a leader in whom they trust. Then the chosen leader says, "Now shut up and obey me." People and party are no longer free to interfere in his business.[53]

This functional division between the elected and the electors is reinforced by two interrelated developments. One is the professionalisation of leadership roles in modern society; the other is the separation of leadership from administration, and the increased specialisation in the latter set of tasks. On the latter development, both Weber and Schumpeter argue for the necessity of a well-trained bureaucracy. According to Weber it is 'the capitalist market economy which demands that official business of the administration be discharged precisely, unambiguously, continuously, and with as much speed as possible'.[54] Moreover, '[b]ureaucracy inevitably accompanies modern mass democracy in contrast to the democratic self-government of small homogeneous units. This results from the characteristic principle of bureaucracy: the abstract regularity of the execution of authority...'.[55] So, to summarise, modern political systems are said to be characterised by a three-

---

48   Ibid 271.
49   Ibid 272.
50   Ibid 282.
51   Held, above n 46, 175.
52   Above n 47, 295. Schumpeter goes so far as to say that even 'less formal attempts at restricting the freedom of action of members of parliament — the practice of bombarding them with letters and telegrams for instance — ought to come under the same ban'.
53   Cited in H Gerth and C Wright Mills (eds and trans), *From Max Weber: Essays in Sociology* (1947) 42. In his essay 'Politics as a Vocation', Weber defined politics as 'any kind of *independent* leadership in action', ibid, 77 (emphasis in original).
54   M Weber, 'Bureaucracy' in ibid 215.
55   Ibid 224.

way division of function: a largely passive electorate, a competitively elected
leadership, and a bureaucracy of specialised administrators.

It is easy to see how this theory might be accommodated within the
formal legal model of the corporation.[56] As I noted earlier, corporate law sets strict
limitations on the role of the members concerning the directors' exercise of
managerial power. Competitive elitism supplies a rationale for those limitations,
and for the grant of plenary management powers to the directors.

However competitive elitism has been criticised on a number of
grounds.[57] The theory has drawn general criticism because of its bleak picture of
political life. In so far as the theory assumes 'the dominion of the elected over the
electors' it can slide easily from elitism towards oligarchy.[58] Another criticism is
the theory's insistence on a passive role for citizens once they have exercised their
vote. The theory has no room in which to develop the idea that members of a
political community can contribute beyond the ballot box. Finally, although
competitive elitism directs attention to questions of process, its focus is narrow. It
does not concern itself with the quality of debate and deliberation that precedes
voting. Provided there is an apparently free competition for the vote, democracy is
satisfied by a majority vote.

The dual decision-making model addresses these points. In particular, it
emphasises the continuing and potentially significant role of members after they
have elected the directors, and it provides a structure for the accountability of
decision-making power. It does not, however, ensure deliberation; this is discussed
in Chapter 5.

Separations of Powers

The dual decision-making model establishes a vertical division of power in the
corporate constitutionalist framework, distinguishing board decisions from those
made by the general meeting of members. Of course, decisions in the boardroom or
at a general meeting are not usually self-contained events. Typically, they are part
of more extended processes that can involve draft proposals, consideration by
board committees, consultations with major shareholders, and so on. In other
words, despite the fact that meetings of directors and of shareholders are only the
legally recognised decision-making forums in a corporation, they are certainly not
the only places in which decisions are made or reviewed in everyday corporate life.

---

[56] This is not surprising. Weber observed that 'things in a private economic enterprise are
      quite similar [to public politics]: the real "sovereign", the assembled shareholders, is
      just as little influential in the business management as is a "people" ruled by expert
      officials.' He went on to note similarities in the dependent relationships of directors
      towards company managers and that between elected leaders and administrators in
      modern state bureaucracies: 'Politics as a Vocation' in Gerth and Mills, above n 53, 91.
[57] For examples of more detailed critiques see Green, above n 46, Part V.
[58] R Michels, 'Political Parties' in Green, above n 46, 69. Weber was critical of Michels'
      'iron law of oligarchy' — see Held, above n 46, 156.

They are also not the most frequently activated decision-making forums: general meetings usually occur only once a year, and board meetings are usually only monthly events. Thus we need to be able to control the decision-making processes that occur outside these formal meetings. We need to recognise the possibility of many separations of decision-making power in the corporation. This is the second feature of structural accountability.

The idea of a separation of power amongst different decision-makers within a governance structure has long been recognised as a key element of effective accountability. Liberal legal and political theory has demonstrated a deep-seated mistrust of concentrations of decision-making power within political communities. Liberal theory requires that these powers should be exercised non-arbitrarily, and that this should be done in ways that are open and accountable. The idea of a separation of powers therefore seeks to achieve the dual aim of the diffusion and the accountability of decision-making power. The exercise of this power is to be broken up into different branches so that no single person or agency has full control over those powers, and so that there are checks and balances on each power-exercising agency or person.

Historically, the separation of powers ideal has developed with reference to the exercise of public power. The concerns of the key writers in this history, Locke, Montesquieu, and Madison, were directed at controlling the potential for state power to impinge unduly on the lives of individual citizens.[59] Lawyers — and constitutional lawyers in particular — have elevated this idea into a formal doctrine that involves a 'holy trinity' of formally distinct public powers: legislative, executive, and judicial. [60] Modern Australian constitutional writing tends to concede that the first two of these powers have merged in practice, due mainly to the operations of the Cabinet system of government. Hence, in the constitutional law literature, discussion about the doctrine of separation of powers tends to be concerned primarily with the separation of the judicial power from legislative and executive power.[61]

As I noted in Chapter 1, significant sites of social, economic and political power are now to be found in the private sector, especially in corporations. The broad idea of a separation of powers should therefore be applied not just to public systems of government but also to corporate systems.[62] In doing this we must

---

[59]   J Locke, *Two Treatises of Government* (1960 ed); Montesquieu, *The Spirit of the Laws* (A Cohler, B Miller and H Stone trans and ed, 1989) especially. Book XI, Pt 6; Alexander Hamilton, James Madison, and John Jay, *The Federalist Papers* (1961 ed), especially Nos 47-51.

[60]   The theological metaphor is noted (but dismissed) by Vile, above n 17, 15.

[61]   Sir Anthony Mason has pointed to the artificiality of this three-way division of powers, because of 'the impossibility of defining each of the three powers in a way that reveals them as mutually exclusive concepts'. Sir Anthony Mason, 'A New Perspective on Separation of Powers' (Reshaping Australian Institutions Australian National University Public Lecture, 25 July 1996) 5.

[62]   On the importance of separations of private power and their role in corporations, see J Braithwaite, 'On Speaking Softly and Carrying Big Sticks: Neglected Dimensions of a

expect that corporate governance systems will be likely to have taxonomies of power that require different separations than the standard legal doctrine recognises.[63] So while I want to preserve the idea that corporate decision-making power should be diffuse and accountable, I am not concerned with a strict application of the traditional classification described above.

There are many governance sites and mechanisms in a large corporation. Thus, as John Braithwaite urges, 'we should be pluralist about what we mean by the nature of the power that is separated. ... Many different kinds of power can be exercised by many different kinds of individual and collective actors'.[64] The exercise of power in a corporation is distributed unevenly, and varies from one corporation to another. There are those for whom it is regular or frequent, and those for whom it is infrequent or sporadic. There are those who are, in information terms, 'on the inside' and there are those who are dependent on others for information. To repeat an earlier example, directors have more regular involvement in the operations of a corporation than do most shareholders, but executive officers have greater daily significance than directors. In corporations we must therefore aim for multiple separations of different decision-making powers that minimises the risk of gaps in the accountability framework. Hence the sub-heading to this part of the Chapter refers to plural 'separations of powers'.

The types of separations that can be found in a corporation include those between the chair of the board and the chief executive officer, between the executive and non-executive or external directors, between the board of directors and its sub-committees, between the board and the non-director executive managers of the corporation, between the corporation and its external auditor, and between corporate managers and the internal auditors.[65] This is not an exhaustive list,[66] and I will address only some of these separations in this Chapter. What the

---

Republican Separation of Powers' (1997) 47 *University of Toronto Law Journal* 305, 307.

[63] The exercise of power and authority in modern government structures is often fragmented and dispersed in complex ways that cannot be adequately caught by the traditional 'three branches of power' model: see E Magill, 'Beyond Powers and Branches in Separation of Powers Law' (2001) 150 *University of Pennsylvania Law Review* 603, 651.

[64] Braithwaite, above n 62, 312. The same idea is implicit in the New York Stock Exchange's image of corporate financial reporting as a 'mosaic' or a 'three-legged stool' (the legs being the board, the financial management team, and the auditors): New York Stock Exchange, *Report of the Blue Ribbon Committee on Improving the Effectiveness of Audit Committees, Overview & Recommendations* (1999) <http://www.nyse.com/about/p1020656067652.html?displayPage=/press/10206560687 11.html> at 19 July 2004.

[65] As Braithwaite notes, this need not be limited to financial auditors, and can extend to environmental, safety, and compliance audits: above n 62, 346.

[66] The list also presumes the single-board structure found in countries such as Australia, the United Kingdom, Canada and the United States. Another form of separation is the management board/supervisory board structure found in countries such as Germany (see ibid 345).

list does indicate is that separations of powers are not limited to hierarchical top-down monitoring, and they may involve overlapping skills and competencies (for example, independent and executive directors). It is important not to be too categorical when designing and instituting divisions and separations of powers within a corporation. It is conceivable, for example, that at some times in some corporations directors might take some hand in the day-to-day management of the company. It is equally conceivable that, in the process of implementing board policies, managers may create further 'subsidiary' policies. This overlap is particularly apparent in the case of executive appointments to the board. So, the aim is not to insist on predetermined separations of power in each and every corporation. Instead, the aim, in each case, is to ensure a plurality of separations that is appropriate to the particular corporation.

The purpose of insisting on these separations of powers is to achieve an institutionalised system of checks and balances which makes it more likely that abuses of power by one part of the corporate governance system can be identified, restrained, corrected, and understood by other parts.[67] This involves a delicate balance. We do not want the different sites of power or decision-making to be so independent or autonomous that they are beyond effective control or scrutiny by other sites. As Vile notes, the idea of checks and balances means that each branch of power must exercise some control over the others by having a limited role in the exercise of the other's functions.[68] That is, we should allow that some decision-makers may have control over others by their partial participation in the others' functions. At the same time, it is important that each site has sufficient independence and autonomy to do its job, to act as an 'outside' monitor of other relevant sites, with the result that that no site is dominated by another or abdicates its responsibilities to another.

Another concern is that a governance system based on multiple separations of powers might lead to institutionalised feelings of distrust. It could be argued that a system in which all are being watched and all are watching, and in which there is an over-emphasis on information reporting and monitoring, is likely to breed distrust and thus be counter-productive. This state of affairs is not, however, an automatic outcome of the separations argument: '[t]rust and control are not polar opposites: they have to co-exist'.[69] Indeed, a system of multiple separations can provide the reassurance necessary for relationships of trust. As Phillip Pettit and John Braithwaite have each argued, a careful institutionalisation of mechanisms of restraint, of challenge, and of accountability is actually necessary to the fostering of trust within — and of — institutions.[70] The purpose of having separations of power is not the division and pigeon-holing of expertise and

---

67 Braithwaite, above n 62, 341-342.
68 Vile, above n 17, 18-19.
69 Philip Stiles and Bernard Taylor, *Boards at Work: How Directors View Their Roles and Responsibilities* (2002) 80.
70 Philip Pettit, 'Republican Theory and Political Trust', John Braithwaite, 'Institutionalising Distrust, Enculturating Trust', both in V Braithwaite and M Levi (eds), *Trust and Governance* (1998) 295 and 343 respectively.

power. Rather, it is to emphasise the nature and function of the relationships between those different sites. Thus a more accurate metaphor would be a web or network of separations of powers.

In the remainder of this Chapter I examine three areas in which separations of powers should be prominent: the board of directors, the role of the auditor, and amongst shareholders. I then consider how a system of separations of powers can be supplemented and reinforced by the encouragement of whistleblowing in corporations.

Separations of Board Power

The need for separations in the allocation and exercise of board power has been a prominent concern in the corporate governance literature. A major Australian case serves as a convenient way of organising the discussion here. The case involved a claim for negligence by AWA Ltd against its auditors and cross-claim by the auditors. The facts centred on the actions of the corporation's chief executive officer/managing director, the non-executive directors, and the auditors. The case was decided at first-instance in 1992 (*AWA Ltd v Daniels*)[71] and then in a subsequent decision by the New South Wales Court of Appeal in 1995 (*Daniels v Anderson*).[72]

At first instance Rogers J referred to a three-way separation of monitoring power from management power. The first separation is between the board of directors and the corporation's senior managers.[73] According to Rogers J:

> A Board's functions, apart from statutory ones, are said to be usually four fold:-
> 1. to set goals for the corporation
> 2. to appoint the corporation's chief executive
> 3. to oversee the plans of managers for the acquisition and organisation of financial and human resources toward attainment of the corporation's goals, and
> 4. to review, at reasonable intervals, the corporation's progress towards attaining its goals.[74]

Justice Rogers went on to note that in a large public company the dictates of 'business necessity' mean that the board cannot be involved in day-to-day management of the corporation's business. Directors must look to others to manage the corporation, which means that those managers are required, amongst other things to:

-   carry out the day to day control of the corporation's business affairs

---

[71] (1992) 10 ACLC 933.
[72] (1995) 13 ACLC 614.
[73] (1992) 10 ACLC 933, 1013.
[74] Ibid (references omitted).

- establish proper internal controls, management information systems and accounting records
- implement the policies and strategies adopted by the Board
- prepare proposals and submission[s] for consideration by the Board
- prepare a budget.[75]

Justice Rogers' recognition of the necessity for board delegations prompted considerable debate about the extent to which directors may rely on others to manage the corporation. The debate was sharpened when the Court of Appeal questioned Rogers J's approach, holding that far from being 'entitled to rely without verification on the judgement, information and advice' of managers, 'directors are under a continuing obligation to keep informed about the activities of the corporation'.[76] They must 'guide and monitor' the management of the corporation,[77] and they are 'obliged' to inform themselves about the financial affairs of the corporation.[78] Subsequently the *Corporations Act* was amended so that the current law states that where directors delegate power they are not responsible for the exercise of power by the delegate provided that they believe on reasonable grounds and in good faith, and after making proper inquiry, that the delegate is reliable and competent.[79] Further, the Act states that a director is entitled to rely on information given by an employee or corporate officer if that reliance is in good faith and follows an independent assessment by the director of the information.[80]

There is debate in the corporate governance literature about whether this separation between board and management is workable, sufficient, or desirable.[81] I do not intend to enter that debate here; my purpose is simply to illustrate one obvious way in which corporate lawyers already understand the importance of the separation of corporate decision-making power. Despite references to 'business necessity', this separation between the board and management is more than just a pragmatic division of labour — it also reveals a concern for accountability and monitoring.

The second separation noted in the *AWA* case (at first instance) was between the non-executive directors and the executive directors, especially the chief executive officer or managing director.[82] The corporate governance literature

---

[75] Ibid 1014.

[76] *Daniels v Anderson* (1995) 13 ACLC 614, 663 and 664 (quoting Pollock J in *Frances v United Jersey Bank* 432 A 2d 814 (1981).

[77] Ibid 662.

[78] *Statewide Tobacco Services Ltd v Morley* (1990) 8 ACLC 827, 832, cited in ibid 661.

[79] *Corporations Act 2001* s 190.

[80] *Corporations Act 2001* s 189.

[81] For a more critical assessment of the division of function between board and management than that in the *AWA* case, see M Eisenberg, 'Legal Models of Management Structure in the Modern Corporation: Officers, Directors, and Accountants' (1975) 63 *California Law Review* 375.

[82] *AWA Ltd v Daniels* (1992) 10 ACLC 933, 1014. Rogers J went on to distinguish between the standard of care owed by non-executive directors and that owed by

suggests that this separation has several dimensions. For example, the basic distinction between executive and non-executive directors (NEDs) is not always useful. In many corporations NEDs are unable to act effectively as a checking mechanism because of past or present affiliations with management. Thus a further distinction is drawn between affiliated and non-affiliated (or independent) NEDs, where affiliation is determined by factors such as whether the NED is a substantial shareholder, a recent employee, a professional adviser, or a significant supplier or customer, to or of the corporation. [83] Internationally, corporate governance guidelines and codes of conduct issued by stock exchanges, directors' associations, institutional investor organisations and other organisations have consistently recommended that boards be comprised of a significant proportion or a majority of independent non-executive directors. [84] The same guidelines also emphasise the importance of establishing board sub-committees to deal with potential conflict of interest issues such as executive and directors' remuneration, the nomination and selection of board positions, and the auditing of the corporation's financial and risk position. The usual recommendation is that those committees should be comprised of independent non-executive directors. For example, in the wake of the Enron and WorldCom collapses in 2001-2002, the New York Stock Exchange and NASDAQ issued new listing rules that require listed companies to have a majority of independent directors on their boards, and to have only independent directors on their audit, remuneration, and selection committees. [85] The requirement for audit committee independence in US listed companies has subsequently been reinforced by s 303(3) of the *Sarbanes-Oxley Act* of 2002. Similar requirements are imposed in Australia by the ASX Listing Rules. [86] As I argued earlier, the aim of this separation of independent directors is not to pigeon-hole their expertise but to focus attention on the relationship between those directors and the executive. In the United Kingdom, the Higgs Review described this as creating 'the potential for a virtuous dynamic in which executive perceptions of the value of non-executive directors' experience and contribution encourage greater executive openness that, in turn, allows for greater non-executive engagement'. [87]

---

executive directors. The Court of Appeal rejected this distinction — see *Daniels v Anderson* (1995) 13 ACLC 614 at 662.

[83] This list is taken from Australian Stock Exchange Corporate Governance Council, *Principles of Good Corporate Governance and Best Practice Recommendations* (March 2003) 20.

[84] For example, ibid recommendation 2.1; Financial Services Authority (UK), *The Combined Code on Corporate Governance* (July 2003) principle A.3.2; OECD, *Principles of Corporate Governance* (2004) principle VI.E.1.

[85] See now NYSE, *Listed Company Manual* (2003) ss 303A.01, 303a.07(b); NASDAQ, *Marketplace Rules* (April 2004) rules 4350(c) and (d).

[86] Australian Stock Exchange, *Listing Rules* (2004) rules 1.1 and 12.7, referring to its *Principles of Good Corporate Governance and Best Practice Recommendations*, above n 83, principle 4.

[87] Derek Higgs, United Kingdom Department of Trade and Industry, *Review of the Role and Effectiveness of Non-Executive Directors* (January 2003) 33.

Again, there is debate about these requirements, particularly the effect which independent directors are presumed to have on corporate operations and performance. Empirical studies show that while a board with a majority of non-affiliated directors does not necessarily have a positive impact on corporate financial performance, it can have a positive impact in monitoring conflicts of interest between executive management and shareholders.[88] But this impact should not be overstated. Whilst the majority of corporate governance guidelines and reports invest great faith in the monitoring capacity of independent directors, actual practice will be affected by a number of factors, including the group dynamics of each particular board and the necessary reliance by those directors on corporate officers for information about the corporation. Indeed, the requirement of independence may, paradoxically, put limitations on the director's capacity to monitor. As Helen Bird has observed:

> To satisfy the definitions of independence recommended by the reports, a high proportion of board candidates will have no experience in the industry in which the company operates, no connection in a commercial or professional capacity with the company, and, in consequence, little experience of the company's management practices. The very circumstances that make their appointment attractive will also cause them to be more beholden to management for assistance and information.[89]

The *AWA* case noted the importance of a third separation, between the role of the board chairperson and the executive directors (particularly the managing director). As described by Rogers J, '[t]he Chairman is responsible to a greater extent than any other director for the performance of the board as a whole and each member of it'.[90] In *ASIC v Rich* Austin J accepted that the chair's role includes leading the board in 'the monitoring of management, the assessment of the company's financial position and performance and the detection and the assessment of any material adverse developments'.[91] A study of Australian directors' attitudes towards corporate governance, conducted between 1990-91, found widespread disapproval of executive chairpersons. As one director put it:

> It is good to have distinct persons in this area. The chief executive is concerned with the day-to-day running of the business and its improvement while the

---

[88] See G Stapledon and J Lawrence, 'Board Composition and Structure in the Top 100' (1996) 12 *Company Director* 80; L Lin, 'The Effectiveness of Outside Directors as a Corporate Governance Mechanism: Theories and Evidence' (1996) 90 *Northwestern University Law Review* 898.

[89] Helen Bird, 'The Rise and Fall of the Independent Director' (1995) 5 *Australian Journal of Corporate Law* 235, 253.

[90] *AWA Ltd v Daniels* (1992) 10 ACLC 933, 1015.

[91] (2003) 21 ACLC 450, 464.

chairmanship has to ensure honesty and look after the interests of shareholders. The chairman is a moderating wise old head.[92]

The need for the board chairperson to be appointed from the ranks of the independent board appointees has become an article of faith in the corporate governance literature in Australia and the United Kingdom since the 1980s.[93] As argued in the Higgs Review in the United Kingdom, '[t]he separation of roles can contribute to the greater achievement of the chief executive as well as being important in creating the conditions for effective performance by the non-executive directors'.[94]

Another aspect of separations of power in and around the board, not relevant to the facts of the *AWA* case, concerns the role of the company secretary.[95] The company secretary is now recognised judicially as the corporation's chief administrative officer.[96] As described by the Institute of Chartered Secretaries and Administrators in the United Kingdom, the company secretary has 'a central role in the governance and administration' of the affairs of the corporation, and is in 'a powerful position of influence'.[97] For the purposes of defining legal duties and liabilities the company secretary is classified in Australia and the United Kingdom as an officer of the company.[98] Nevertheless, the secretary's role in providing 'independent impartial guidance and advice' to the board in general and to the independent directors and the board chairperson in particular,[99] especially where this involves briefing directors on the work of senior executive officers, suggests that this is another point at which the separations argument should be considered. That is, the secretary ought to stand separately from the senior executives and from the board.[100]

[92] R Tomasic and S Bottomley, *Directing the Top 500: Corporate Governance in Australian Public Companies* (1993) 56.

[93] The situation is different in the United States, where the CEO is usually also the chair of the board. There are some calls to change this: see, eg, California Public Employees' Retirement System, Corporate Governance Core Principles and Guidelines (1998) <http://www.calpers-governance.org/principles/domestic/us/page01.asp> at 21 July 2004.

[94] Above n 87, 24.

[95] In Australia a public company must have at least one secretary: *Corporations Act 2001* s 204A(2).

[96] *Club Flotilla (Pacific Palms) Ltd v Isherwood* (1987) 12 ACLR 387.

[97] Institute of Chartered Secretaries and Administrators (United Kingdom), *Duties of a Company Secretary Best Practice Guide* (1998) 2.

[98] *Corporations Act 2001* (Aust) s 9; *Companies Act 1985* (UK) s 744.

[99] Higgs, above n 87, 51.

[100] It is common in smaller public companies for the finance director to be appointed as the company secretary: ibid 51.

Audit and Separations of Powers

A further separation of power, which was a prominent aspect of the *AWA* litigation but has been of greater significance since then, concerns the role of a corporation's external auditor. Corporations legislation requires public corporations to have their financial affairs audited annually.[101] The basic statutory requirement of an auditor is to provide an independent and expert assessment as to whether the corporation's financial accounts comply with the relevant accounting and auditing standards and give a true and fair view of the corporation's financial situation.[102] This statutory framework is restricted to audits within the regular annual and half-yearly financial timetable, and it does not involve any assessment of 'the prudence of business decisions made by management'.[103]

Crucially, as a matter of law the appointment of a corporation's auditor is a decision of the shareholders at an annual general meeting of the corporation.[104] Furthermore, an auditor may only be removed from office by a resolution passed at a general meeting, initiated by the directors or members of the corporation.[105] It is true that as a matter of practice the shareholders' decision on auditor appointment or removal will usually be determined by the recommendation of the board (acting on the recommendation of the audit committee). It also appears, in Australia at least, that the removal power is not often used.[106] Nevertheless, the strict legal position continues to emphasise the auditor's role as a key component in an accountability process in which the members monitor the performance of the directors and managers.

There is an obvious link between the ideas of accountability and audit, that is, between providing information about the use of resources, and having that information checked and verified by an independent expert. But we have seen that the idea of accountability can go beyond simple processes of verification or 'accounting for'; it can also be understood as a key part of democratic processes. Just like accountability, the idea of auditing has many dimensions. Michael Power points out that:

---

[101] See, eg, *Corporations Act 2001* (Aust) s 301 (mandatory audit for all corporations except small proprietary companies); *Companies Act 1985* (UK) s 235 (mandatory audit report for all companies).

[102] See, eg, *Corporations Act 2001* (Aust) ss 307-308; *Companies Act 1985* (UK) s 235 (true and fair view).

[103] Ford, Austin, and Ramsay, above n 23, 589.

[104] The directors may appoint the company's initial auditor, who then holds office until the first AGM (s 327(2)).

[105] In Australia, see *Corporations Act 2001* s 329.

[106] A study of annual general meetings in 271 Australian listed companies found that the removal of the auditor had not been an agenda item in any of the meetings held between 2001 and 2003: S Bottomley, The Role of Shareholders' Meetings in Improving Corporate Governance (Research Report, Centre for Commercial Law, Australian National University, 2003) 36.

distinctions can be formulated between ex post and ex ante auditing, between verification and review, between the audit of transaction regularity and value for money, between private and public sector audits, between financial and non-financial audits, between auditing, evaluation, assessment and inspection, between big and small audits, between auditing and other forms of assurance services, between financial and environmental audits, between internal and external audits.[107]

And just as accountability can have a democratic role, a similar role can be claimed for audits — indeed, Power refers (albeit critically) to 'the democratizing potential of audit'.[108] That is, an audit report can provide the basis for questioning and further investigation, for moving from 'accountability as verification' to 'explanatory accountability' and even to 'accountability as responsibility'. In this way, audits can form an important part of a framework of separations of power in corporations. At the same time it is important not to over-emphasise or to be idealistic about the 'accountability value' of the audit process. Although the connection between audit and accountability may seem obvious, the two ideas may also come into conflict. Power notes how the intention behind many audit reports is to end scrutiny and inquiry, to bring the processes of accountability to a conclusion. The irony, as he puts it, is that 'the fact of being audited deters public curiosity and inquiry. ... Audit is in this respect a substitute for democracy rather than its aid'.[109] Thus, when audit becomes tied to a narrow conception of accountability it can impede broader conceptions of accountability.

One impediment to the capacity of audits to provide accountability within a separations of power framework is the perception — and in many instances the reality — that auditors are not independent of the corporations that they are auditing. These are longstanding concerns. For example, in the 1970 case of *Pacific Acceptance Corporation Ltd v Forsyth*, Moffitt J, in the NSW Supreme Court, noted that while the statutory auditor is appointed by the shareholders, most frequently it is the corporation's managers who determine that appointment. Moffitt J went on to observe that for the auditor:

> there must often be a real and practical conflict ... between his duty to the shareholders and his interest not to take action which may prejudice his reappointment or his relations with those with whom he works.[110]

There were strong criticisms of audit practices and auditor independence after the corporate crises of the 1980s.[111] And, of course, the prominent corporate collapses

---

[107] M Power, *The Audit Society: Rituals of Verification* (1999), 5-6.
[108] Ibid 123.
[109] Ibid 127.
[110] (1970) 92 WN(NSW) 29, 131.
[111] In addition to the *AWA* case, above n 71, see Commonwealth of Australia, Royal Commission of Inquiry into the Activities of the Nugan Hand Group, *Final Report - Volume 2* (1985); National Companies and Securities Commission, *Special Investigation into Affairs of the Trustees Executors & Agency Company Ltd and*

that occurred between 2001 and 2002[112] prompted renewed investigation into the lack of auditor independence.[113]

In Australia the Federal Government-commissioned Ramsay Report on auditor independence noted that independence is 'an imprecise and ambiguous concept' but concluded, nevertheless, that 'the terms "independent" and "auditor" can no longer be separated - independence appears to be endogenous to auditing'.[114] The two key professional accounting bodies in Australia define audit independence in terms of 'freedom from bias, personal interest, prior commitment to an interest, or susceptibility to undue influence or pressure'.[115] The Ramsay Report noted several factors that may erode the independence, or the apparent independence, of an audit[116] including: the provision to the corporation by the audit firm of other non-audit services (thereby building a broader commercial relationship between firm and corporation); the employment of former auditors by the corporation or appointment to the board (creating the possibility that continuing auditors will then be dealing with ex-colleagues); and lengthy terms of appointment (increasing the possibility that over time the auditor will become more tolerant of the corporation's practices). The Ramsay Report contributed to a significant rewriting of the audit provisions in the Australian *Corporations Act 2001*.[117]

Different reasons are advanced for requiring auditors to be independent. One rationale is that an independent audit adds value to the corporation's financial report:

the auditor's objective is to enhance, through the expression of an independent opinion, the credibility of the reported financial information of an entity. The

---

Related Corporations, *Fourth Interim Report* (1985); Western Australia, *Report of Inspection on a Special Investigation into Rothwells Ltd* (1990).

[112] For example, Enron corporation in late 2001, WorldCom Inc in mid-2002, and in Australia, One.Tel Ltd in May 2001 and HIH Insurance Ltd in March 2001.

[113] For example, in Australia, I Ramsay, *Independence of Australian Company Auditors: Review of Current Australian Requirements and Proposals for Reform* (2001) (hereafter, the Ramsay Report); Joint Standing Committee on Public Accounts and Audit, Parliament of Australia, *Review of Independent Auditing by Registered Company Auditors* (2002); Department of Treasury, *Corporate Disclosure: Strengthening the Financial Reporting Framework* (2002); Commonwealth of Australia, The HIH Royal Commission, *The Failure of HIH Insurance Volume 1* (2003) 162-184; in the United Kingdom, Co-Ordinating Group on Audit and Accounting Issues, *Final Report to the Secretary for Trade and Industry and the Chancellor of the Exchequer* (2003); in the United States, the New York Stock Exchange, above n 64.

[114] Ramsay Report, above n 113, 8.01 and 8.15.

[115] Australian Society of Certified Practicing Accountants and The Institute of Chartered Accountants in Australia, 'Statement of Auditing Practice AUP32 "Audit Independence"' in *Auditing Handbook, Volume 2 of the Accounting and Auditing Handbook* (2001) 955-956, cited in ibid, 8.06.

[116] Ramsay Report, above n 113, 8.26-8.91.

[117] See Schedule 1 to the *Corporate Law Economic Reform Program (Audit Reform and Corporate Disclosure) Act 2004* (Cth).

> value of the independent audit lies both in the fact that the auditor is, and is seen to
> be, independent of the audited entity, and hence is able to carry out the audit free
> of any externally imposed constraints.[118]

Independent audits are also said to have a role in enhancing the integrity of
financial markets by aiding in the detection of fraud or malpractice and promoting
investor confidence. It is also argued that independent audits reduce the
information asymmetry that exists between corporate managers and shareholders,
improving the investment decisions made by the latter.[119] Auditors thus serve as
'reputational intermediaries', assisting the efficient operation of the market for
corporate information,[120] and so their perceived independence promotes confidence
in the audit process.

    The argument advanced here is that alongside these claimed benefits,
auditor independence is a necessary component in an accountability framework
that is based on the idea of separations of powers. Having said that, it is also the
case that no matter how well-founded the concern about lack of auditor
independence is, a separations of power framework should try to ensure that
auditors do not become so independent that they are beyond effective scrutiny of
their work by others in the separations of power framework. There have been many
solutions offered to the problem of balancing auditor independence and
accountability. These include:

- splitting auditing work and consulting work between different accounting firms;[121]
- compelling the disclosure of non-audit services provided to the corporation by the auditor. In Australia the *Corporations Act* requires the directors of a listed corporation to include in the annual report a statement that describes the dollar amount paid to the auditor for non-audit services during the year, explains whether the directors are satisfied that the provision of those services is compatible with the general standard of independence for auditors, and gives reasons why the directors are satisfied about this;[122]
- mandating the periodic rotation of auditors to avoid a relaxation of audit procedures due to over-familiarity with the audit client. In Australia, an

---

[118] Statement of Auditing Practice AUP 32, quoted in Ramsay Report, above n 113, 4.09.
[119] Ramsay Report, above n 113, 8.22.
[120] See A Corbett, 'The Rationale for the Recovery of Economic Loss in Negligence and the Problem of Auditors Liability' (1994) 19 *Melbourne University Law Review* 814, 850, referring to R Gilson and R Kraakman 'The Mechanisms of Market Efficiency' (1984) 70 *Virginia Law Review* 549.
[121] D Kitney and R Buffini, 'Directors target audit overhaul' *The Australian Financial Review*, 4 March 2002, 1. In the United States the *Sarbanes-Oxley Act* of 2002 (Pub. L. No. 107-204, 116 Stat. 745 (2002)) prohibits auditors from providing certain non-audit services contemporaneously with the audit (s 201).
[122] s 300(11B).

individual who plays a significant role[123] in the audit of a listed corporation for five successive years cannot play a significant role in the audit of that corporation for another two years;[124]

- imposing a cooling-off period for ex-auditors who wish to join a former client as a director or officer;[125]
- ensuring that audit committees are properly constituted and have clear responsibilities for oversight of the audit function and, in particular, for recommending to the board the appointment, remuneration or removal of the external auditor;[126]
- requiring, or encouraging, the attendance of the auditor at the annual general meeting,[127] and giving members a reasonable opportunity to ask questions about the audit, the accounting policies used in preparation of the audit, and the independence of the auditor.[128]

The *Corporations Act 2001* in Australia also imposes general and specific independence requirements for auditors. The general requirement focuses on the need to avoid 'conflict of interest situations'[129] in which an auditor is not capable of exercising objective and impartial judgement in conducting the audit, or a reasonable person would conclude that this is the case. This involves looking at the relationship between the auditor and the corporation, its current or former directors and managers.[130] One implication of this general requirement is that an auditor must have in place a quality control system that is reasonably capable of making them aware that a conflict of interest situation exists. The specific independence requirement focuses on particular relationships that constitute a breach of the auditor's independence when they are engaged in audit activity. The Act defines nineteen such relationships. Some are role relationships (eg where the auditor is an officer or employee of the audited corporation); others are property relationships

---

[123] A person 'plays a significant role' if they are appointed and act as the auditor or prepare the audit report for the company, or if they are the lead or review auditor for a firm or company that is appointed as auditor (s 9).

[124] *Corporations Act 2001* s 324DA. If the auditor is a firm or a corporation, and the lead or review auditor has played a significant role in audits for the past five successive years, then the firm or corporation may continue to act as auditor, provided that it uses another person in the lead or review capacity (ss 324DC and DD). See also *Sarbanes-Oxley Act* of 2002 (Pub. L. No. 107-204, 116 Stat. 745 (2002)) s 203 (audit rotation period of five years).

[125] In Australia, the cooling-off period is two years – *Corporations Act 2001* ss 324CI and CJ.

[126] Ramsay Report, above n 113, 6.59 and 6.105; Australian Stock Exchange, above n 83, recommendation 4.4; United Kingdom, Financial Services Authority, *The Combined Code on Corporate Governance* (July 2003) principle C.3.6.

[127] See, for example, *Corporations Act 2001* s 250RA (mandatory auditor attendance at AGM of listed company), and s 249V (right of auditor to attend AGM).

[128] *Corporations Act 2001* s 250T.

[129] ss 324CA-CC.

[130] s 324CD.

(eg where the auditor has an asset that is an investment in the audited corporation); the remainder are financial relationships (eg where the auditor owes money to, or is owed money by, the audited corporation).[131]

The independence requirements listed above are largely concerned with what Power calls organizational independence.[132] That is, they define the independence problem in terms of the relationship between the corporation and the auditor, focusing, for example, on the auditor's impartiality and the way in which the auditor is appointed. A similar concern is expressed in the idea that the auditor must be independent not only as a matter of fact but also in appearance.[133]

Power argues that there is a second dimension to audit independence — operational independence — which focuses on the process of the audit rather than on the auditor.[134] This idea is further sub-divided into what Power calls informational and epistemic independence. Informational independence draws attention to the fact that regardless of their degree of organisational independence, an auditor must depend, at least to some extent, on information supplied by the corporation that is being audited. This is the problem discussed in the *Pacific Acceptance* case, noted earlier,[135] and it has been a constant concern of the courts. For example, in defining the common law duties of auditors, the courts have concentrated on the obligation to look behind the corporation's books and determine its true financial position.[136] Acknowledging that auditors must be dependent, at least to some extent, on information supplied by the corporation, the second sub-category — epistemic independence — is concerned with whether the auditor is nevertheless able to draw independent conclusions from this information.[137] Power argues that for this to be possible, auditors must have a knowledge base that is independent of the audited party on which to assess information provided by that party.[138] This reduces the impact of negotiations with the audited party about what should and should not be noted in the audit report. This aspect of operational independence highlights the use of auditing (and accounting) standards. For example, the *Corporations Act* s 307A requires an audit to be conducted in accordance with the auditing standards that are made by the Auditing and Assurance Standards Board, a statutory authority.[139]

Each of the auditor independence mechanisms described above (and the list is not exhaustive) has generated debate on questions of practicability and effectiveness. Without rehearsing those debates here, my argument is that these ideas should be assessed by their potential to contribute to a separation of powers

---

[131] ss 324CE-CH.
[132] Power, above n 107, 132.
[133] See Ramsay Report, above n 113, 8.08.
[134] Power, above n 107, 132.
[135] *Pacific Acceptance Corporation Ltd v Forsyth* (1970) 92 WN(NSW) 29.
[136] For example, *Arthur Young & Co v WA Chip & Pulp Co Pty Ltd* (1988) 13 ACLR 283; *AWA Ltd v Daniels* (1992) 10 ACLC 933.
[137] Power, above n 107, 132-133.
[138] Ibid 133.
[139] Established by s 227A *Australian Securities and Investments Commission Act 2001*.

form of accountability. None of these reforms by itself provides a guarantee of accountability. For example, while the evidence suggests that in Australia auditors already attend AGMs as a matter of course, shareholder questioning of auditors is often either non-existent or is hampered by inadequate understanding of the financial data. But misgivings about the practice of audits and auditors should not negate their role as one part of a system of corporate checks and balances that is achieved by separations of powers. Furthermore, it must be remembered that the separation of powers is only one part of the wider framework of corporate constitutionalism in which problems in one aspect of that framework (such as poor audit practices) have every chance of being detected and remedied by another aspect.

Shareholders and Separations of Powers

I argued earlier in this Chapter that shareholders, via the general meeting, occupy one of the two key decision-making sites in a corporation. But the general meeting is not the only mechanism through which shareholders can have contact with directors and managers.[140] We can therefore consider separations of powers within the ranks of the shareholders outside the general meeting. Some shareholders have the capacity to monitor and influence management. Indeed, institutional shareholders (such as superannuation funds, insurance companies, managed investment funds, and banks) are now being urged to play a role as catalysts for improved governance practices in listed public companies. The OECD Principles of Corporate Governance argue that:

> The effectiveness and credibility of the entire corporate governance system and company oversight will ... to a large extend depend on institutional investors that can make informed use of their shareholder rights and effectively exercise their ownership functions in companies in which they invest.[141]

The OECD urges that institutions should 'establish a continuing dialogue' with their portfolio corporations. Similarly, in the United Kingdom the Institutional Shareholders' Committee (a lobby group representing four major institutional associations) has published principles that urge institutional shareholders to monitor and, where necessary, enter into 'active dialogue' with the boards and senior managers of portfolio corporations.[142] In Australia the Federal Parliamentary Joint Committee on Corporations and Financial Services has noted that:

---

[140]   Higgs, above n 87, 15.11.
[141]   OECD, above n 84, 37.
[142]   Institutional Shareholders' Committee, *The Responsibilities of Institutional Shareholders and Agents – Statement of Principles* <http://www.abi.org.uk/Display/File/38/Statement_of_Principles.pdf> at 30 July 2004. This Statement of Principles is supported in the FSA Combined Code, above n 126, Principle E.1, and endorsed in the Higgs Review, above n 87, 15.25.

there are growing expectations that institutional investors will take an active part in monitoring and influencing the companies in which they invest especially through exercising their vote at meetings. For example, the Australian Chamber of Commerce and Industry urges institutional investors to be mindful of their fiduciary duty to their clients and to 'take a greater degree of active interest and engagement in the affairs of those companies where they, on behalf of their clients, have substantial economic interests'.[143]

Institutional shareholders can perform this task in a number of ways (including indirect methods such as lobbying for law reform), but chiefly it is done through the exercise of voting rights at general meetings or through private meetings and the exchange of information with senior managers of portfolio corporations. Australian research suggests that institutions prefer the latter method, although the exercise of voting rights by institutional shareholders has increased since the corporate collapses of 2001-02.[144] Another study of institutional shareholders in Australia found that many institutions maintain regular contact with the corporations in which they own shares, providing an opportunity to monitor financial matters, strategic planning and management issues.[145] Similarly, the Higgs Review in the United Kingdom reported that 'three-quarters of chairmen discuss company business with some of their investors at least once a year'.[146]

As with other separations of powers, it is important not to place too much reliance on the role of institutional shareholders. The interests of institutional shareholders will not necessarily accord with those of other shareholders — as John Coffee observes, '[i]nstitutional investors should not be mistaken for financial saints'.[147] Despite the fact that institutional shareholders can — and sometimes do[148] — vote contrary to the recommendations of the directors or senior managers of a corporation, it is equally possible that these private forms of monitoring and persuasion may result in alliances that resist outside scrutiny. Requiring institutions to disclose their voting policy and record is a partial response to this particular

[143] Parliamentary Joint Committee on Corporations and Financial Services, Parliament of Australia, *CLERP (Audit Reform and Corporate Disclosure) Bill 2003 - Part 1* (2004) 168.

[144] Investment & Financial Services Association Ltd, *Shareholder Activism Among Fund Managers: Policy and Practice*, (2003) — submission to Parliamentary Joint Committee on Corporations and Financial Services, Parliament of Australia, Canberra, <http://www.aph.gove.au/senate/committee/corporations_ctte/clerp9/submissions/sub044a1.pdf> at 30 July 2004.

[145] I Ramsay, G Stapledon and K Fong, 'Corporate Governance: The Perspective of Australian Institutional Shareholders' (2000) 18 *Company and Securities Law Journal* 110, 124.

[146] Higgs, above n 87, 67.

[147] J Coffee, 'Liquidity versus Control: The Institutional Investor as Corporate Monitor' (1991) 91 *Columbia Law Review* 1277, 1334.

[148] Ramsay, Stapledon and Fong, above n 145, 121; Investment & Financial Services Association Ltd, above n 144, 13.

problem, though one that is resisted by some institutions.[149] Furthermore, there is no reason to assume that all institutional shareholders will share similar concerns. As John Farrar notes, '[i]nstitutional investors are ... not a monolithic whole with one investment objective'.[150] Finally, there are significant legal limitations on the extent to which institutional investors can play an active role in the governance of portfolio corporations, including takeover laws and insider trading prohibitions.[151]

Whistleblowers

A system of separations of powers cannot guarantee that every instance or pattern of illegal, improper or illegitimate behaviour will be brought to light and dealt with. It may simply be impossible for (say) the external audit team to discover what is happening in some parts of the corporation. One way of supplementing a separations framework is to encourage those who know of problems, and who know that those problems are unlikely to be detected or dealt with through normal channels, to voice their concerns. We should encourage whistleblowing.[152] The Royal Commission of Inquiry into the collapse of the HIH insurance group urged this:

> Those responsible for the governance of a company should have an interest in inculcating within the company a culture and processes that enable instances of questionable conduct to be brought to attention outside normal reporting lines without fear of retribution.[153]

Typically, a whistleblower protection scheme offers some form of protection from liability or retaliation for certain types of disclosure about wrongdoing in an organisation.[154]

I emphasise that whistleblowing should be regarded as a supplement to the formal system of corporate accountability, not as a key component of it. For

---

[149] Eg, Parliamentary Joint Committee on Corporations and Financial Services, above n 143, recommendation 23. Research in the UK suggests that fund managers oppose the public disclosure of voting: see above n 87, 13.

[150] J Farrar, *Corporate Governance in Australia and New Zealand* (2001) 319.

[151] P Ali, G Stapledon and M Gold, *Corporate Governance and Investment Fiduciaries* (2003) chapter 3.

[152] Corporate whistleblowing has many contexts, for example the employee who 'goes public' regarding illegal dumping of toxic waste or price-fixing. This present discussion concerns questions of corporate governance.

[153] HIH Royal Commission, above n 113, 131. Encouragement for whistleblowing can also be found in the Australian Stock Exchange's corporate governance code, above n 83, recommendation 10.1, and in the OECD Principles of Corporate Governance, above n 84, principle IV.E.

[154] The *Corporations Act 2001* (Aust) Part 9.4AAA gives qualified privilege and provides immunity from civil or criminal liability for a disclosure made on reasonable grounds and in good faith by an officer or employee of a corporation or by a person (or their employee) who has a contract for the supply of services or goods with the corporation.

one thing, corporate leaders would presumably prefer to reduce the need for whistleblowing and encourage the prospect of detecting problems through regular internal channels. [155] Another reason is that the choice facing a potential whistleblower is always difficult, notwithstanding the positive attention that whistleblowing often receives in the press. The personal consequences can be significant, and many will consider the risks to be too high. Nevertheless, encouraging whistleblowing can be an important supplement — a safety net that may operate when other forms of accountability fail. [156]

The consequences when this is not done can be significant. As Alan Greenspan, Chair of the United States Federal Reserve Board, commented in 2002:

> In recent years, shareholders and potential investors would have been protected from widespread misinformation if any one of the many bulwarks safeguarding appropriate corporate evaluation had held. In too many cases, none did. Lawyers, internal and external auditors, corporate boards, Wall Street security analysts, rating agencies, and large institutional holders of stock all failed for one reason or another to detect and blow the whistle on those who breached the level of trust essential to well-functioning markets. [157]

As this quote suggests, whistleblowers can come from within a corporation (employees, corporate officers) or be external to it (eg professional advisers, consultants, related corporations). [158] The aim in having a wide base of potential whistleblowers is to maximise the likelihood that people who are not beholden to power bases within the corporation will voice their concerns. [159] Similarly, the recipients of their information can be internal to the corporation (eg the audit committee[160]) or external (eg the relevant corporate and securities regulator). [161]

Whistleblowing can be an obligation that is attached to a particular position. The external auditor is the most common example of a 'role-prescribed whistleblower'. [162] In Australia an auditor is required to notify the Australian and

---

[155] M Miceli and J Near, *Blowing the Whistle: The Organizational and Legal Implications for Companies and Employees* (1992), 282.

[156] M Winfield, 'Whistleblower as Corporate Safety Net' in G Vinten (ed), *Whistleblowing: Subversion or Corporate Citizenship?* (1994) 21, 22.

[157] Statement to United States Senate Committee on Banking, Housing and Urban Affairs (July 2002), quoted in P Latimer, 'Whistleblowing in the Financial Services Sector' (2002) 21 *University of Tasmania Law Review* 39, 42.

[158] This is recognised in *Corporations Act 2001* s 1317AA.

[159] See Braithwaite, above n 62, 349ff for more detailed discussion of this point.

[160] For example, in the United States s 10A(m)(4)(b) of the *Securities Exchange Act of 1934* requires each audit committee to establish procedures for the confidential, anonymous submission by employees of concerns regarding questionable accounting or audit matters.

[161] As an example, the *Corporations Act 2001* (Aust) s 1317AA protects disclosures that are made to the Australian Securities and Investments Commission, the auditor, a director or senior manager, the corporate secretary, or to a person authorised by the corporation to receive those disclosures.

[162] This term comes from Miceli and Near, above n 155, 21.

Securities Investments Commission (ASIC) if the auditor has a reasonable suspicion that the *Corporations Act* has been contravened or that someone has attempted to unduly influence, coerce, manipulate, mislead or interfere with the conduct of the audit.[163] This requirement is an expanded version of a previous section that had little effect. A Treasury discussion paper in 2002 noted an 'almost total absence of reports made to ASIC by auditors' under the old section.[164] At the time of writing it is too early to comment on the impact of the redrafted section, but the earlier experience does underline the point that for whistleblowing to be an effective safety net there must be many different categories of person who are potential sources of disclosure.

There are other factors that can affect the likelihood that a formally sanctioned system of whistleblowing will effectively supplement a separations of powers system.[165] One factor is the type of misconduct that can be reported under whistleblower protections — is it restricted to contraventions of a specific statute (or statutes), or does it include breaches of ethical or best-practice codes? Is it enough that the whistleblower is aware of a probable violation or must there be a stronger suspicion? Must the discloser be shown to have acted in 'good faith', or is an 'honest and reasonable belief' sufficient? Can the disclosure be made anonymously? What is the scope of protection for disclosers — does it cover forms of in-house retaliation or victimisation as well as immunity from law suits?

Conclusion

The idea of separations of powers operates within a framework of dual decision-making. To put it another way, the distinction between the board of directors and the general meeting of shareholders is not just another form of power separation, even though we can identify power separations within both of these decision-making sites. The idea of dual decision-making is a constant in all public corporations, while separations of powers will not necessarily be the same between one corporation and another or within one corporation over time. Separations of powers can occur amongst people or groups who are parts of a single decision-making process (eg separations in the board of directors). In comparison, the dual decision-making model begins from the premise that the shareholders and the board (and managers) engage in quite different types of decisions. Shareholders have interests that are categorically distinct from those of directors and managers. The point of the dual model is to preserve those distinct interests.

---

[163] s 311. See also s 1289, giving an auditor qualified privilege in respect of a notification under s 311.

[164] Commonwealth of Australia, Department of Treasury, *Corporate Disclosure: Strengthening the Financial Reporting Framework* (2002) 10.2; see also R Tomasic and S Bottomley, *Directing the Top 500: Corporate Governance and Accountability in Australian Companies* (1993) 107.

[165] See the discussion in Parliamentary Joint Committee on Corporations and Financial Services, above n 143, Chapter 2.

Furthermore, separations and divisions of power alone are insufficient and, by themselves, may be counter-productive, breeding mistrust and a compliance-oriented, 'tick the box' approach to corporate governance. Braithwaite, drawing on the work of Charles Sabel, argues that the potential inefficiencies from separations of power can be resolved through an emphasis on each separate site of power learning from the know-how of other sites.[166] In Sabel's terms the trick is to reconcile 'the demands of learning with the demands of monitoring'.[167] In Braithwaite's terms, separations of powers must be supplemented with reliance on the idea of deliberation: 'the separation of powers creates a world where dialogue can displace sanctioning as the dominant means of regulating abuse of power'.[168] The role and importance of deliberation — of explanation, justification, questioning and criticism — in corporate governance is the subject of the next Chapter.

---

[166]   Braithwaite, above n 62, 359.
[167]   Ibid.
[168]   Ibid 361.

Chapter 5

Corporate Decisions and Deliberation

As I noted in Chapter 1, we readily think of public corporations as economic entities because of the fundamental role they play in the economy. Corporations accumulate, convert, produce and disperse economic resources. But as I argued in Chapter 3, it is equally important to emphasise that these activities are predicated on processes of decision-making within each corporation, and those decision-making processes have a political dimension. I argued in Chapter 4 that our system of corporate law is based on a system of dual decision-making. In corporate constitutional terms, decisions made by directors are ultimately subordinate to decisions made by the general meeting of shareholders. This is emphasised in the exclusive power of the general meeting to amend the constitution,[1] to dismiss directors,[2] and to ratify what would otherwise be a breach of duty by the directors.[3] It is crucial to the legitimate operation of this dual system that the role of the general meeting should not be reduced to that of a rubber-stamp or a mere procedural hurdle. It is also essential that directors should actually exercise their decision-making powers rather than simply signing off on proposals put by management. Directors should also exercise their powers responsibly.

In this Chapter I argue that one way we can address the potential risks of general meeting decisions being taken for granted, or of boards ignoring their responsibilities, is by insisting on the idea of deliberative decision-making. That is, we can assess the legitimacy of corporate decisions not simply by asking whether they command the support of the requisite majority of votes or whether they produce desirable outcomes, but also by assessing the extent to which the processes leading to the formal adoption of those decisions are based on the deliberative input of the persons concerned.

This is an interdisciplinary argument and so a brief explanation is needed. The idea of deliberation has received a lot of attention in the past fifteen years or so. Different strands of deliberative theory have emerged, ranging from conservative

---

[1] See, eg, *Corporations Act 2001* (Cth) s 136(2); *Companies Act 1985* (UK) s 9; Canada Business Corporations Act s 173. In the United States, the power to amend a corporation's bylaws is usually shared between the directors and the shareholders: see, eg, *Revised Model Business Corporations Act* s 10.20 (2002).

[2] See, eg, *Corporations Act 2001* (Cth) s 203D; *Companies Act 1985* (UK) s 303; *Canada Business Corporations Act*, RSC 1985, s 109.

[3] See, eg, *Bamford v Bamford* [1970] Ch 212; *Winthrop Investements Ltd v Winns Ltd* [1975] 2 NSWLR 666.

liberal views to critical and radical perspectives.[4] Deliberative theorists debate with each other (as, of course, they should) the differences and the commonalities in their perspectives. I do not propose to enter these debates or to offer a particular theory of deliberation. Instead, I take some of these deliberative ideas and apply them to the context of corporate decision-making. This is a context that has received little, if any, attention from deliberative theorists. Nevertheless, my reading of the literature suggests that deliberative ideas do have a role to play in corporate governance. I have tended to borrow widely from the deliberative literature. Particular deliberative theorists may baulk at some of what they read here, but any damage I do to particular theories of deliberation is due to the unique characteristics of the corporate context.[5]

The Idea of Deliberative Decision-Making

In this part of the Chapter I make the general argument that the idea of deliberative decision-making can be applied to corporations. Later on, I address some more specific aspects of deliberative decision-making in board-rooms and the general meetings.

I use the term 'deliberative decision-making'[6] to describe the idea that *as far as possible* there should be processes prior to reaching decisions (whether in the board-room or the general meeting) that are *open and genuine*, and that these processes should lead to decisions that represent a *collective judgement* about the issue at hand.

By *open and genuine* I mean that corporate decisions ought to be reached as a consequence of processes of inquiry and be made in the light of all relevant

---

[4]   A useful review of the literature, written from a critical perspective, can be found in J Dryzek, *Deliberative Democracy and Beyond: Liberals, Critics, Contestations* (2000).

[5]   In particular, the corporate context of countries such as Australia and the United Kingdom.

[6]   I refer to 'deliberative decision-making' rather than 'deliberative democracy' because I want to highlight the process of deliberation as a necessary prelude to decision-making. That is, I do not want to characterise deliberation as a good in and of itself — a claim that is sometimes associated with the term 'deliberative democracy'. My ideas on deliberative decision-making draw on a variety of sources, but in particular: Joshua Cohen, 'Deliberation and Democratic Legitimacy' in A Hamlin and P Pettit (eds), *The Good Polity: Normative Analysis of the State* (1989); Bernard Manin, 'On Legitimacy and Political Deliberation' (1987) 15 *Political Theory* 338; Philip Pettit, *Republicanism: A Theory of Freedom and Government* (1997) (hereafter, 'Republicanism'); Cass Sunstein, *The Partial Constitution* (1993) (hereafter 'The Partial Constitution'); C Sunstein, *Democracy and the Problem of Free Speech* (1993) (hereafter, 'Democracy and Free Speech'); Iris Young, 'Communication and the Other: Beyond Deliberative Democracy' in M Wilson and A Yeatman (eds), *Justice and Identity: Antipodean Practices* (1995). This Chapter is an adaptation of these ideas because none of these arguments has specifically applied the idea of deliberation to corporate decision-making.

arguments. Decision-making in the general meeting and in the board room ought to involve 'recourse to methods of discussion, consultation, and persuasion' prior to the counting of votes and the adoption of a resolution.[7] Adapting Cass Sunstein's description, corporate decisions should be the outcome of processes of 'deliberation and discussion, in which new information and new perspectives are brought to bear'.[8] The legitimacy of a decision is not determined simply by the results that it produces. A decision 'inherits most of its legitimation from the preceding deliberation'.[9] This accords with wider research showing that people evaluate their experiences in decision-making forums by focusing on the fairness of the procedures, rather than on the personal consequences of the decision.[10]

The idea of deliberative decision-making emphasises process as much as outcome. It also emphasises reason rather than authority.[11] Deliberative decisions are based on the critical assessment of reasoned argument, not on managerial edict, deference to the authority or expertise of directors or to the votes of powerful shareholders, nor by appeal to pre-existing assumptions about what is reasonable, feasible, or appropriate.[12] Moreover, during deliberation there should be an 'equality of input'. For example, the views of small or minority shareholders should not be discounted simply because of the size of their potential vote. This was put nicely in *Re Compaction Systems Pty Ltd*, where Bowen CJ in Eq pointed out that:

> [t]he right to receive notice of a meeting and to attend and to be heard is not an insubstantial right. The right to advance arguments and to influence the course of discussion may in some circumstances have an effect, even a decisive effect, on the decision reached.[13]

The requirement that decisions be open and genuine entails, therefore, that there should be practices and structures in place to ensure that participants in the decision-making forum have the opportunity to have their point of view heard before the decision is made. A brief note of caution is needed here: the argument about deliberation should not be read as an argument about participation, except to the extent that it insists that the general meeting and the board room should be forums in which decisions are actually made, rather than being procedural showpieces that merely formalise or ratify decisions that have effectively been

---

[7]   J Dewey, 'The Public and Its Problems', in D Morris and I Shapiro (eds), *John Dewey: The Political Writings* (1993) 187. See also Sunstein, Democracy and Free Speech, above n 6, 242.

[8]   Sunstein, The Partial Constitution, above n 6, 134.

[9]   A Tschentscher, 'Deliberation as a Discursive Feature of Contemporary Theories of Democracy: Comment on John S. Dryzek' in A Van Aaken, C List, and C Luetge (eds), *Deliberation and Decision: Economics, Constitutional Theory and Deliberative Democracy* (2004) 72, 76.

[10]   See Tom Tyler, *Why People Obey the Law* (1990).

[11]   Young, above n 6, 136.

[12]   See Cohen, above n 6, 22; Young, above n 6, 137.

[13]   (1976) 2 ACLR 135, 142.

made elsewhere. Deliberation is intended to counter decisions being made through 'rubber stamping' and 'back-room deals'. I return to the relationship between deliberation and participation in more detail later in this Chapter.[14]

So much for the requirement that decision-making should be open and genuine. My definition of deliberative decision-making also requires that decisions represent a *collective judgement* about the issue at hand. Corporate decision-making is legitimate insofar as it is a consequence of processes of discussion and debate in which shareholders and/or directors (depending on the particular forum), move beyond self-interest and reflect on the corporate interest. That is, members of the decision-making group should be encouraged to move from a preoccupation with their individual preferences towards the formulation of a collective opinion about a given proposal. As I note later, this approximates the legal standard for directors.[15] Shareholders are under a more vaguely defined obligation, under certain circumstances, to exercise their voting power for a proper purpose.[16]

This is not to suggest that individuals must, or will, abandon their private interests and concerns. It is undeniable that private interest will often supply the motivation for a person's input to a corporate decision. As Richard Buxbaum notes, there is a continuing tension between 'collective decision making by egoists and collective decision making by altruists'.[17] But in a deliberative system private interests *alone* are not sufficient to legitimate the final decision. Considerations of the corporate interest are a necessary ingredient for decision-making.[18] There is an important difference between a decision that is based on an aggregation of antecedently formed and unchanged individual preferences, and the situation where a vote reflects the result of a debate about what is in the corporate interest.[19] To paraphrase Sunstein again, in a deliberative political process even the most venal or self-interested participants must feel encouraged to invoke corporate justifications in their support, even if they do not actually mean it.[20] Put less cynically, during the process of deliberation each participant should be able to encounter competing perspectives and interests, and thus realize that appeals to individual preference alone are unlikely to attract the support of others. Ideally, then, arguments ought to be framed in ways that will attract the support of a diversity of interests.

Deliberation is, therefore, a process in which individual interests are exposed to competing perspectives that are debated and transformed into a collective judgement concerning the corporate interest in the issue at hand. Even if there are no significant differences of opinion about an issue, deliberation is still

---

[14]   See below n 36 and accompanying text.

[15]   The law prescribes that directors must act in the general corporate interest: see below n 36 and accompanying text.

[16]   This is discussed later: see below n 52 and accompanying text.

[17]   R Buxbaum, 'Corporate Governance and Corporate Monitoring: The Whys and Hows' (1996) 6 *Australian Journal of Corporate Law* 309, 312.

[18]   Young, above n 6, 143.

[19]   Young, above n 6, 137.

[20]   Sunstein, Democracy and Free Speech, above n 6, 244.

important in transforming the several similar individual views into a group opinion. There will, of course, be competing versions of what is in the corporate interest, and different views of the criteria to be used in assessing it. Indeed, some interpretations may require the articulation of other interests as well, eg employees, consumers, the environment. It is one purpose of deliberative decision-making to encourage this sort of debate.

Deliberation and Majority Decisions

None of this means that corporate decisions must of necessity be based on consensus or unanimity. Indeed, insisting on consensus could work against the idea of deliberation; it would risk producing decisions based on the lowest common denominator. As I noted in Chapter 3, the idea of deliberation is consistent with majority decision-making.[21] Importantly, however, it is inconsistent with majority domination of the decision-making process. From a deliberative perspective we can be comfortable with a majority vote, provided that the minority has had an open and genuine chance for input.

Deliberation therefore provides a standard by which the legitimacy of a majority decision can be assessed. As John Dewey once pointed out, what is important is how the majority on a given issue comes to be a majority.[22] Manin adds to this: a majority vote that is based on deliberation necessarily involves a recognition that there were also good reasons *not* to support the decision which was finally adopted.[23] There is a strong theme in Tom Tyler's research on procedural justice which supports this idea. When people feel that they have had an opportunity to present their arguments and have been listened to — when they feel that 'they have had a hand in the decision' — they are more likely to accept the outcome, even if the decision goes against them.[24]

In the corporate context there is an important qualification to be noted about this: a majority vote in a general meeting does not necessarily mean the same thing as a vote by the majority of voting shareholders. It is important to keep in mind the way in which corporate voting systems operate.

Using Australian law as an example,[25] the *Corporations Act* presumes that each share in a corporation will have one vote unless the corporate constitution provides otherwise.[26] The Act nevertheless provides that in the first instance a vote

---

[21] There are issues to be addressed in the procedures used to achieve a decision by majority vote: see Philip Pettit, 'A Dilemma for Deliberative Democrats' in Van Aaken, List and Luetge, above n 9, 91.

[22] Dewey, above n 7, 187.

[23] Manin, above n 6, 359.

[24] Above, n 10, 163 (Tyler's research concerns people's experience with decisions made by police and courts).

[25] These are similar to statutory provisions in other countries, eg the United Kingdom and Canada.

[26] *Corporations Act 2001* (Cth) s 250E (a replaceable rule). The comparable provision in the *Companies Act 1985* (UK) s 370(6) is said to be based on 'a presumption of equality between shareholders': P Davies, *Gower and Davies' Principles of Modern*

on a resolution will be decided on a show of hands.[27] This has long been common corporate practice,[28] and most resolutions are decided in this way.[29] This suggests that, initially at least, corporate decision-making places some value on the political ideal of one person – one vote or, as Ratner puts it, the idea that 'votes are decisions, decisions are made by people, and one person's decision should not be given greater weight than another's unless some important reason of policy supports the distinction'.[30] Of course there is a countervailing policy: corporate law has an underlying preference for the principle of one share – one vote, which directly correlates voting power to the size of a shareholder's financial stake in the corporation.[31] Voting at a general meeting ultimately becomes an expression of economic interests; the shareholder who owns more share capital in a corporation has a greater opportunity to have a say in the corporation's affairs.[32]

The legislation provides that on or before the declaration of a result on a show of hands, a specified proportion of shareholders may demand that the resolution be decided on a poll (or ballot).[33] When a poll is taken, each voting shareholder is able to exercise the actual votes per share that they hold.[34] This

---

Company Law (7th ed, 2003) 618. The Australian Stock Exchange Listing Rules *require* a listed company to allocate one vote per share as a prerequisite to listing: Listing Rule 6.9. In an unlisted company, there is no legal impediment to the creation of voting rights that are unrelated to the size of the member's shareholding (see eg *Amalgamated Pest Control Pty Ltd v McCarron* (1994) 12 ACLC 171, 173). Shares can be given multiple voting rights that can operate either generally or on particular types of resolution (see eg *Bushell v Faith* [1970] AC 1099).

[27] s 250J (a replaceable rule). Unless the corporation's constitution says otherwise, a proxy may vote on a show of hands (s 249Y).

[28] It was described by Lindley LJ in *Ernest v Loma Gold Mines Ltd* [1896] 1 Ch 1, 6 as a 'well known mode of conducting business'.

[29] S Bottomley, The Role of Shareholders' Meetings in Improving Corporate Governance (Research Report, Centre for Commercial Law, Australian National University, 2003), 38.

[30] D Ratner, 'The Government of Business Corporations: Critical Reflections on the Rule of "One Share, One Vote"' (1970) 56 *Cornell Law Review* 1, 19.

[31] Earlier companies legislation provided a slightly different formulation. For example, in New South Wales, the *Companies Act 1874* s 84 provided that every member shall have one vote unless the Articles said otherwise. The model Articles set out a variable voting scale: one vote per share for the first 10 shares held; one additional vote for every extra 5 shares up to 100 shares; and one additional vote for every 10 shares over 100. This appears to have been taken from the *Companies Act 1862* (UK). In New South Wales reference to one vote per share in the model articles was not introduced until the *Companies Act 1936*.

[32] See H Manne 'Some Theoretical Aspects of Share Voting — An Essay in Honor of Adolf A. Berle' (1964) 64 *Columbia Law Review* 1427, 1430 for an explanation of the relationship between what he describes as the voting and investment components of the voting share.

[33] The demand must be made by either the chairperson of the meeting, or by a sufficient number of members as specified: s 250L

[34] On a poll a member does not have to exercise all of their votes, nor need they cast all their votes in the same way: s 250H.

means that reference to 'a majority vote' at a general meeting may mean a majority of the shareholders or it may mean a majority of the votes that were actually cast (which, depending on the spread of shares, may or may not be the same as a majority of shareholders).

One problem that may impede the effective operation of deliberative processes in a decision-making system that is based on allocating votes per share and in which voting is voluntary is that holders of large parcels of voting shares may decide to exercise their voting power regardless of the deliberative process. Because their vote will carry the day, they may shun deliberative input. My response to this potential problem begins from the premise that shareholders cannot — and should not — be forced to deliberate. Instead, shareholders should be encouraged — in ways that I will describe — to consider the benefits for the corporation as a whole that can result from quality deliberative input from as many shareholders as possible. On some matters, as we will see in the case of minority share expropriations,[35] the law supports this, setting firm guidelines that are intended to encourage consideration by majority shareholders of the interests of others.

Deliberation and Participation

The deliberative process requires input from varying perspectives, such as (depending on the forum) individual shareholders, institutional and corporate shareholders, executive and independent directors. But as I noted before, the requirement for deliberation in corporate decisions does not mean that each and every person must participate in every decision-making process. For one thing, corporate decision-making takes place within the dual framework described in the previous Chapter. Nor does it presume any particular method of participation (for example, as I argue later, absentee or proxy voting at a general meeting can be consistent with deliberative decision-making). It is easy to see that we could render corporate decision-making processes unworkable by insisting on full participation in all instances.[36] The aims of deliberation in a corporate context can be satisfied in the absence of full-scale participation, provided that there are appropriate mechanisms to ensure that points of view can be put and heard, that interests can be made known, and that perspectives can be brought to bear. Attention must be given to matters such as voting processes and structures, and to the conduct of meetings. Meetings should have procedures that allow, as far as possible, that all present 'have a right to express their opinions and points of view, and all ought to listen'.[37]

Of course in large corporations shareholders frequently have only a limited engagement with corporate affairs. As law and economics analysis has stressed, gaining even a rudimentary understanding of corporate affairs (for

---

[35] See below n 65, and accompanying text.
[36] Here I depart from some formulations of deliberative theory that require participation by *all* those who are subject to the decision — eg Manin, above n 6, 352.
[37] Young, above n 6, 142.

example, which directors to vote for, whether to vote for or against a constitutional amendment) can take a lot of work, and may require specialised knowledge. There are many factors leading to shareholder passivity, not all of which will be influenced or altered by deliberative structures and processes. On any given occasion, a shareholder may not participate in decision-making for a number of reasons: not being aware that a decision is being made; not understanding the issues; not being personally affected by the issues; indecision; or plain indifference. But while we can acknowledge the real pressures towards inaction, a constitutionalist framework should have rules, structures and processes that permit and encourage shareholders to exercise their capacities as members and to seek to influence the decision-making process, rather than acting as purely passive investors or 'residual claimants'.

Thus, while one goal of deliberative decision-making is to improve the quality of corporate decision-making by increasing the potential range of viewpoints that are brought to bear on a decision, it can also have a broadly educative function, whereby members learn that their personal interests are linked to those of the corporation, and that as a consequence they are corporate as well as private actors.[38] Whatever reason shareholders have for not exercising their right to vote, it should not be due to a feeling that there is no point, that passivity is encouraged, and that general meetings are mere formalities or public relations exercises.

Deliberation and Pluralism

My definition of deliberation stresses that *as far as possible* the processes of corporate decision-making should be open and genuine, and they should be aimed at decisions that represent a collective judgement about the issue at hand. The qualification is important, particularly when we are referring to large public corporations with widely-held share registers.

This type of corporation faces a number of problems in maintaining a legitimate system of corporate decision-making. For one thing, shareholders are often dispersed geographically and demographically and, as I have just noted, not all shareholders possess the skills, expertise or interest to become involved in detailed deliberations on all occasions. Deliberation is therefore likely to be incomplete because not all shareholders will have their say, and so not all values, aspects, opinions or arguments will necessarily be heard. Shareholder decisions are

---

[38]   This draws on Rousseau's theory of participation, as discussed by Carole Pateman, *Participation and Democratic Theory* (1970) 24-25. Pateman argues that the educative function is the major purpose of participation — see 42-43. On the distinction between instrumentalism and other goals such as political and moral education see G Parry, 'The Idea of Political Participation' in G Parry (ed) *Participation in Politics* (1972) 19-31. It is easy to overstate the impact of this educative function in the corporate context. Membership of a widely-held public company does not tend to 'produce strong community ties constitutive of the member's self-understanding' — W Bratton, 'Public Values and Corporate Fiduciary Law' (1992) 44 *Rutgers Law Review* 675, 695.

therefore likely to be only an approximation of the corporate interest. The aim, then, is to achieve the best approximation. We can do this by adopting a wide, multi-leveled concept of deliberation. We do not need to restrict our deliberative focus to the general meeting or the board room, although these are the central forums. Instead we should also recognise the plurality of roles, the plurality of discursive perspectives, and the plurality of opinions and arguments that can be found within a public corporation and that can, potentially, be brought to bear on a decision.[39]

First, there is a *plurality of roles*. The corporate governance literature has abandoned the one-dimensional archetype of the 'shareholder as owner' that underpinned corporate law regulation for most of the 20th century. It now acknowledges that shareholders occupy a variety of roles, including the shareholder as active participant, as passive investor, or even as de facto managerial partner.[40] The distinction between small retail shareholders and large and institutional shareholders, discussed in Chapter 4, is another example. Similarly, board rooms demonstrate a plurality of directors' roles — for example, in the distinction between executive and independent positions.

Secondly, there is a *plurality of discursive perspectives*. At different times, different persons and groups in a corporation may highlight different values and aspects of an issue, as well as different criteria for assessing the validity of the outcome of the deliberation. For example, there are debates about whether the criterion for 'good' corporate-decision-making should be fairness or efficiency, or whether shares should be regarded as 'property' or simply as 'capitalized dividend streams'.[41] Deliberative procedures should seek to ensure that no particular set of values is privileged during the discussion that occurs prior to a decision. All relevant values and perspectives on an issue ought, potentially, to be able to be taken into account. Again, this is not a requirement that a decision can only be made after each and every angle has been pursued. But at the same time, one-dimensional decisions should be suspect where it is reasonable to think that there are other aspects which might have been considered. The legitimacy of a decision can be measured not solely by what perspectives were actually brought to bear, but also by considering the extent to which different perspectives had a real possibility of being brought to bear. It may be that at the final stage of making the decision

---

[39] This threefold categorisation is taken from William Rehg and James Bohman, 'Discourse and Democracy: The Formal and Informal Bases of Legitimacy in Habermas' *Faktizität und Geltung*' (1996) 4 *The Journal of Political Philosophy* 79, 86-88.

[40] J Hill, 'Visions and Revisions of the Shareholder' (2000) 48 *American Journal of Comparative Law* 39.

[41] In Australia these debates were prompted by the High Court's decision in *Gambotto v WCP Ltd* (1995) 182 CLR 432. See, for example, Ian Ramsay (ed), *Gambotto v WCP Ltd: Its Implications for Corporate Regulation* (1996); Peta Spender, 'Guns and Greenmail: Fear and Loathing after *Gambotto*' (1998) 22 *Melbourne University Law Review* 96.

one set of values or perspectives will carry the day, but this should be an outcome of a deliberative process rather than a predetermined conclusion or strategy.

Finally, we can expect a *plurality of opinions and arguments* on any given issue, even amongst those who share a common discursive perspective. The greater the range of conflicting opinions and arguments that are put, the more likely it is that the resulting decision, reflected in a majority vote, will be acceptable to, and can be said to be authored by, the general body of decision-makers.

Being Realistic About Deliberation

What I have said so far about deliberative decision-making is, perhaps, an idealised description that establishes a benchmark against which actual corporate practices may be evaluated. Deliberation aims to enhance the *quantity* and *quality* of information which is brought to bear upon a decision, thereby enhancing the quality of the decision itself. But the reference to *quantity* does not imply that more information is necessarily better. It is a characteristic of most deliberative systems that 'it is not possible to deliberate everything, or all the possibilities permitted by a given situation'.[42] Clearly there are practical limits to the number and range of inputs that a decision-making process can sustain, and deliberative structures and processes must allow for this. I explore some ways in which this might be done later in this Chapter. There are also limitations imposed by the constitutional framework within which deliberation occurs. Not just anything can go onto the agenda of a general meeting or a board meeting, and not just anything can be decided about the agenda items.

Similarly, the reference to *quality* does not mean that deliberative processes alone will guarantee contributions of greater calibre, nor that decisions will always be reasonable. Deliberative structures and processes are not of themselves guarantees against the problems of domination, oppression or unfairness in corporate affairs. Indeed, as Schauer has noted, it *is* possible that sometimes deliberation:

> lowers rather than raises the quality of consideration, increases the likelihood that bad arguments will be accepted and good ones rejected, overly empowers the rhetorician and the demagogue, and exacerbates the disempowerment of those already disempowered on the basis of race, gender, class, wealth, physical attractiveness, and all of the other features that distinguish the empowered from the disempowered.[43]

Corporate meetings (especially general meetings of shareholders) are not inherently egalitarian. In thinking of deliberation in a corporate context we must avoid using idealized models of the town-hall or the local community meeting. Moreover the norms of deliberation in a corporate setting may sometimes privilege

---

42　　Manin, above n 6, 356-357.

43　　F Schauer, 'Deliberating about Deliberation' (1992) 90 *Michigan Law Review* 1187, 1200.

certain forms and styles of contribution over others, and there will be differing levels of expertise and differing capacities to put an argument.[44] The processes of corporate deliberation will not always be mannered and polite; they may be tense, uneven, and at times, unpleasant. All of this reminds us, again, that deliberation is only one aspect of the corporate constitutionalist framework; deliberation alone is not sufficient, and other mechanisms, such as appropriate separations of power, and avenues for contesting decisions (dealt with in the next Chapter), must also be considered.

Corporations as Deliberative Entities

There is every reason to be optimistic that public corporations can be deliberative entities, at least to some extent. For one thing, corporate law is built around rules and doctrines that are premised on this idea. I will review some of these rules in a moment, but first I want to note a further reason for optimism. Typically, large corporate organisations exhibit features that are considered by deliberative theorists to be necessary for effective deliberative processes. A corporation meets the desideratum that a deliberative organisation is 'an ongoing and independent association, whose members expect it to continue into the indefinite future'.[45] Furthermore, large corporations usually embody the plurality of interests and preferences necessary for deliberative processes: '[d]eliberation requires not only multiple but conflicting points of view because conflict of some sort is the essence of politics'.[46] Finally, as we saw in Chapter 4, corporate practice and corporate law assume that the two formal decision-making groups — the directors and the shareholders — will exercise their powers through meetings which are open to their respective constituencies.

But perhaps the best way to illustrate the relevance of deliberative decision-making to corporations is to examine some of the ways in which corporate law doctrine already embodies, or is at least compatible with, deliberative ideas. In other words, there is a doctrinal foundation upon which more detailed deliberative arguments can be built. I begin by considering some examples of corporate law rules (drawing on Australian law) that seek to make directors engage in processes of deliberation before making a decision.

Deliberation, Corporate Law and Directors

There is good reason why directors should be expected to behave deliberatively, and why there should be common law and statutory rules to enforce this. Directors are charged with deciding corporate policy, setting goals, establishing guidelines, and monitoring the implementation of these decisions on a regular basis.[47]

---

[44] See Young, above n 6, 138-139.
[45] Cohen, n 6, 21.
[46] Manin, above n 6, 352.
[47] See, eg, *AWA Ltd v Daniels* (1992) 10 ACLC 933, 1013-1014.

The deliberative standard is clearly evident in case law concerning the duty of care and diligence owed by directors. In Australia a succession of decisions since 1990[48] has stressed the legal obligation of directors to hold and attend board meetings, and to participate actively in the board's decision-making processes. These cases have emphasised the importance of inquiry into the background and reasons for board decisions. The idea of deliberation also underpins the standards that directors are expected to meet in these processes.

In *Vrisakis v Australian Securities Commission*, Malcolm CJ noted that '[t]oday, a director is expected to attend all meetings unless exceptional circumstances, such as illness or absence from the State prevent him or her from doing so'.[49] The courts have held, however, that mere attendance at board meetings is not enough to satisfy the required legal standard. A director is obliged to obtain a general understanding of the corporation's business. This is necessary because, in the words of Rogers J in *AWA Ltd v Daniels*, '[d]irectors should bring an informed and independent judgement to bear on the various matters that come to the board for decision'.[50]

The law also emphasises a further aspect of deliberation: the need for collective decision-making. In *Daniels v Anderson*, a majority in the NSW Court of Appeal noted that a director's common law duty to take reasonable care 'includes that of *acting collectively* to manage the company'.[51] The necessity for collective decisions is further reinforced by general fiduciary duties that insist that directors should not base their deliberative input on personal or sectional interests. Regardless of who has nominated or appointed them to their position, directors are required to consider the best interests of the corporation as a whole.[52]

The requirement for collective decision-making holds even though the courts are prepared to allow board meetings to be held through the use of telecommunications technology. Regardless of the mode by which a meeting is conducted, there must be 'a meeting of minds'.[53] A clear explanation of this point was made in *Re GIGA Investments Pty Ltd*. The case examined the validity of a decision made at a directors' meeting in which one director had participated by telephone. Upholding the validity of the meeting, Branson J posed a question about the purpose of a requirement in the corporation's constitution that the directors must 'meet together'. Her Honour answered:

---

[48]   This line of cases is usually taken to have begun with the judgement of Ormiston J in *Statewide Tobacco Services Ltd v Morley* (1990) 8 ACLC 827 but note should also be made of Kirby P's dissenting judgement in *Metal Manufacturers Ltd v Lewis* (1988) 13 ACLR 357.
[49]   (1993) 11 ACSR 162, 170.
[50]   (1992) 10 ACLC 933, 1013.
[51]   (1995) 13 ACLC 614, 666 (emphasis added). See also *Northside Developments Pty Ltd v Registrar-General* (1990) 8 ACLC 611, 645.
[52]   *Greenhalgh v Arderne Cinemas Ltd* [1951] Ch 286; *Levin v Clark* [1962] NSWR 686; *Re Broadcasting Station 2GB Pty Ltd* [1964-1965] NSWR 1648.
[53]   *Bell v Burton* (1994) 12 ACLC 1037, 1038; see also *Wagner v International Health Promotions* (1994) 12 ACLC 986.

The purpose, in my view, is to ensure that directors taking part in a directors' meeting are able to deliberate together concerning the affairs of the company and ultimately resolve upon action to be taken. Deliberation in this sense, in my view, involves each director:

    (a) being able to know of the matters of fact and opinion articulated by all other directors participating in the meeting; and

    (b) being free to seek to persuade such other directors to particular views with respect to the matters properly before the meeting.[54]

As I argued earlier in this Chapter, a key part of 'being free to persuade' other directors is that decisions should be based on the critical assessment of reasoned argument, not on deference to the authority of others. In the words of Catherine Walter, a prominent Australian director who resigned from the board of one of Australia's leading banks after publicly voicing concerns about the board's processes:

> Boards need to be meritocratic, not autocratic, not bureaucratic. They should evaluate ideas according to their quality, and not the standing of the person who has raised them.[55]

The separation of powers within the board — especially between the roles of chairperson and CEO — is one way to encourage board decisions that are based on reason rather than hierarchy. Of course this is not sufficient by itself. The basic requirement, as Ford, Austin and Ramsay put it, is that directors are required 'to exercise an active discretion; they will be in breach of duty for letting things slide or for improperly acting blindly at the directions of another person'.[56]

The case law on directors' decisions therefore emphasises the processes that should precede a decision. This can be reinforced by statutory requirements. In Australia, for example, the *Corporations Act* contains a business judgement rule[57] which provides that a 'business judgement' made by a director (or officer) of a corporation will be taken to satisfy the duty of care and diligence, provided that the judgement meets certain criteria. One criterion is that the director has informed him or herself about the subject matter of the judgement to the extent they reasonably believe is appropriate.[58] Furthermore, the protection of the rule is only available if the director *actively* makes a business judgement— that is, there must be a decision to take or not to take action about a matter that is relevant to the

---

[54] (1995) 13 ACLC 1047, 1050.
[55] ABC Radio, 'Ex NAB Board member Catherine Walter speaks out', *AM*, Wednesday 1 September 2004, <http://www.abc.net.au/am/content/2004/s1189565.htm> at 1 September 2004.
[56] H Ford, R Austin and I Ramsay, *Ford's Principles of Corporations Law* (12th ed, 2005) 373.
[57] Section 180(2). This rule is based upon a similar provision in the American Law Institute's Principles of Corporate Governance: Analysis and Recommendations.
[58] Section 180(2)(c).

corporation's business operations.[59] Passivity, inattention, and failure to act will not qualify. In this way the statute seeks to reinforce the idea that directors should *make* decisions, and should engage in consideration of issues prior to making decisions.

Deliberation, Corporate Law and Shareholders

Members of a corporation do not owe fiduciary duties to the corporation.[60] Although there are rules that give members the opportunity to deliberate at general meetings (some of which are discussed later in this Chapter), there are no rules or duties that require them to do this. The basic legal presumption is encapsulated in long-standing dicta such as that of Jessel MR in *Pender v Lushington*:

> There is, if I may say so, no obligation on a shareholder of a company to give his vote merely with a view to what other persons may consider the interest of the company at large. He has a right, if he thinks fit, to give his vote from motives or promptings of what he considers his own individual interest.[61]

There are, however, occasions on which the courts have imposed constraints on the exercise of majority voting power in a general meeting, and the principles enunciated in these cases are consistent with aspects of the deliberative ideal.

A court may declare that a decision made by a majority of members that constitutes an abuse of power is void. This is done on the grounds that the majority must not exercise its voting power for a purpose that lies outside the implied scope of purposes for which that power was conferred by the corporation's constitution.[62] In one explanation of this doctrine Templeman J said that it applies when majority shareholders 'use their powers, intentionally or unintentionally, fraudulently or negligently, in a manner which benefits themselves at the expense of the company'.[63] To this extent the doctrine enjoins the majority members to exercise their votes by having regard to matters that lie outside, and may be inconsistent with, their personal interests.

This requirement is also found in cases concerning the power of members to amend the corporate constitution by special resolution. For many years the courts circumscribed the power of the majority members in this situation by requiring that their vote 'must be exercised ... bona fide for the benefit of the company as a whole'.[64] This broad requirement proved to be unhelpful in situations where the proposed constitutional amendment would alter or abrogate the rights of some members against their will. In *Gambotto v WCP Ltd*, a case involving an

---

[59]   Section 180(3).
[60]   *Peters' American Delicacy Co Ltd v Heath* (1939) 61 CLR 457, 504 (Dixon J).
[61]   (1877) 6 Ch D 70, 75-76.
[62]   Ford, Austin and Ramsay, above n 56, 618. This is sometimes referred to as the doctrine of fraud on the minority.
[63]   *Daniels v Daniels* [1978] Ch 406, 414.
[64]   *Allen v Gold Reefs of West Africa Ltd* [1900] 1 Ch 656, 671 per Lindley MR.

expropriation of minority shares, the High Court of Australia enunciated a revised test, requiring that the power of amendment must be exercised for a proper purpose and that it must not be used to oppress minority shareholders.[65] Despite debate about the precise meaning of this test,[66] its underlying purpose is clear: the exercise of majority voting power at a general meeting is not to be regarded solely as an expression of private or personal interest when the interests of other shareholders are at stake. Put another way, any interference with another member's interests must be genuinely referenced to the interests of the members as a whole rather than to sectional interests (the proper purpose requirement), and it must 'track the interests and ideas of the person suffering the interference' (the avoidance of oppression requirement).[67]

Disclosure of Information

A precondition for shareholders to be able to contribute effectively to deliberative debate is that they have access to information about the management, business and performance of the corporation. Corporate law contains a variety of disclosure rules that stipulate requirements for periodic reporting, [68] special-occasion reporting[69] and continuous reporting.[70] There are three broad arguments put in favour of these mandatory reporting requirements: they allow investors to make informed investment decisions; they assist corporate regulators in monitoring corporate behaviour and taking action when necessary; and, by enhancing shareholder scrutiny, they constrain the possibility of managerial and boardroom misbehavior.

The imposition of mandatory disclosure rules has been contested in the literature. Many of the arguments against mandatory disclosure rely on claims about the capacity of a semi- (or strongly-) efficient securities market to provide adequate information about corporations in the absence of regulation.[71] My suggestion is that a deliberative system of corporate decision-making supplies an important non-regulatory and non-economic argument in favour of disclosure rules.

---

[65]   (1995) 13 ACLC 342, 348.

[66]   See above n 41. There is also debate about the application of the test to the facts in *Gambotto*, where the majority shareholder (with 99.7% of the shares) had refrained from voting, the resolution being passed by a majority of the remaining shareholders.

[67]   The words quoted come from Pettit, Republicanism, above n 6, 55. There are interesting similarities between the *Gambotto* test and Pettit's idea of freedom as non-domination.

[68]   In Australia, Chapter 2M of the *Corporations Act 2001* specifies requirements for preparation and publication of annual financial reports and conduct of annual audits.

[69]   For example, takeovers (*Corporations Act 2001* Chapter 6), and public offers of securities (*Corporations Act 2001* Chapter 6D).

[70]   Australian Stock Exchange Listing Rule 3.1, backed up by Chapter 6CA of the *Corporations Act 2001* imposes continuous disclosure requirements on listed entities.

[71]   See the review of these debates in I Ramsay, 'Models of Corporate Regulation: The Mandatory/Enabling Debate' in C Rickett and R Grantham (eds), *Corporate Personality in The 20th Century* (1998).

The disclosure of information permits members to make informed assessments of, and contributions to, corporate debates. That is, disclosure can enhance corporate decision-making insofar as it provides an information basis for effective deliberation. The prospects of deliberative involvement in corporate decision-making might persuade at least some shareholders to see the disclosure of information not merely in terms of what it might reveal about the value of their investments, but also in terms of its capacity to inform debate.

This disclosure *should* be mandatory. As I argue in Chapter 6, a crucial aspect of corporate constitutionalism is that members should have clear and useable avenues for contesting corporate decisions and actions. Contestability is assisted to the extent that corporate information is produced in an identifiable format, is produced by identifiable persons, and is made available to all of the corporation's shareholders equally. Leaving it solely to the market to produce information, or insisting that all relevant information about a corporation is represented in the market price of its securities, reduces this capacity.

Deliberation may also help shareholders identify missing information. Even where mandatory disclosure rules operate, there is a risk that corporate managers may still conceal or distort information that would be useful to shareholders in assessing the corporation and its management. This is partly because disclosure rules can never be sufficiently detailed and prescriptive to cover all eventualities, and partly because the general standards for corporate reporting may be incomplete. This problem is unlikely to be solved simply by increasing the volume of regulatory requirements. A system that is based on deliberative debate can increase the opportunities for shareholders to discover what they don't know. It has the potential to elicit further information, to reveal gaps and insufficiencies in published information. Deliberative debate can therefore supplement a mandatory disclosure framework; it can 'fill the gaps' in a way that is more attuned to the needs of members of a particular corporation than is the case with detailed external regulation.

Not all information that is disclosed will promote deliberation, and not all shareholders will use or read the information that is produced. The response to this is to look for mechanisms whereby information can nevertheless be brought to bear on deliberative debate. I explore one such mechanism later in this Chapter. But more generally we should encourage a predisposition towards disclosure — a view that disclosure is beneficial not just because it staves off market suspicion or regulatory inquiry, but because it promotes good decision-making processes.

The continuous disclosure regime in Australia emphasises many of the elements necessary to support a deliberative system. A combination of statutory rules, stock exchange requirements and codes of conduct requires a listed corporation to disclose any materially price sensitive information to the stock exchange[72] immediately the corporation becomes aware of that information. The test for determining what information should be disclosed (that is, whether a reasonable person would expect the information to have a material effect on the

---

[72]   In certain circumstances, an unlisted corporation is required to make disclosure to the Australian Securities and Investments Commission.

price or value of the corporation's securities[73]) means that disclosure can be tied to the circumstances of the particular corporation. As explained by O'Loughlin J in *Flavel v Roget*:

> Much will depend upon the identity of the particular company; what one company should advise the Stock Exchange might not have to be advised by a second company; what should be advised by a company at one stage in its career might not have to be advised at another stage of its career because of changed circumstances.[74]

Corporations are encouraged[75] to establish written disclosure polices that (amongst other things) explain what type of information will be disclosed, how it will be disseminated (eg via corporate websites, press release, email, mail-out), and identify which officers within the corporation have authority to make these public disclosures.[76]

Deliberation at General Meetings

There are more specific statutory rules that are intended to give members the opportunity to deliberate at the general meetings of public corporations. These rules may be supplemented by provisions in a corporate constitution (and, in the case of listed corporations, by stock exchange rules). The statutory rules seek to ensure that members are given adequate notice of a meeting and of the business to be conducted so that they can make informed choices about attendance and voting. Typically there are requirements concerning the timing of annual general meetings, [77] notice requirements, [78] as well as provisions dealing with voting procedures, quorum, proxies and minutes.[79] The Australian legislation also requires

---

[73] See, eg, *Corporations Act 2001* (Cth) s 674(2)(c).

[74] (1990) 8 ACLC 237 243-245.

[75] See Australian Stock Exchange, *Guidance Note 8: Continuous Disclosure: Listing Rule 3.1* (2003); Australian Securities and Investments Commission, *Better Disclosure for Investors — Guidance Rules*,
<http://www.asic.gov.au/asic/pdflib.nsf/LookupByFileName/better_disclosure.pdf/$file/better_disclosure.pdf> at 1 September 2004.

[76] Some professional and industry groups now give annual awards to corporations, determined by reference to the quality of corporate continuous disclosure polices and practices. See, eg, the Australasian Reporting Awards < www.arawards.com.au > at 18 February 2005.

[77] Eg, *Corporations Act 2001* (Cth) s 250N; *Companies Act 1985* (UK) s 366; *Canada Business Corporations Act*, RSC 1985, s 133.

[78] Eg, *Corporations Act 2001* (Cth) ss 249H – L (s 249R requires a meeting to be held at a reasonable time and place); *Companies Act 1985* (UK) s 369; *Canada Business Corporations Act*, RSC 1985, s 135.

[79] Eg, quorum: *Corporations Act 2001* (Cth) s 249T, *Companies Act 1985* (UK) s 370A, *Canada Business Corporations Act*, RSC 1985, s 139; voting procedure: *Corporations Act 2001* (Cth) s 250J, *Companies Act 1985* (UK) s 370, *Canada Business Corporations Act*, RSC 1985, s 141; right to appoint proxy: *Corporations Act 2001*

that the chairperson of an annual general meeting must allow a reasonable opportunity for the members as a whole to ask questions about, or to comment on, the management of the corporation.[80] In the same vein, the members must be allowed a reasonable opportunity to ask questions about the conduct of the audit, the preparation and content of the auditor's report, the accounting policies used, and the independence of the auditor.[81]

Some of these statutory provisions are the product of recent reviews of the law governing shareholder meetings.[82] In Australia, these inquiries were prompted, in part, by concerns in the business community about amendments to the corporations legislation that were made in July 1998.[83] Those amendments included rules governing the notice requirements for general meetings of listed public companies, the disclosure of information about proxy votes, and the power of individual directors to call general meetings. But it is important to note that these inquiries also took place in a context of public concern about levels of directors' remuneration and performance,[84] and growing activism by environmental, labour, and human rights groups using strategic shareholdings to file resolutions at the annual general meetings of mining and other multinational companies.[85]

The report of one of the Australian inquiries into shareholder participation in general meetings began with the statement that:

(Cth) s 249X, *Companies Act 1985* (UK) s 372, *Canada Business Corporations Act*, RSC 1985, Pt XIII; minutes: *Corporations Act 2001* (Cth) ss 251A, 251B, *Companies Act 1985* (UK) s 382.

[80] s 250S.

[81] s 250T. The auditor is required to attend the AGM of a listed corporation (s 250RA).

[82] In Australia, see Companies and Securities Advisory Committee, *Shareholder Participation in the Modern Listed Public Company*, Final Report (2000); Joint Statutory Committee on Corporations and Securities, Parliament of Australia, *Report on Matters Arising from the Company Law Review Act 1998* (1998); in the United Kingdom, see Company Law Review Steering Group, *Company General Meetings and Shareholder Communication*, Consultation Document (1999).

[83] *Company Law Review Act 1998* (Cth). Some of the new rules had been introduced in the Senate by the Democrat and Labor Parties against the Government's wishes.

[84] See, eg, Catherine Fox, 'Shareholders keeping their eyes glued on boards' *The Australian Financial Review*, 5 November 1999, 19. Another example is the forced resignation of the chair of the board of AMP Ltd (one of Australia's largest insurance companies) in April 2000: *The Australian Financial Review*, 4 April 2000, 1.

[85] For example, in 1999 the Australian mining company North Ltd faced legal action brought by a group of shareholders (North Ethical Shareholders) to compel the corporation to consider a resolution concerning the environmental impact of the activities of one of its subsidiaries. The action was settled out of court after North agreed to consider the resolution at the same time as its annual general meeting: *The Age* (Melbourne) 13 September 1999. Shareholders in the transnational mining company, Rio Tinto Ltd/Plc faced action from international union-backed shareholders seeking changes to board structure and company compliance with ILO conventions: *The Australian Financial Review*, 8 March 2000, 1; *The Sydney Morning Herald* (Sydney) 12 May 2000, 10.

the rules governing shareholder participation, through physical meetings or electronic communications, should facilitate *the efficient determination of the will of the majority* of shareholders in defined areas, with all proper safeguards to ensure *informed decision-making*. All shareholders should have an equal right to all appropriate information and an opportunity to express their views, with voting rights proportionate to their shareholding.[86]

This juxtaposing of 'efficiency' and 'informed decision-making' is evident throughout the contemporary debate on general meetings. Amongst the issues in this debate, we find:

- a tension between the idea that the public listed corporation is primarily — if not exclusively — an economic institution, and the idea that general meetings can and should be deliberative forums;
- concerns about the proper division of decision-making functions between the general meeting and the board of directors;
- assumptions about the deliberative capacity (one way or the other) of general meetings; and
- divergent opinions about the relative worth of minority and majority shareholder views.

At one extreme there are arguments tending towards either the abolition of general meetings[87] or, less dramatically, limiting the role of general meetings in corporate governance. Shareholder meetings are depicted as expensive, time consuming, and often poorly attended events where the outcomes on key resolutions are usually predetermined by proxy votes.[88] At the other extreme there are arguments that favour the use of general meetings as forums in which members can voice both corporate and wider economic, political, environmental, or social concerns. In this view, shareholder meetings are seen as one method whereby the concerns of majority and minority shareholders and other stakeholders in a corporation can be brought to the attention of the corporation's managers. The theoretical bases for this argument are aligned with a variety of communitarian or stakeholder theories.[89]

We are thus presented with a choice between privileging the efficiency of decision-making at the expense of deliberation, or promoting vague notions of

---

[86] CASAC Final Report, above n 82, 1 (emphasis added).

[87] For example, 'Commonwealth Bank chief executive David Murray told a group of newspaper executives in 1998 that the important question about AGMs was not how they were run, but whether they should be held at all.' *The Weekend Australian*, 27-28 May 2000, 36 (the Commonwealth Bank is one of Australia's largest listed corporations).

[88] See G Stapledon, S Easterbrook, P Bennett, and I Ramsay, *Proxy Voting in Australia's Largest Companies*, Research Report, Centre for Corporate Law and Securities Regulation, University of Melbourne, 2000.

[89] See, eg, D Millon, 'Communitarianism in Corporate Law: Foundations and Law Reform Strategies' in L Mitchell (ed) *Progressive Corporate Law* (1995) 1.

democracy at the cost of effective decision-making.[90] Neither view has taken hold. The image of corporations as democratic communities does not take sufficient account of the great dispersion and diversity of shareholders' interests in public corporations. The abolitionist arguments underestimate the value (even if only symbolic) that many shareholders and directors continue to place on the general meeting as an occasion for accountability. The remainder of this Chapter attempts to chart an intermediate path between these choices, avoiding the undesirable extreme of general meeting minimalism and the unworkable ideal of town-hall meeting inclusiveness. The challenge is to link the value of deliberation, the need for effective decision-making, with the concept of corporate membership.

The Limits of Deliberation in Corporations

While I think that a good case can be made for the deliberative ideal as an existing theme in current corporate law, the claim should not be overstated. The deliberative prospects are greater for boards than for general meetings because typically a board is a small,[91] relatively homogeneous group that, in practice, has a degree of control over its membership.[92] A general meeting is a larger assembly of often disparate membership interests.

There is ample evidence that general meetings in public corporations can be desultory affairs, characterised by relatively low rates of member attendance and input. A survey of 217 Australian public company annual general meetings held between 2001 and 2003 ('the AGM study') found that in 98 per cent of meetings shareholders attending in person or participating by proxy represented no more than 20 per cent of all shareholders in the corporation.[93] Even if higher rates of attendance can be achieved, the deliberative options in a general meeting are constrained by a number of factors. The formal agenda, which sets the decision-making parameters of the meeting, is determined prior to the meeting. As Black describes it, in large corporations, '[m]anagers control what the shareholders get to vote on, when they get to vote, what order proposals are offered in, and when the shareholders learn what's on the agenda'.[94] Corporate decision-making is a

---

90   Rehg and Bohman, above n 39, 85.

91   The average board size in Australia is seven, with the majority of corporations having between four and nine directors: Korn/Ferry International, *Boards of Directors Study in Australia and New Zealand* (2003) 14. In the UK the average board sized for a listed company is approximately seven: Derek Higgs, United Kingdom Department of Trade and Industry, *Review of the Role and Effectiveness of Non-Executive Directors* (January 2003), 18.

92   In most corporations the board has the power to fill casual vacancies. Such an appointment must then be confirmed by resolution of the shareholders at the next annual general meeting, with the person at the advantage of having been given the board's imprimatur.

93   Above n 29, 25.

94   B Black, 'Shareholder Passivity Reexamined' (1990) 89 *Michigan Law Review* 520, 592.

cumulative process involving many stages.[95] By the time a proposal is included in the meeting agenda it will already have been researched, debated, defined, and its legal compliance and financial viability assessed by many people in the corporation, most of whom are not involved in the final decision at the general meeting. A shareholder either votes for or against, or abstains from voting on, pre-determined resolutions. There is no scope for members to put alternative proposals from the floor of the meeting,[96] and any amendments to a motion must be consistent with the general purpose of the original motion.[97] The ordering of the agenda items can affect the outcome of decisions[98] and the extent of deliberation. For example, if the election and re-election of directors is placed on the agenda ahead of the presentation and discussion of the corporation's financial reports, members may well complain that they are being asked to cast their votes before having the opportunity to hear explanations of, and comment on, the performance of the candidates.[99] At general meetings of large corporations it is likely that there will be limits on the number of times and the amount of time that a member is permitted to speak.[100] Other factors, such as the number of proxy votes,[101] the duration of the meeting,[102] the length and complexity of the agenda,[103] and the location and lay-out of the venue will also affect the quantity and quality of deliberative input from members.

Given this combination of legal and practical limitations, a scheme for effective deliberation by shareholders must be supplemented by methods outside the general meeting. Importantly, though, this should not be in substitution for direct participation at meetings. Meetings are important: notwithstanding the low levels of shareholder turn-out, the AGM study found considerable support for general meetings at which shareholders and directors see each other face to face: directors take meetings seriously.[104] As one director put it, 'there's nothing like the

---

95 Parry, above n 38, 6.

96 *Corporations Act 2001* (Cth) s 249N: members with at least 5 per cent of the total votes, or 100 members with voting rights, may give notice of a resolution prior to a meeting.

97 E Magner, *Joske's Law and Procedure at Meetings in Australia* (8th ed, 1994) 46.

98 C Plott and M Levine, 'A Model of Agenda Influence on Committee Decisions' (1978) 68 *American Economic Review* 146.

99 As occurred, for example, at the 2001 AGM of Telstra Ltd: <http://workers.labor.net.au/119/news93_telstra.html> at 17 December 2004.

100 I have observed meetings held in large auditoriums where members are required to speak via microphones, with power to the microphone being controlled by the persons running the meeting.

101 This is discussed below at n 117 and accompanying text.

102 The average length of a meeting in the AGM study was 1.25 hours, with 38 per cent taking less than one hour: above n 29, 42-43.

103 The AGM study, above n 29, 36-37, found that 87% of AGM agendas dealt with no more than four matters, although these may have been broken up into a larger number of agenda items.

104 AGM study, above n 29. A United Kingdom study reaches the same conclusion: P Stiles and B Taylor, *Boards at Work: How Directors View Their Roles and*

threat of angry shareholders from the floor to hold directors accountable'. Another described the value of the general meeting in the following terms: 'if someone is asking you a question, looking [you] in your eye, face to face, and you don't want to answer it, there's some pressure there'. [105] Nevertheless, there should be mechanisms that give members the opportunity to deliberate outside the general meeting and, perhaps, influence the matters which might be decided prior to the formulation of the agenda. Under the next heading I explore what this might mean.

Shareholder Deliberation Outside the General Meeting

A plausible model of shareholder deliberation must take account of the dispersed and pluralistic nature of most public corporation share registers. This means acknowledging that, of those shareholders who choose to, not all will deliberate in the same way, and these varied deliberative methods will be dispersed across different forums. Therefore we need a wide, multi-layered model of shareholder deliberation that is not restricted to the formal decision-making authority of the general meeting. A resolution at a general meeting should be the end-point in series of deliberative processes that begins well before the agenda for the meeting is settled. Good decision-making in a general meeting — that is, achieving decisions which command the respect of members even though they may disagree with the actual outcome — depends upon the availability of informal opinions and ideas that develop informally outside and prior to the general meeting. Jurgen Habermas' description of deliberative politics is useful here: 'Deliberative politics', he says, 'lives off the interplay between democratically institutionalized will-formation and informal opinion-formation. It cannot rely solely on the channels of procedurally regulated deliberation and decision making'. [106]

Spheres of Deliberation

Borrowing from Habermas, we might think of corporate deliberation and decision-making in terms of a series of concentric 'spheres of influence', with the general meeting of shareholders at the centre. The outer sphere — call it 'the business world' — is populated by shareholders (small and large), market analysts, proxy advisory services, shareholder associations, regulatory agencies, [107] stock exchanges,

---

Responsibilities (2001) 93. See also Business Council of Australia, *Company and Shareholder Dialogue: A Discussion Paper* (2004) <http://www.bca.com.au/upload/Fresh_Approaches_to_Communication_Betweeen_Companies_and_their_Shareholders.pdf> at 2 December 2005.

[105] AGM study, above n 29, 41-42.

[106] J Habermas, *Between Facts and Norms: Contributions to a Discourse Theory of Law and Democracy* (1996) 308.

[107] The Australian Securities and Investments Commission operates a Company Alert service that enables a person to nominate companies in which they are interested and to then be notified by email of changes to the Commission's database on those companies.

media commentators, and others. This sphere consists of continuous informal exchanges of information. It is characterised by unstructured deliberation, or 'unregulated talkativeness'.[108] Moving towards the centre, we find in the next sphere the more structured processes of deliberation and decision-making that non-director managers and other corporate employees engage in on a daily basis. Then, in the next sphere, there are the less frequent but more formalised deliberative processes of the board of directors (usually meeting once a month). And finally, as indicated, we come to the highly structured decision-making in the annual general meeting of shareholders.

This image of concentric spheres[109] has two characteristics that I want to emphasise. First, deliberation becomes less frequent and more structured as we move from the periphery to the centre.[110] Moreover, the presentation of information being considered becomes more structured and constrained (compare, for example, discussion on an internet bulletin board with information published in the notice papers for a general meeting). The second characteristic is that in the outermost sphere the processes of deliberation and opinion formation occur outside the parameters of the corporate constitution; they do not substitute for formal decision-making. It is only in the centre — in the board room and at the general meeting — that binding decisions are made. Deliberation on the periphery will be biased, subjective, and sometimes impractical. That is why it cannot be a substitute for the formalised processes at the core, and why there is a need for the board to act as a filter of inputs from the periphery. Nevertheless, what goes on at the periphery is important because it can inform (though it cannot determine or usurp) the decisions that are made at the centre. While it is correct to say that '[i]f binding decisions are to be carried out with authority, they must pass through the narrow channels of the core area',[111] it is also the case that 'the legitimacy of decisions depends on processes of opinion- and will-formation at the periphery'.[112] The task of a deliberative model of corporate decision-making is to create possibilities for communication and information flow between the periphery and the core, in both directions. Later in this Chapter I consider some ways in which this might be done.

Because deliberation becomes less frequent as decision-making becomes more formalised, the attention of those on the 'inside' should be directed to monitoring and ensuring the quality of deliberation by those on the periphery.[113]

Since January 2000 the Australian Stock Exchange has conducted a free email alert service that provides summaries of major announcements by participating companies. See E Boros, 'Corporations Online' (2001) 19 *Companies & Securities Law Journal* 492, 501.

[108] B Noveck, 'Designing Deliberative Democracy in Cyberspace: The Role of the Cyber-Lawyer' (2003) 9 *Boston University Journal of Science and Technology Law* 1, 6-7.

[109] This is an explanatory device, not a descriptive model of corporate organisational structure. The image of concentric spheres (or circles) coincides with Habermas' argument, but a pyramid or hierarchical model could just as easily be used.

[110] Thanks to John Braithwaite for this observation.

[111] Habermas, above n 106, 356.

[112] B Peters, *Die Integration moderner Gesellschaften* (1993), quoted in Habermas, ibid.

[113] This point is also prompted by an observation made by John Braithwaite.

Thus, the general meeting should seek assurances about the quality of the board's deliberations; the board should monitor the quality of deliberation by the corporation's managers; and both the board and management will want to ensure that deliberation in the business world is properly informed so that directors and managers receive effective feedback about their decisions.[114]

To make this picture more concrete, consider the range of possibilities that might arise when there is an issue to be decided at the general meeting of a public corporation. We can begin with two extremes. Some (perhaps many) shareholders, through reasons of indifference or the pursuit of a passive investment strategy, will have *no input* at all. This can be consistent with the ideals of good corporate decision-making, provided that a shareholder's decision not to participate is voluntary, that the shareholder has been adequately informed about the proposed decision and is aware that there are realistic opportunities for involvement.[115] This means that on any given issue, deliberation will be incomplete to the extent that not all shareholders will have their say. At the other end of the spectrum, some shareholders will have a *direct and formal* involvement in the decision-making process at the general meeting. This is consistent with good corporate decision-making provided that the processes at the meeting are open and genuine, as I explained earlier in this Chapter. But it is what happens between these two extremes that is of greater interest. A deliberative corporate decision-making model should allow for other possibilities. On a given corporate issue we may be able to distinguish between three other groups of shareholders.

First, for some shareholders involvement in the decision-making process will be *informal and peripheral* to the formal process of decision-making. These shareholders will monitor corporate issues, seek information, participate in informal discussions, and, possibly, debates. However they will not seek to exert any direct influence on the outcome, nor will they participate in a formal way in the decision-making process. This may be due to lack of time or other resources, or because (after consideration) the issue is not one they wish to pursue. This is consistent with the ideals of good corporate decision-making, provided that the formal processes of decision-making are receptive to inputs from this informal and peripheral sphere of corporate discourse.

A second group of shareholders comprises those whose involvement in the corporate decision is *informal but influential*. The impact of institutional shareholders on corporate decision-making is the obvious example here. As I noted in Chapter 4, many large shareholders prefer to keep in regular contact with their portfolio corporations as a way of monitoring financial matters and management issues.[116] This is consistent with good corporate decision-making provided that it

---

[114] This can be done, for example, through the continuous disclosure requirements, and via company websites. The majority of large public companies in Australia now have websites: Boros, above n 107, 502. A 2004 discussion paper released by the Business Council of Australia urges greater use of websites by corporations: above n 104, 49.

[115] The purpose of rules requiring notice of meetings and of resolutions to be passed at meetings is to ensure that decisions are not made without the knowledge of members.

[116] See Chapter 4 n 144 and accompanying text.

does not preclude the involvement of other shareholders, and provided that it does not define the decision-making agenda or outcome in a conclusive or exclusive way.

Thirdly, there is a group of shareholders who will participate in a *formal but limited* way, through the use of proxy votes. Proxy voting has some anti-deliberative consequences. There is evidence in Australia that most shareholders do not give their proxies discretion about how to cast the votes. The AGM study found that in 88 per cent of corporations more than half of the shareholders who gave proxies specified the way in which the proxy-holder should vote.[117] In that situation the shareholder's vote is not susceptible to change in response to any arguments that might be put at the general meeting. Where voting discretion is granted by the shareholder, the proxy holder is usually the chairperson of the meeting, meaning that the votes are nearly always cast in favour of board-initiated resolutions and against shareholder-initiated resolutions.[118] Despite this, proxy voting can nevertheless be consistent with deliberative decision-making, provided that shareholders who choose to attend the meeting and vote in person are not denied reasonable opportunities to ask questions and obtain explanations, and provided that those voting by proxy have had the opportunity for some form of deliberation prior to appointing their proxy.

The first of these two provisos means that the weight of proxy votes should not be used as an excuse to truncate the consideration of arguments at the general meeting. This might happen where the chairperson discloses the state of the proxy votes on a proposal before there has been any discussion. Proxy votes will usually determine the outcome of resolutions at a general meeting; for example, the AGM study found that in 99 per cent of corporations, shareholders participating by proxy constituted more than half of all voting shareholders, and in 48 per cent of corporations proxies accounted for over 90 per cent of the voting shares represented at the meeting.[119] As I have emphasised, deliberation is not about counting votes; it is about exposing arguments to question and influence, and testing the strength of each argument and counter-argument. In Australia the *Corporations Act* contains a replaceable rule that requires the chair to inform the meeting before the vote is taken whether any proxy votes have been received and how they are to be cast.[120] This leaves open the possibility that proxies may be revealed to the meeting before there has been any discussion on a proposed resolution.[121] The AGM study found a range of practices and opinions concerning the timing of proxy disclosures in meetings, although most corporate officers

---

[117] Above n 29, 28. Even so, a proxy who is not the chair of the meeting need not vote on a show of hands or on a poll: *Corporations Act 2001* (Cth) s 250A(4). The draft Corporations Amendment Bill (No 2) 2006 proposes to amend this.

[118] Stapledon et al, above n 88, 21.

[119] Above n 29, 28.

[120] Section 250J(1A).

[121] The CASAC Final Report recommended that the question of when proxy voting details should be disclosed should be left as a matter of discretion for the chair of the meeting: above n 82, 57.

indicated a preference for disclosure by the chair after discussion but before the vote is taken.[122]

The second proviso carries two requirements. First, the information sent out with the proxy voting forms should present the full range of arguments on each resolution as far as they can be identified ahead of the meeting. There is some indication in Australia that the courts will insist on this. In *Fraser v NRMA Ltd* the Federal Court dealt with a claim that information sent to members of NRMA Ltd, concerning the proposed demutualisation of the corporation, was false and misleading under the *Trade Practices Act 1974*. The Court held that members should receive information about the disadvantages as well as the advantages of the demutualisation proposal:

> the failure to identify and inform the members about disadvantages of which the directors making the recommendation were aware was to leave the members in a half light which had the potential to lead them to think that the unidentified disadvantages, whatever they might be, must be ones that they would not treat as significant ...[123]

The second requirement is that a proxy should be required by statute to cast the proxy votes, and where the proxy has received directions on how to cast the votes, to do so in accordance with those directions.[124]

Where a shareholder stands on this continuum of involvement will vary from one corporation to another, and within a given corporation, from one issue to the next. It will also vary depending on the type of shareholder: large institutional shareholders are likely to be located closer to the centre of decision-making because of their de facto power to influence outcomes.[125] In contrast, individual or retail shareholders are more likely to be involved only in the informal processes that operate at the periphery. The task, as I have noted already, is to encourage these peripheral processes of opinion formation and to ensure that they have an impact on the processes of decision-making in the board room and the general meeting.

---

[122] Above n 29, 39 (interviews were conducted with officers from 21 corporations).
[123] (1995) 15 ACSR 590, 621.
[124] In Australia this would require the amendment of s 250A(4) of the *Corporations Act 2001*, as per the draft Corporations Amendment Bill (No 2) 2006.
[125] See I Ramsay, G Stapledon, K Fong, 'Corporate Governance: The Perspective of Australian Institutional Shareholders' (2000) 18 *Companies & Securities Law Journal* 110, reporting that intervention by institutional shareholders on corporate governance issues is common. See the discussion in Chapter 4 at ns 141-151 and accompanying text.

Deliberation on the Periphery

Deliberation on the periphery requires that shareholders should have timely access to relevant information about the corporation and the decisions that they are being invited to make, and that there are means whereby they can then engage in discussion about this information in ways that will come to the attention of the decision-makers in the 'inner spheres'.

There are well known obstacles confronting individual shareholders in achieving these aims. The costs involved in obtaining, understanding and acting upon corporate information will often exceed the benefits to the individual shareholder, making it less likely that individual shareholders will seek it out themselves. One way of responding to this, discussed in the corporate governance literature, is to encourage the work of 'information intermediaries' who collect corporate information, analyse it, and then publicise their conclusions or recommendations for shareholders to act upon. Auditors play their part here, but the primary role is played by the market analysts, proxy advisory services and internet services mentioned previously. [126] There are, of course, issues to be confronted in maintaining an effective system of information intermediaries, including questions about who will, or should, pay for the supply of information.[127] I want to focus, however, on an issue that has received less attention: what shareholders do once they have received the information.

The common assumption is that armed with the information supplied by intermediaries, shareholders will then be in a position to make informed individual choices about exercising their votes, either directly or by proxy. This two-step process — the supply of information followed by voting (or other action)[128] — either omits or downplays the possibility of deliberation as an intermediate step. In what follows I consider some ways in which shareholders might be encouraged to deliberate outside the parameters of the general meeting. This is not intended as an exhaustive or a prescriptive list: my aim is simply to explore briefly some of the possibilities and acknowledge some of the difficulties.

Internet discussion sites for shareholders provide one option. These might be run by the corporation on its own web-page, or by shareholder associations or activist groups. They permit the exchange of information and opinions about the corporation and its performance. Caroline Bradley notes the many hundreds of bulletin boards and chat rooms specialising in corporate and investment issues that

---

[126] See above n 107 and accompanying text.

[127] Shareholders are unlikely to supply sufficient levels of funding to ensure an adequate supply of information. An alternative is for the corporation to pay. The issue then becomes how to give shareholders a say in how the corporation directs this funding. There are various proposals about how this might be achieved: see below n 145.

[128] There is evidence that the ready availability of information via the internet has prompted retail investors to engage in more active and speculative trading, rather than retaining their shareholdings: B Barber and T Odean, 'Online Investors: Do the Slow Die First?' (2002) 15 *The Review of Financial Studies* 455.

are available through the Yahoo internet portal.[129] She also points out that notwithstanding the proliferation of these sites, not all shareholders utilize this access to online information:

> some investors are more comfortable with new technology than others; some investors have the financial resources to invest in computers and software that others do not have (or would prefer to spend on investing than on technology)…Investors may have different levels of ability to evaluate the information they can obtain about their investments.[130]

We should be careful not to overestimate the quality of deliberation that occurs in these forums. There is no guarantee that enhanced avenues and opportunities for deliberation will produce enlightened discussion that focuses on the wider corporate interest. Indeed, Bradley's review of internet postings found 'varying degrees of coherence and control', ranging from opinion, to unsubstantiated rumor and false information.[131] But this is the nature of deliberative processes — they are not about guaranteeing substance but about improving process. Even if much of the discussion that occurs is of doubtful quality or is focused on short-term concerns, the point is to encourage the prospect of informed debate.

It may therefore be necessary to consider ways of regulating what occurs on these sites.[132] For example, the Australian Securities and Investments Commission permits internet discussion sites to operate outside the licensing requirements[133] provided that the purpose of the site is to enable people who are not securities market professionals to exchange information, opinions or advice about securities, that the postings are clearly separated from commercial material that may be on the site, and that users are warned that the posted material is not professional investment advice.[134]

Another way of effecting 'peripheral deliberation' is to build on the role played by information intermediaries. In some instances groups such as shareholder associations, trade associations,[135] alliances of shareholders within a

---

[129] C Bradley, 'Online Financial Information: Law and Technological Change' (2004) 26 *Law and Policy* 375, 388.

[130] Ibid 380.

[131] Bradley, ibid; see also D Kingsford Smith 'Decentered Regulation in Online Investment' (2001) 19 *Companies & Securities Law Journal* 532, 535.

[132] See, eg, Symposium on Online Investing and the Online Consumer (2004) 26 *Law & Policy*.

[133] Australian law imposes licensing requirements on any person who conducts an investment advice business — see *Corporations Act 2001* Pt 7.6.

[134] Australian Securities and Investments Commission, *Interim Policy Statement – Exposure Draft: Internet Discussion Sites*, IPS 162, 15 August 2000.

[135] Stapledon notes that trade associations are active in the UK, describing some as major players in areas of shareholder protection and corporate governance: G Stapledon, *Institutional Shareholders and Corporate Governance* (1996) 49ff.

corporation,[136] or even groups advocating consumer or environmental concerns, might act as *deliberative* intermediaries. These groups — call them corporate interest groups, or CIGs[137] — can monitor corporate issues, facilitate discussion and debate in the informal and peripheral sphere, and, via the proxy voting system, be direct conduits for the deliberative input of shareholders into the corporation's general meeting. A proxy has the right to speak at the meeting[138] and, in a public corporation, it is not necessary for a person who is appointed as proxy to be a member of the corporation.[139]

The sorts of issues in which CIGs can be involved range from board elections ('control contests'), to constitutional amendments, share restructures, or directors' remuneration ('issue contests'), to questions concerning social and other issues ('policy contests'). [140] The larger and more widely dispersed the corporation's business and shareholding, the more desirable it is that there should be a range of CIGs who seek to represent different shareholder interests around these sorts of issues. Indeed, CIG representation should be contestable.[141] That is, we should encourage different CIGs to compete with each other for the privilege of acting in that capacity. Moreover, there should be no long-standing grants of proxy: the contest between CIGs should be re-opened before each general meeting. What different CIGs will offer in their efforts to secure the capacity to represent other shareholders is a particular idea of what is in the corporate interest. A shareholder's choice of one CIG over others can then be read as an attenuated form of deliberation about the particular issue(s) over which the CIGs are competing. That is, the grant of proxy voting power to a particular CIG is a means whereby a shareholder communicates their concerns and interests to the managers of the corporation.

This idea means introducing the practice of proxy solicitation, found in the United States and Canada but less common in Australia and the United Kingdom, in an overt way. There are, of course, legal issues to be addressed in implementing this idea. As with other information given to shareholders in connection with corporate matters, it is necessary to regulate the form and content

---

[136] For example the Friends of ANI, a group of small shareholders in Australian National Industries Ltd, formed in late 1996 in response to issues raised at the company's annual general meeting. See B Frith, 'Friends of ANI make good case for pooling of votes' *The Australian* (Sydney), 27 November 1996.

[137] The term is prompted by I Ayres and J Braithwaite, *Responsive Regulation: Transcending the Deregulation Debate* (1992) 56.

[138] Eg, *Corporations Act 2001* (Cth) s 249Y; *Canada Business Corporations Act*, RSC 1985, s 152(2).

[139] *The NSW Henry George Foundation v Booth* (2002) 20 ACLC 736, applying *Corporations Act 2001* s 249X. See also *Canada Business Corporations Act*, RSC 1985, s 148(1); *Companies Act 1985* (UK) s 372(1).

[140] The labels are taken from L Bebchuk and M Kahan, 'A Framework for Analyzing Legal Policy Towards Proxy Contests' (1990) 78 *California Law Review* 1071.

[141] I Ayres and J Braithwaite, *Responsive Regulation: Transcending the Deregulation Debate* (1992) 57.

of information supplied by CIGs. [142] It is also necessary to allow for communications between shareholders, and between shareholders and CIGs, to facilitate the effective choice of a CIG and to avoid the unnecessary application of rules that regulate unpublicised accumulations of voting power. [143] For example, the Australian Securities and Investment Commission has granted relief from the application of the takeover provisions in cases of collective action by institutional investors. [144] The policy is designed to allow institutions to enter into short-term voting agreements, provided that those agreements are confined to:

(a) holding discussions or meetings about voting at a specific or proposed meeting of a corporation;
(b) discussing issues about the corporation, including problems and potential solutions;
(c) discussing and exchanging views on a resolution to be voted on at a meeting;
(d) disclosing individual voting intentions on a resolution; or
(e) recommending that another institution votes in a particular way.

The same policy could be applied in the case of discussions with a CIG and any subsequent grant of a proxy to that CIG.

There are also practical issues. As with information intermediaries, a key question is 'who pays for the work done by CIGs'? Proxy solicitation can be expensive. Some interest groups may be self-sustaining (because of their commitment to a particular cause, for example). Others will require financial input. For the same reasons that individual shareholders may decide not to exercise their voting rights, they may not supply sufficient financial support to sustain a competitive field of CIGs. A number of commentators have explored options that involve the provision of funding to intermediary groups by the corporation itself, with the final allocation being determined by the shareholders (eg by resolution at a general meeting, or through the operation of a voucher system). [145] The idea of corporate funding of CIGs is not as novel as it may first seem: corporations already pay for or subsidise certain forms of intermediary activity, for example through

---

[142] See, eg, the requirement for a 'proxy circular' in *Canada Business Corporations Act*, RSC 1985, s 150.

[143] Rules governing takeovers and substantial shareholdings are examples, eg *Corporations Act 2001* (Cth) Chapter 6 (takeovers), Chapter 6C (substantial shareholdings). The *Corporations Act* excludes proxies from the associate and relevant interest provisions which form the basis of the takeover and substantial shareholder provisions ss 16, 609(5).

[144] Australian Securities and Investments Commission, *Collective action by institutional investors*, Policy Statement 128, 14 January 1998.

[145] See T Baums and P von Randow, 'Shareholder Voting and Corporate Governance: The German Experience and a New Approach' in M Aoki and H-K Kim (eds), *Corporate Governance in Transitional Economies: Insider Control and the Role of Banks* (1995) 405; S Choi and J Fisch, 'How to Fix Wall Street: A Voucher Financing Proposal for Securities Intermediaries' (2003) 113 *Yale Law Journal* 269; M Latham, 'Democracy and Infomediaries' (2003) 11 *Corporate Governance* 91.

compulsory auditor appointments, or by paying for the inclusion and dissemination of shareholder sponsored resolutions in notices of general meetings.[146]

Conclusion

There is clearly more to be considered in constructing a deliberative system of corporate decision-making than has been discussed in this Chapter. My purpose has been to explain the importance of, and to sketch some options for, a deliberative model, not to provide a detailed blueprint. In particular there are details of CIG representation which require more attention: how closely, and in what way, should CIGs be monitored in their 'lobbying' activities? Other aspects of corporate general meetings also need to be considered, including the process by which the agenda of the general meeting is determined and structured (including the practice, adopted by some corporations, of inviting shareholders before the meeting to nominate matters for discussion at the meeting),[147] the conduct of the meeting (including the question of who should chair the meeting), and the possibility of allowing shareholders to pass advisory resolutions.[148]

Deliberative processes will not always be easy to introduce, and they will sometimes fall short of the description in this Chapter. Decisions may still be made that do not adequately track the interests of shareholders (or other relevant persons). For these reasons, a move towards better deliberative processes in corporations must be augmented with systems of accountability, as discussed in the previous Chapter, and possibilities for contestation, as I explain in the next Chapter.

---

[146] Eg *Corporations Act 2001* (Cth) s 249O; *Companies Act 1985 (UK)* s 376;

[147] See Business Council of Australia, above n 104, 19-20 (describing this practice in Australian corporations).

[148] The CASAC Final Report rejected the idea of advisory resolutions – see above n 82, 37. The *Corporations Act 2001* has since been amended to require an advisory resolution prior to the adoption of the remuneration report at a listed company's AGM (s 250R(2) and (3)).

Chapter 6

Contesting Corporate Decisions

Notwithstanding opportunities for deliberation, it is possible that majority shareholders, directors or managers will still act solely out of self-interest. Some shareholders may be disadvantaged because of the deliberative indifference of the majority. A corporate governance system that relies, in addition to deliberation, on the checks and balances supplied by separations of powers (as I argued in Chapter 4) will go some way towards guarding against this, but only so far. A further mechanism is required. In this Chapter I explain how the idea of contestability — the third of the three principles elaborated in this book — can fulfil this role.

Why is Contestability Important?

In Chapter 4 I examined the division of corporate decision-making power between the board of directors and the general meeting of members, with managerial decision-making power being vested in the directors (and, through them, the corporation's executive officers). Shareholders, appropriately, do not have direct daily control over matters of corporate policy. Two ideas are commonly used to justify this arrangement, and they are fundamental to the way in which modern corporate law is structured. The first idea is majority rule: corporate decisions, including decisions to grant managerial power to the directors, are legitimated by receiving the approval of a majority of the voting shareholders. The second idea is that shareholders give their consent to the division of power and to the idea of decision by majority rule. In some instances this consent may be actual (eg where shareholders actually vote on the adoption of a constitutional provision that vests managerial power in the directors), but more often consent is said to be implicit in each shareholder's act of purchasing shares and thereby accepting the pre-existing terms of the corporate constitution.

These two related ideas — majority rule and consent — exercise a powerful hold on the thinking of corporate lawyers and legislators.[1] But, as I noted in Chapter 3, corporate lawyers and legislators also recognise that these ideas can create and disguise problems, including a lack of accountability and oppressive or self-serving behaviour by directors or majority shareholders. These problems can arise when, for example, majority rule slides into majority domination or self-

---

[1] Examples can be found throughout corporate law statutes, including general meeting approval mechanisms for reductions of share capital, share buy backs, and financial assistance transactions.

interested rule, or when an absence of debate or protest is misinterpreted as implied consent.

The law's response to the possibility of these problems is to impose standards on decision-makers in particular circumstances and to require procedures aimed at ensuring that each member's consent continues as informed and that majority voting power is exercised properly. For example, as I noted in previous Chapters, corporate statutes impose mandatory disclosure and reporting requirements and courts impose proper purpose requirements on majority shareholders in certain instances.[2] These processes and standards are clearly necessary but, equally clearly, they have a limited capacity to protect shareholders (or directors) from the risk of arbitrary or self-interested behaviour by others.

A further legitimating mechanism is needed, and an appropriate mechanism is found in the idea of contestability, which I have taken from Philip Pettit's work on republican political theory.[3] In the remainder of this part of the Chapter I explain the idea of contestability in more detail, and I explore how the idea of contestability affirms the importance of shareholder 'voice' alongside the 'exit' as an appropriate response to corporate problems. In subsequent parts of the Chapter I examine how corporate law already recognises the importance of contestability, and how these existing mechanisms might be improved or given greater effect.

Contestability in More Detail

Adapting Pettit's idea to the corporate context,[4] contestability refers to the permanent possibility that a decision which does not track the relevant interests and ideas of the shareholders (or directors[5]) who are affected by the decision can be effectively contested.[6] Contestability operates as a legitimating mechanism insofar as each decision is made against the factual possibility that it might be contested and thereby be subject to some form of review. The requirement that corporate decisions should track the interests and ideas of the affected shareholders means

---

[2]   For example, *Gambotto v WCP Ltd* (1995) 13 ACLC 342 (proper purpose and fairness requirements when corporate constitution is amended in order to expropriate minority shares).

[3]   Particularly P Pettit, *Republicanism* (1997); 'Republican Freedom and Contestatory Democracy' in I Shapiro and C Hacker-Cordón (eds), *Democracy's Value* (1999) 163; 'Democracy, Electoral and Contestatory' in I Shapiro and S Macedo (eds), *Designing Democratic Institutions: Nomos 42* (2000) 105.

[4]   Pettit's idea of contestability is developed by reference to decision-making in larger political communities. It therefore has different components and goes further than contestability in a corporate context.

[5]   Although my focus is on contestation by members, in some instances a director may want to contest a decision made by directors and members. In *Talbot v NRMA Ltd* (2000) 18 ACLC 600 the court stated that before taking such a step, a director must believe that the litigation will be in the corporation's best interests and that he or she would be in breach of his or her duties by not taking the action.

[6]   Compare Pettit *Republicanism*, above n 3, 63 and 184-185.

that we want a form of decision-making that shareholders can 'own and identify with' and in which they can see their interests furthered and their ideas respected.[7]

There is an important difference between this idea and the more commonly encountered argument that those who control corporate decision-making must be given incentives, through the threat of legal action, to act in the best interests of the corporation.[8] The incentive argument is concerned with persuading directors and managers to act in accordance with the shareholders' interests by deterring undesirable managerial behaviour. Deterrence is said to work either specifically, where legal action is brought against directors or managers for actual instances of misbehavior, or generally, where the prospect or possibility of legal action deters managers from misconduct. Either form of deterrence requires that directors and managers should be monitored so that shareholders will know when to take action. Moreover, the directors must know or suspect that they are being monitored so that they are aware of the risk of action being taken. The incentive/deterrence argument therefore takes the perspective of the directors and managers. It is concerned with achieving decision-making legitimacy by monitoring and controlling the actions of directors and managers who, it is presumed, are otherwise apt to misbehave. As we will see later in this Chapter, while the incentive/deterrence argument cannot be discounted it is difficult to measure the extent to which it works in practice, and its effect is easy to overstate.

Recognising this, the argument developed here emphasises another reason for insisting on contestability, one that is concerned with the legitimacy of corporate decision-making processes as perceived *by the shareholders*. The contestability argument emphasises that shareholders should know that action can be taken if their interests are not being tracked. As a consequence shareholders can have a measure of confidence in the decision-making process, and they will be more likely to view that process as legitimate.[9] This means that the contestation of corporate decisions must be a real option for shareholders, and that avenues for contestation not be overly restrictive, too cumbersome or remote.

There are four further points of clarification. First, contestability does *not* mean giving each shareholder a right of veto over corporate business, and it does not mean that minority interests must always be satisfied. Courts have confirmed repeatedly that there is nothing oppressive about being a minority shareholder.[10] Merely being out-voted on an issue does not activate the idea of contestability — but having one's interests (including interests in proper and fair decision-making

---

[7]   Ibid 184.
[8]   The managerial incentive argument has been adopted by many commentators on derivative suit legislation, especially those writing from a law and economics perspective. See, eg, D Fischel and M Bradley, 'The Role of Liability Rules and the Derivative Suit in Corporate Law: A Theoretical and Empirical Analysis' (1986) 71 *Cornell Law Review* 261; R Romano, 'The Shareholder Suit: Litigation Without Foundation?' (1991) 7 *Journal of Law, Economics and Organization* 55.
[9]   This aspect of the argument relies on Tom Tyler's work on the importance of perceptions about procedural fairness: see Chapter 5 n 24 and accompanying text.
[10] See, eg, *Re G Jeffrey (Mens Store) Pty Ltd* (1984) 9 ACLR 193.

procedures) improperly excluded from consideration does. Even then, as Pettit notes, 'not every contestation can be satisfied';[11] the legitimate interests of a dissenting shareholder (or group of shareholders) may properly be judged to be secondary to the wider interests of the corporation.

Secondly, there need not be contestation of every corporate decision. For one thing, actual contestation is not a necessary precondition to demonstrating that all relevant interests have been tracked by a decision. What *is* required is that as decisions are being made the possibility of contestation is realistic and that this is understood by all involved. As Pettit says, what is important is 'the possibility of contestation'.[12] Furthermore, too much contestation would make corporate operations unworkable. Corporations, perhaps more so than the wider political systems at which Pettit's argument is directed, are susceptible to the adverse consequences of frivolous or vexatious challenges. These consequences include financial costs, lost business opportunities, and damage to a corporation's reputation.

One way in which the risk of needless contestation can be avoided is by ensuring that decision-making processes are properly open and deliberative in the first place. Contestability is about ensuring that the corporation tracks the interests and ideas of its members, and so those interests must be brought to the attention of the decision-makers in the organisation. A key purpose of deliberation — as I argued in Chapter 5 — is to give those who will be affected by a decision the opportunity to inject their particular interests and ideas into the decision-making process. In effect, deliberation can operate as a form of contestation prior to a decision being reached.[13] Another way of avoiding, or at least reducing, the adverse consequences of unnecessary contestation is to encourage the use of options such as general meetings rather than immediate use of options such as court process. I explain this idea shortly.

The third point of clarification is that despite my reference to corporate decisions as the focal point of contestation, it is just as feasible that a failure to make decisions or to take action should be contestable. Patterns of managerial behaviour that ignore or avoid relevant interests can give rise to the same concerns as arbitrary or improper decisions and so should be subject to the corrective influence that the possibility of contestation supplies.

Fourthly, it should not be thought that contestability is limited to the pursuit of shareholders' individual interests or the protection of their personal rights. As will be seen later in this Chapter when I look at the statutory derivative action, contestability can be concerned to protect the corporate interest in situations where there is little or no immediate gain to the person who initiates the contestation.

Contestability is important to the legitimacy of the corporate constitutional system because it offers those who are in the minority the prospect that a fairer or better result is achievable. It offers the possibility of change and

---

[11]   Pettit, Republicanism above n 3, 197.
[12]   Ibid 185.
[13]   Pettit, 'Democracy, Electoral and Contestatory', above n 3, 122.

thus contributes to a sense that the corporate system merits support, despite any perceived flaws. More importantly, a system that is open to the possibility of change is more likely to command the respect of its participants than one that appears to stand 'pat, smug and self-satisfied'.[14]

Voice Rather Than Exit

Contestability relies on the capacity and willingness of members to challenge decisions that do not meet their relevant interests, rather than simply selling their shares and doing the 'Wall Street walk'. In other words, contestability promotes the exercise of 'voice' over the option of 'exit'.

The classic analysis of 'exit' and 'voice' as responses to poor organisational performance is provided by Albert Hirschman.[15] Hirschman defines voice as:

> ... any attempt at all to change, rather than to escape from, an objectionable state of affairs, whether through individual or collective petition to the management directly in charge, through appeal to a higher authority with the intention of forcing a change in management, or through various types of actions and protests, including those that are meant to mobilize public opinion.[16]

Hirschman notes that there is a strong alignment between exit and economic behaviour on the one hand, and voice and political behaviour on the other. Exit involves shareholders using the market to defend or improve their position:

> [Exit] is the sort of mechanism economics thrives on. It is neat – one either exits or one does not; it is impersonal – any face-to-face confrontation ... with its imponderable and unpredictable elements is avoided and success and failure of the organization are communicated by a set of statistics; and it is indirect – any recovery on the part of the declining firm comes by courtesy of the Invisible Hand...[17]

Exit is the common response of many shareholders in large corporations because it is faster and more impersonal than voicing one's concerns.[18] In contrast, voice involves personal and direct action. It requires the articulation of reasons, and the

---

[14]   The quote and the argument in this paragraph comes from J Balkin, 'Respect-Worthy: Frank Michelman and the Legitimate Constitution' (2004) 39 *Tulsa Law Review* 485, 496.

[15]   Albert O Hirschman, *Exit, Voice, and Loyalty: Responses to Decline in Firms, Organizations and States* (1970).

[16]   Ibid 30.

[17]   Ibid 15-16.

[18]   Ibid 33 and 76. Exit is not always an easy option. Large or institutional shareholders cannot readily liquidate or transfer their holdings. Small shareholders must consider the costs of brokerage fees and other transaction costs.

defence of one's position. Hirschman describes voice as 'political action par excellence'.[19]

Voicing one's concerns requires time and planning, and involves some level of face-to-face interaction. The exercise of voice will therefore be conditioned by the influence and bargaining power which shareholders estimate that they can bring to bear on the corporation, and by the members' willingness to trade the certainty of exit for the uncertainties of improvement due to voice.[20] As Hirschman observes, in large business corporations the availability of the exit option tends to drive out the voice option; voice is the subsidiary mode of reaction.[21]

Provided that voice is a genuine option, I suggest that this balance between exit and voice is appropriate. In fact it is necessitated by the business environment in which most public corporations operate, taking into account the necessary division of managerial functions, the need for directors to discharge the managerial oversight function that shareholders have given to them, and the need for managers to get on with the day-to-day job of management. And exiting a corporation can, depending on the circumstances, send powerful signals to the market and to the corporation's managers about shareholder sentiment. In this sense, exit can be an indirect means of voicing concerns. But this does not mean that corporate law should ignore or abandon the direct exercise of voice, or that the importance of voice options should be down-played. The task is to ensure that 'the art of voice' (to use Hirschman's phrase)[22] is not lost or underestimated. Why should corporate law be built upon the presumption that shareholders are always looking for reasons to exit the corporation? Why not allow for the possibility that sometimes — perhaps quite often[23] — shareholders have reasons to stay with a corporation and, perhaps, voice their concerns in an effort to change the corporation's performance or behaviour? Why should we construct our corporate law system around the assumption that exit is the best option, rather than allowing for the possibility of voice?

Different Forms of Corporate Contestability

I have emphasised that there must be realistic opportunities for effective contestation. I have also acknowledged that in the corporate context too much

---

[19] Ibid 16.
[20] Ibid 77.
[21] Ibid 76.
[22] Ibid 31.
[23] Evidence in Australia suggests that many individual shareholders are not active market traders. A survey found that 49 per cent of shareholders had not engaged in any trading (selling or buying) during 2003; the other 51 per cent of shareholders had an average of six trades during the same period: Australian Stock Exchange, *2003 Australian Share Ownership Study* (2004).

contestation can be counterproductive. One way of responding to both of these concerns is to have available a range of contestability options.

Corporate law is quite familiar with court-based forms of contestation. These include the shareholders' action for oppressive or unfair conduct,[24] the statutory derivative action,[25] and actions for the protection of class rights.[26] But corporate contestation does not always have to begin or end in the courtroom. An over-reliance on judicial forums for contestation might, conceivably, have adverse effects. For example, faced with too great an emphasis on external challenge and review, a board of directors might develop a 'groupthink' mentality that fails to explore alternatives and is not sufficiently critical about the performance of individual members.[27] Conversely, a board might adopt an 'every person for themselves' approach which impedes the interpersonal relationships that foster good group decision-making.[28]

A system of corporate contestability can encourage shareholders to consider non-judicial options, at least as a first resort. Depending on the nature of the disagreement,[29] other forms of contestation include: questioning directors and senior managers at general meetings; proposing resolutions for consideration at the annual general meeting;[30] or complaining to the relevant regulatory agency and asking it to take action.[31] The nature of the contestation — how it is conducted, who controls the process, who decides the outcome, and what range of outcomes is possible — varies with these different options. This will be another factor in the choice of contestability method. With options such as courts, tribunals and resort to regulatory agencies, the contestation becomes more public and control over the outcome is removed from the hands of those whose actions are the subject of complaint. There is an increased prospect of a final decision that is independent of the self-interest of the contestants, and of an outcome 'in which relevant interests are taken equally into account and only impartially supported decisions are

---

24   In Australia, *Corporations Act 2001* (Cth) Part 2F.1.

25   In Australia, *Corporations Act 2001* (Cth) Part 2F.1A.

26   In Australia, *Corporations Act 2001* (Cth) Part 2F.2.

27   As summarised by Bainbridge, the term 'groupthink' describes the psychological phenomenon where 'cohesive groups with strong civility and cooperation norms value consensus more than they do a realistic appraisal of alternatives...[These] groups may strive for unanimity even at the expense of quality decision-making.' S Bainbridge, 'Why a Board? Group Decisionmaking in Corporate Governance' (2002) 55 *Vanderbilt Law Review* 1, 32.

28   Ibid 49-50.

29   Other factors include the size and distribution of the shareholding in the corporation.

30   *Corporations Act 2001* (Cth) s 249N (members with 5 per cent of total votes or 100 members may give notice of a resolution to be moved at a general meeting).

31   This option may have limited utility. A study of the court-based enforcement patterns of the Australian Securities and Investments Commission found that penal enforcement predominated over civil enforcement: H Bird, D Chow, J Lenne and I Ramsay, 'ASIC Enforcement Patterns' (Research Report, Centre for Corporate Law and Securities Regulation, The University of Melbourne, 2003).

upheld'.[32] This does not, however, rule out the use of 'in-house' options, such as questioning at a general meeting. Recall that the underlying idea of contestability is to encourage the deliberative resolution of issues against the background possibility that other more independent and more public modes can always be invoked. In this light 'in house' forms of contestation may produce effective results.

In the remainder of this Chapter I examine 'in house' and external forms of corporate contestation. I do this by looking at how the idea has played out in recent debates concerning extraordinary general meetings (an instance of 'in-house' contestability), and the statutory derivative action (a form of court-based contestation).

Contestability Within the Corporation

General meetings are not impartial forums of review and, as was seen in Chapter 5, the course of deliberation at a general meeting can be constrained and manipulated. Nevertheless, there are several reasons why it might be appropriate for contestation to take place via a general meeting. The issue being contested may be one of internal or commercial policy for which the law provides no effective remedy. Even where legal remedies are available, disaffected shareholders may still prefer to keep the matter 'in house' for reasons such as cost or to reduce reputational damage to the corporation. Deliberating a matter within the corporation may help to define the problem more clearly. Further, as I noted in Chapter 5,[33] despite low attendance by shareholders, many directors do take the threat of critical questioning at a general meeting seriously. Finally, the courts continue to express a long-held preference for the resolution of internal corporate disputes via general meetings. As Lindley LJ put it in *Isle of Wight Railway Company v Tahourdin*, 'this Court has constantly and consistently refused to interfere on behalf of shareholders, until they have done the best they can to set right the matters of which they complain, by calling general meetings'. [34] Much more recently, Campbell J in the Supreme Court of New South Wales said that:

> Questions of what is, or is not, in the interests of the members as whole are often best left to be decided by the officers, organs and procedures of the company itself, or by the court deciding, after events have happened, whether those events fall short of a legally required standard of conduct...[35]

With these points in mind, I want to look at the clearest instance where a general meeting can be used as a form of contestation: the right of members to require that

---

[32] Pettit, Democracy's Value, above n 3, 179.

[33] See Chapter 5, n 104 and accompanying text.

[34] (1884) 25 Ch D 320, 333; cited in *NRMA v Parkin* (2004) 22 ACLC 861, 868.

[35] *Turnbull v NRMA* (2004) 22 ACLC 1094, 1105.

an extraordinary (or special) general meeting of the corporation be convened. This has been a topic of some debate in Australian corporate governance law reform.[36]

The Right to Requisition a General Meeting

Corporate law statutes commonly provide that a certain number or proportion of members may require the directors of a corporation to convene a general meeting of the corporation.[37] Using the Australian statute as an example, the request must state the purpose of the meeting and include any resolution that is to be proposed at the meeting. The meeting must be held for a proper purpose,[38] and if the proposed resolution is not one that can lawfully be passed by a general meeting then the directors can refuse to include it in the notice of the meeting.[39] This statutory right implies that the meeting must be conducted in a manner that allows the business for which it was convened to be dealt with fully, adequately, and for matters to be fairly discussed.[40] If the directors do not act upon the request within 21 days, then the members who have requisitioned the meeting (or, at least, those holding more than half of the votes held by the requisitioning members) can convene the meeting themselves, with the corporation bearing their reasonable costs.[41]

This right can used to challenge the board of directors by putting resolutions for the removal and replacement of directors. In Australia it has also been used on a very small number of occasions to put resolutions concerning corporate investment in uranium mining operations[42] or the environmental impact of timber logging activities.[43] The use of this procedure to raise environmental or human rights concerns, or to seek to direct board policy has prompted debate about the proper purpose of the right to requisition meetings, and whether there should be stricter threshold requirements before it can be exercised.

In Australia the threshold requirement (as at early 2006) is that the request must be made by members with at least five per cent of the votes that might be cast at the general meeting, or by at least 100 members who are entitled to vote at the general meeting.[44] In 1999 a Federal Parliamentary Committee recommended that

---

[36]   See below n 43 to 48 and accompanying text.

[37]   See *Corporations Act 2001* (Cth) s 249D; *Companies Act 1985* (UK) s 368; *Revised Model Business Corporations Act* §7.02 (2002). While it is the directors' responsibility to call the meeting, it is the corporation which holds the meeting: *ASIC v NRMA* (2003) 21 ACLC 186, 190. In Australia it is also possible for the members to call and convene a general meeting themselves, bearing the costs (s 249F).

[38]   *Corporations Act 2001* (Cth) s 249Q.

[39]   *NRMA v Parker* (1986) 4 ACLC 609 (members cannot pass a resolution that purports to control the exercise of power vested in the board of directors).

[40]   *John J Starr (Real Estate) Pty Ltd v Robert R Andrew (Australasia) Pty Ltd* (1991) 6 ACSR 63, 84.

[41]   *Corporations Act 2001* (Cth) s 249E; *Companies Act 1985* (UK) s 368(4)-(6).

[42]   As occurred with North Ltd in June 1999.

[43]   As occurred with Wesfarmers Ltd in July 1999, and Gunns Ltd in February 2003.

[44]   *Corporations Act 2001* (Cth) s 249D(1). Prior to 1998, the statute required each of the 100 members to have an average paid-up capital of at least $200. In the UK the

the statute be amended to make the sole criterion for requisitioning an extraordinary general meeting that the requisitioning members hold five per cent of the issued share capital.[45] This recommendation was endorsed one year later by the Companies and Securities Advisory Committee (CASAC).[46] The Parliamentary Committee accepted arguments against the 100 members rule that were put by some prominent publicly-listed corporations (including the mining corporations Rio Tinto Ltd and North Ltd, and the large retailer Coles Myer Ltd) and by organisations such as the Law Council of Australia, the Investment and Financial Services Association Ltd,[47] the Business Council of Australia, and the Australian Institute of Company Directors. These arguments can be summarised as follows: the 100 members rule is too easily satisfied, with the result that shareholders with only a nominal or insignificant economic interest in a corporation can put the corporation and other shareholders to the cost and disruption of holding a meeting, distracting directors and managers from their core functions. Furthermore, the procedure is open to abuse by disgruntled minorities, single-issue groups and activists who are motivated by concerns that are at odds with the financial interests of the corporation. Similarly, the CASAC recommendation was based on the argument that eliminating the 100 members rule would ensure that 'the cost of convening an extraordinary general meeting is only incurred when it is requisitioned by shareholders who collectively have a material economic interest in the company'.[48] The inability of would-be requisitioners to satisfy the remaining five per cent shareholding test 'would call into serious question the prospects of their proposed resolution succeeding'.[49] In early 2005 the Federal Government released the draft of its proposed amendments for public consultation, in which the 100 members rule was removed.[50] Following public hearings, a Parliamentary

---

requisitioning members must hold a minimum of ten per cent of the paid-up voting shares in the corporation: *Companies Act 1985* (UK) s 368(2); the Company Law Review Steering Group, *Final Report*, Volume 1 (June 2001) recommended that this be retained: 153-156.

[45] Joint Committee on Corporations and Securities, Parliament of Australia, *Report on Matters Arising From the Company Law Review Act 1998* (1999) 164.

[46] Companies and Securities Advisory Committee (CASAC), *Shareholder Participation in the Modern Listed Public Company* (June 2000).

[47] The Investment and Financial Services Association Ltd represents most major institutional investors in Australia.

[48] CASAC, above n 46, 11-12.

[49] Ibid 12.

[50] Corporations Amendment Bill (No. 2) 2005 Exposure Draft. Prior to this, in April 2000 the Federal Government introduced a regulation (under s 249D(1A)) that reflected these recommendations. The regulation was disallowed by the Senate in June 2000. In response the Federal Minister for Financial Services and Regulation released a proposal in December 2000 that retained the five per cent requirement but added, as an alternative, a minimum number requirement calculated as the square root of the total number of shareholders in the corporation. The proposal was later withdrawn from consideration.

Committee recommended that this be enacted and in December 2005 the Government announced its intention to proceed in this way.[51]

Despite these reforms, there is no evidence, in Australia at least, of widespread 'abuse' of the right to requisition a general meeting. The AGM study referred to in Chapter 5 found in a sample of 217 corporations that there were only five extraordinary general meetings requisitioned by shareholders in the four years between July 1998 and June 2002.[52] The 1999 Parliamentary Committee inquiry heard (but chose not to act on) submissions from organisations including the Institute of Chartered Accountants in Australia, the Australian Society of Certified Practicing Accountants, and the Association of Superannuation Funds of Australia Ltd that the 100 members rule had not given rise to any significant problems, and that the threshold was in fact difficult to achieve (the latter argument being put by shareholder groups in certain corporations, such as the Boral Green Shareholders, Amcor Green Shareholders, BHP Shareholders for Social Responsibility, and North Ethical Shareholders). Concerns about the disruptive potential of the 100 members rule overlook the fact that it is just as feasible for a corporation to be needlessly disrupted by the self-interest of a single shareholder who controls a five per cent parcel (or more) of shares. Indeed, the impact of either the five per cent rule or the 100 members rule varies depending on the total number of shareholders in the corporation. For example, in a corporation with 1000 members the five per cent rule is more easily satisfied than the 100 members rule. The reverse is true for a corporation with more than 2,000 members.[53] There is, in other words, no 'correct' threshold requirement that can apply to all corporations and in all situations.

The debate about the threshold is really one about control over management of the corporation, and about the proper place of shareholders in that process. The arguments for a more restrictive threshold have strong echoes of the political arguments put by Joseph Schumpeter and Max Weber (discussed in Chapter 4)[54] according to which the job of voters is to elect their leaders and then refrain from interfering with the job of running the polity. In the corporate context this is translated into the maxim 'let the managers manage' or, in the specific context of the debate about the 100 members rule, 'let only those voters with significant economic interests have a say'.

In the absence of any evidence that the 100 members threshold is being abused in any significant way there is no reason to change it. Indeed, the fact that it

---

[51] Joint Committee on Corporations and Financial Services, Parliament of Australia, *Inquiry into the Exposure Draft of the Corporations Amendment Bill (No. 2) 2005* (2005) 6; Hon. Chris Pearce MP, 'Pearce Announces Corporate Governance Reforms' (Press Release, 8 December 2005).

[52] S Bottomley, The Role of Shareholders' Meetings in Improving Corporate Governance (Research Report, Centre for Commercial Law, Australian National University, 2003) 47.

[53] M Whincop, 'The Role of The Shareholder in Corporate Governance: A Theoretical Approach' (2001) 25 *Melbourne University Law Review* 418, 449.

[54] See Chapter 4, n 46 to 55 and accompanying text.

attracts the attention of corporate managers demonstrates its usefulness in contestability terms. Recall, it is the factual possibility of contestation[55] that provides the legitimating mechanism for corporate decisions. A threshold that is perceived (with or without any empirical basis) to be too low or too 'easy' can supply a constraining effect on managerial behaviour. More significantly, the 100 members threshold appeared to achieve the right balance between offering a realistic avenue for contestation (to the extent that the 100 members rule is easily met) while not resulting in over use of this contestability option (as evidenced by its low level of use).

Contestability Outside the Corporation: The Statutory Derivative Action[56]

Many countries make statutory provision for a derivative action (SDA),[57] allowing a person to commence proceedings on behalf of a corporation against those who have caused harm to the corporation in a situation where the corporation is unable or unwilling to bring the action itself.[58] The SDA is used to pursue the corporation's interests, with any remedy that is awarded by the court going to the corporation. The standard case arises where directors have breached their duties causing loss to the corporation, with the board declining to cause the corporation to bring an action to recover that loss. More generally, the SDA is appropriate where the majority's control of the corporation prevents the minority from effective contestation through internal means such as the general meeting.

The statutory provision of a right of derivative action thus provides a mechanism for contestation, emphasising the exercise of 'voice' rather than the use of 'exit'. However, as I will argue, while it is necessary for good corporate governance the SDA works best by not being used with great frequency.

---

[55] Pettit, Republicanism, above n 3, 185.

[56] This part develops ideas from S Bottomley, 'The Relative Importance of the Statutory Derivative Action in Australia' in F Macmillan (ed) *International Corporate Law Annual Vol 2* (2003) 141-166.

[57] B Welling, *Corporate Law in Canada: The Governing Principles* (2nd ed, 1991) 534 and 544, prefers the term 'representative actions'. Similarly Wedderburn describes this form of action as representative: K W Wedderburn, 'Shareholders' Rights and the Rule in Foss v Harbottle' [1957] *Cambridge Law Journal* 194 and [1958] *Cambridge Law Journal* 93.

[58] Eg *Corporations Act 2001* (Cth) ss 236-242; *Canada Business Corporations Act*, RSC 1985, s 239; in New Zealand the *Companies Act 1993* (NZ) ss 165-168. In the United Kingdom the Company Law Reform Bill, introduced in November 2005, makes provision for a derivative action. In the United States provisions for derivative actions are found in State corporations legislation, with variations between States. Rule 23.1 of the Federal Rules of Civil Procedure regulates derivative actions brought in federal courts; it is also a model for some State statutes: L Ribstein, *Business Associations*, (2nd ed, 1990) 578. The American Law Institute's *Principles of Corporate Governance* (1994) Part VII contain standards and procedures for derivative actions.

The Statutory Derivative Action in Australia

In this section I use the Australian legislation to outline the main features of the SDA. This will set the basis for assessing the role of the SDA as a mechanism for contestability.

In Australia the SDA expressly replaces the limited and uncertain common law rules regarding the availability of derivative actions as exceptions to the rule in *Foss v Harbottle*.[59] The statute defines a derivative action as one in which a person either brings proceedings on behalf of and in the name of a corporation, or intervenes in proceedings to which the corporation is a party for the purpose of taking responsibility for those proceedings on behalf of, and in the name of, the corporation. This can be done by a current or former member of the corporation or a related body corporate (or someone entitled to be registered as a member), or by a current or former officer of the company.[60]

The statute does not define or limit the type of matter which can be the subject of a derivative action.[61] The only prerequisite to commencing a derivative action is obtaining leave from the court. The court must grant leave if five criteria are all satisfied.[62] The criteria are as follows:

1. *It is probable that the corporation will not bring the proceedings itself or take responsibility for them.* One way of determining this is to look at how the board of directors has responded if the applicant has served on the corporation a notice of intention to apply for leave (discussed at point five, below). Another factor to take into account is the extent to which any decision by the corporation against commencing an action has been influenced by the people whose conduct is the subject of the potential derivative suit.

2. *The applicant is acting in good faith.* The purpose of this requirement is to rule out suits in which the applicant's substantive goal is a personal rather than a corporate remedy. The applicant must demonstrate an honest belief that there is a good cause of action that has a reasonable prospect of success, and that there is no

---

[59] *Corporations Act 2001* (Cth) s 236(2). The rule in *Foss v Harbottle* (1843) 2 Hare 461; 67 ER 189 states that (i) the corporation is the proper plaintiff in any situation in which a wrong is alleged to be done to the corporation, and (ii) the actions which constitute the alleged wrongdoing can be made binding on the corporation by a majority vote at a general meeting of shareholders. The classic discussion of the rule and its exceptions is found in Wedderburn, above n 56.

[60] See *Corporations Act 2001* (Cth) s 236. An officer is defined to include a director, secretary, executive officer or employee of the company (s 82A).

[61] This is similar to Canada and New Zealand. In contrast the UK Company Law Reform Bill Law (see above n 58) restricts the statutory derivative action to breaches of directors' duties or directors' negligence: cl 239(3).

[62] *Corporations Act 2001* (Cth) s 237(2). The *Canada Business Corporations Act*, RSC 1985, s 239(2) specifies three criteria, similar to points 2, 3 and 5 in the text. In New Zealand the *Companies Act 1993* specifies either criterion 1 or 3 as alternative prerequisites to bringing a derivative action: s 165(3). The UK Bill (see above n 58) lists five criteria, three of which are similar to points 1, 2 and 3 in the text (proposed s 242(3)).

collateral purpose in bringing the action.[63] To the extent that this catches frivolous or vexatious suits, this overlaps with the 'serious question' criterion, discussed at point four below.

     3. It is in the corporation's best interests for the court to grant leave.[64] This criterion lies at the heart of the derivative action because it is the corporation's separate and independent interests which are at stake rather than those of the applicant or any group of directors or shareholders.[65] Welling's description of the equivalent Canadian provision puts it nicely: 'what the complainant is really doing is presenting the court with 'a corporation in need of protection'.[66] This criterion encourages the court to regard the corporation 'as a continuing concern which must encompass the interests of past, present and future shareholders, creditors and (one would hope) employees'.[67] It is not left to either the board of directors or the general meeting of shareholders to decide what is in the corporation's best interests. While the views of these two groups are clearly relevant, the corporation's interests in commencing legal action are a matter for judicial determination, taking into account the character of the corporation, its business (if any), whether redress can be achieved by other means, and whether the defendant can meet any judgement made in the corporation's favour.[68] This emphasises the point that corporate governance is not to be regarded solely as a matter of private intra-corporate agreement.

     The 'best interests' criterion has a further implication. Even if the corporation has suffered a wrong which could, in theory, be subject of a derivative suit, it may nevertheless not be in the corporate interest for action to be taken. For example, it may be that the benefit to the corporation of the potential remedy will be significantly outweighed by the financial or reputational costs of the action.[69] It may also be that the actions of the directors, whilst constituting a breach of duty, have not had a material effect on the corporation.

     4. There is a serious question to be tried. This criterion is intended to import the test which is used regularly by Australian courts in determining interim injunction applications.[70] In other words, the court must determine whether the applicant's claim is frivolous or vexatious, whether it has a real prospect of succeeding, and whether the balance of convenience favours granting leave.[71]

---

[63] *Swansson v Pratt* (2002) ACLC 1594, 1601.

[64] In Canada the Court must be satisfied that the proposed action 'appears to be' in the corporation's interests: *Canada Business Corporations Act*, RSC 1985, s 239(2)(c). In New Zealand the Court must 'have regard to' the interests of the corporation: *Companies Act 1993* s 165(2).

[65] *Charlton v Baber* (2003) 21 ACLC 1671.

[66] Welling, above n 57, 535.

[67] M A Maloney, 'Whither the Statutory Derivative Action?' [1986] 64 *Canadian Bar Review* 309, 328.

[68] *Swansson v Pratt* (2002) 20 ACLC 1594, 1604-1605.

[69] *Metyor Inc v Queensland Electronic Switching Pty Ltd* (2002) 20 ACLC 1517, 1523.

[70] Explanatory Memorandum, Corporate Law Economic Reform Bill 1998 (Cth) para 6.46.

[71] *Nicholas John Holdings Pty Ltd v ANZ Banking Group Ltd* [1992] 2 VR 715, 722-723.

5. *Whether the applicant has notified the corporation of the application.*
Although this is the last criterion in the list, as a matter of procedure it precedes the others. Before applying for leave, the applicant should give the corporation fourteen days written notice of the intention to apply, together with the reasons for the application. Obviously this notice will give the board of directors the opportunity to decide whether the corporation should commence the action in its own right, thereby avoiding the need for a derivative suit. Alternatively, receipt of the notice might lead to the settlement of the dispute out of court, thereby avoiding the need for any litigation. The Court may still grant leave in the absence of such notice provided that it is 'appropriate' to do so,[72] and provided that the other four criteria have been satisfied. This will be appropriate where giving notice 'is not practical or expedient, thus allowing for an ex parte hearing where there is a need for urgent litigation'.[73]

Neither the right to apply for leave to commence a derivative action, nor the right to bring the action once leave has been granted, is determined by the fact that a majority of shareholders in the corporation has voted to ratify or approve the conduct in question.[74] The court may take a ratification into account in deciding what order to make in the leave application or in the resulting proceedings, but it must be satisfied that the ratification or approval was well-informed and that the members were acting for proper purposes. This reverses the common law position in which a proper ratification by members had the effect of negating the possibility of derivative suit.[75] The message here is that the principle of majority rule does not necessarily provide a justification for corporate actions, and that 'in some circumstances judicial action is preferable to action by the shareholders'.[76]

The Rationale for a Statutory Derivative Action

There are two rationales that are commonly given for providing shareholders with a right of derivative action.[77] One is that the SDA is concerned with compensating the corporation for harm that has been caused by corporate wrong-doers. The second rationale is that the derivative action deters directors and managers from wrongful or improper behaviour. Commentators seem to agree that, of these two rationales, '[d]eterrence is the major reason for and principal effect of derivative

---

[72] *Corporations Act 2001* (Cth) s 237(2)(e).
[73] Explanatory Memorandum, Corporate Law Economic Reform Bill 1998 (Cth) para 6.50.
[74] *Corporations Act 2001* (Cth) s 239. The *Canada Business Corporations Act*, RSC 1985, s 242 is similar. In contrast the proposal in the UK is that the court must refuse leave if the act or omission has been ratified: Company Law Reform Bill cl 242(2).
[75] *Hogg v Cramphorn* [1967] Ch 254.
[76] Companies and Securities Advisory Committee, *Report on a Statutory Derivative Action*, July 1993, 21.
[77] J Coffee and D Schwartz, 'The Survival of the Derivative Suit: An Evaluation and a Proposal for Legislative Reform' (1981) 81 *Columbia Law Review* 261, 302-309.

suits'.[78] This is not to say that compensation is an 'illusory or insignificant goal'.[79] Indeed it has been emphasised by the courts; in *Karam v ANZ Banking Group Ltd*, for example, Santow J noted that 'the statutory derivative action ... was intended to be remedial'.[80] However, the argument goes that the SDA is an imperfect compensation device because, for example, of the dissonance between the corporation's gains and losses and those of the shareholders. Deterrence was certainly the accepted motivation behind the Australian reforms. The 1999 legislative amendments which enacted the SDA were based on a recommendation of the Federal Government's Corporate Law Economic Reform Program (CLERP).[81] They were apparently introduced as a trade-off for shareholders in light of the enactment of a statutory business judgement rule that was intended to protect directors. The policy and concerns which underpinned the CLERP recommendation can be seen in the following passage:

> Any enhancement of members' rights must be assessed against the need to encourage managerial risk-taking which is an essential element in the pursuit of profit. The conferral of rights on members should not work against their interests by causing management to avoid commercial risk-taking because of the risks of personal liability. The overall goal of conferring rights on investors *is to provide an incentive for management* to exercise its powers appropriately and discharge its functions for the ultimate advantage of the providers of the corporation's capital.[82]

The CLERP recommendation assumed a corporate model in which directors and managers act as agents for shareholders in the pursuit of commercial risk, and in which there is therefore a need for the law to supply incentive mechanisms so that directors will act in the shareholders' interests.

---

[78]   D Schwartz, 'In Praise of Derivative Suits: A Commentary on the Paper of Professors Fischel and Bradley' (1986) 71 *Cornell Law Review* 322, 331. See also Coffee and Schwartz, ibid, 302.

[79]   Coffee and Schwartz, above n 77, 305. Compensation supplies the primary rationale when, as in some Australian cases, the SDA is brought by shareholders of a corporation that is in liquidation to recover property – see, eg, *Charlton v Baber* (2003) 21 ACLC 1671.

[80]   (2000) 18 ACLC 590, 597.

[81]   Corporate Law Economic Reform Program (CLERP), *Directors' Duties and Corporate Governance: Facilitating Innovation and Protecting Investors*, Paper No 3 (1997). The CLERP recommendation was the latest in a number of reform proposals: Companies and Securities Law Review Committee, *Enforcement of the Duties of Directors and Officers of a Company by Means of a Statutory Derivative Action*, Report No 12 (1990); House of Representatives Standing Committee on Legal and Constitutional Affairs, Parliament of Australia (the Lavarch Committee), *Corporate Practices and the Rights of Shareholders* (Canberra, AGPS, 1991); Companies and Securities Advisory Committee, *Report on a Statutory Derivative Action*, July 1993; Commonwealth Attorney-General's Department, *Proceedings on Behalf of a Company (Statutory Derivative Action) Draft Provisions and Commentary* (1995).

[82]   Corporate Law Economic Reform Program, above n 31, 31 (emphasis added).

As I argued earlier in this Chapter, however, contestability is not just about providing deterrence-based incentives towards proper managerial performance. It is also about establishing mechanisms that allow shareholders to 'own and identify with' decision-making processes such that they can see their interests furthered and their ideas respected.[83] There is, then, a third rationale for the SDA: it offers a legitimacy mechanism for decision-making processes.

I want to assess how the SDA measures up on this legitimacy rationale by looking at three criticisms that have been directed at the statutory right of derivative action. They are: that institutional shareholders are a better means of correcting poor managerial behaviour; that the SDA increases the risk of wasteful strategic litigation by minority shareholders; and that the SDA is not important because it is rarely used and is ineffective.

Institutional Shareholders as Monitors

One criticism of the SDA is that it permits small or minority shareholders to commence legal action, disturbing the economically preferred view that monitoring and correcting corporate management is best left to large or institutional shareholders. As Fischel and Bradley explain it, '[b]ecause shareholders with the largest stakes will gain the most from good performance and bear most of the costs of bad performance, they have the best incentives to maximize the value of the firm'.[84] This is similar to the argument, encountered earlier, that the right to requisition extraordinary general meetings should be limited to those shareholders with a sufficiently large stake in the corporation.

There are at least three problems with this argument. First, institutional shareholders are constrained by the effect of legal rules that impede or limit the extent of their overt intervention in corporate management.[85] Secondly, as we saw in Chapter 4, when institutional shareholders do take steps 'to maximize the value of the firm' their power is usually exercised informally through private meetings and direct communications with senior corporate officers.[86] If contestation is left to these shareholders alone then the risk is that information about critical corporate governance issues and decisions becomes the preserve of large corporate insiders, rather than a matter of wider corporate knowledge. As a consequence the confidence of other shareholders in the operation of the corporate decision-making system may be reduced. Contestability is not divorced from concerns for accountability, and as far as possible the processes of contestation ought to be open

---

[83]   Pettit, *Republicanism*, above n 3, 184.

[84]   Above n 8, 271.

[85]   See G Stapledon, *Institutional Shareholders and Corporate Governance* (1996) 271ff discussing the impact of laws on insider trading and takeovers. In Australia, the Australian Securities and Investments Commission has granted limited relief from the application of the takeover provisions in cases of collective action by institutional investors: *Collective action by institutional investors*, Policy Statement 128, 14 January 1998.

[86]   See Chapter 4 n 144 to 146 and accompanying text.

and transparent. Thirdly, as I also noted in Chapter 4, there is no reason to assume that the interests and concerns of institutional shareholders will necessarily accord with those of other shareholders.

Action by institutional investors does have a role in corporate governance, as was seen in Chapter 5, but it is not a substitute for contestability via the SDA. Along with intervention by institutional shareholders, the SDA should operate as a necessary component of a larger scheme comprising formal and informal, internal and external contestability mechanisms.

The 'institutional investor as monitor' argument usually includes two further claims: it is argued that minority or small shareholders either have 'very little incentive to consider the effect of the action on other shareholders', preferring to engage in strategic or selfish litigation[87] or, conversely, that minority or small shareholders lack sufficient incentive to bring any actions. These criticisms of the SDA are considered under the next two subheadings.

Strategic Behaviour by Minority Shareholders

The criticism here is that providing a statutory mechanism for bringing derivative actions increases the risk of frivolous, self-serving, or strategic law suits by minority shareholders, distracting corporate managers from their proper tasks.[88] While this risk cannot be discounted entirely, it is easily overstated, at least in the Australian context. The risk of strategic lawsuits is met by the effective use of judicial screening devices such as the good faith, best interests of the company, and serious question criteria found in the Australian SDA, described above. The cumulative effect of these criteria is to limit the occasions on which leave is granted. In the words of one judge: '[i]t is clearly the intent of [the Act] that leave to bring a derivative action must not be given lightly'.[89]

In the United States, where most of the concerns about overuse and misuse of the derivative procedure have been raised,[90] some incentive towards shareholder suits is provided by cost rules[91] and the use of contingency fee arrangements whereby the plaintiff lawyer's fees are calculated as a percentage of the amount awarded by the court in a successful action.[92] Contingent fee

---

[87]   Eg, Fischel and Bradley above n 8, 271.

[88]   For example, ibid 272; Romano above n 8, 55-56.

[89]   *Swansson v Pratt* (2002) 20 ACLC 1594, 1600.

[90]   One explanation for this is that 'the US is more permissive towards derivative litigation' in the framing of its procedural rules – G Miller, 'Political Structure and Corporate Governance: Some Points of Contrast Between the United States and England' (1998) *Columbia Business Law Review* 51, 52.

[91]   See J Coffee, 'The Unfaithful Champion: The Plaintiff as Monitor in Shareholder Litigation' (1985) 48 *Law & Contemporary Problems* 5, 16.

[92]   J Macey and G Miller, 'The Plaintiffs' Attorney's Role in Class Action and Derivative Litigation: Economic Analysis and Recommendations' (1991) 58 *University of Chicago Law Review* 1.

arrangements of this sort are not permitted in Australia.[93] Furthermore the Australian legislation gives the court full discretion regarding costs orders in relation to the initial leave application and the subsequent derivative action. This includes discretion about the timing of any such order.[94] Thus a shareholder plaintiff faces the risk of having to bear at least some of the legal costs of the derivative litigation. Of course, assurances that the SDA will not result in a flood of strategic lawsuits raise a potentially more telling criticism.

Under-use of Derivative Actions

Recall that the SDA is said to be a deterrence mechanism, both specifically, when liability rules are applied by courts in derivative actions, and generally, through the threat that such cases might be brought. Some critics point out, however, that shareholder litigation is a relatively rare occurrence. Shareholders are regarded as investors who seek to maximise the returns on the capital that they have invested, who are keen to protect that investment, and who therefore weigh the costs and benefits of legal suits according to a criterion of net personal return. The argument goes that shareholders are discouraged from using the SDA by the fact that any benefits from a derivative action will flow to the corporation while the risks of the suit remain with the applicant shareholder. Furthermore, the amount recovered by the corporation will translate into relatively small benefits on a per share basis. Shareholders will also be discouraged by the prospect of other inactive shareholders getting a free ride on any benefits (however small and indirect) that do flow through to shareholders.[95] Derivative actions, it is argued, therefore have little direct effect because of under-use and consequently, contrary to the claims about the role of the SDA noted earlier, the deterrent effect is also reduced. One assessment of the Canadian experience thus concludes that 'the statutory derivative action has, on balance, not made the impact on Canadian corporate law which might have been expected'.[96] Even in the United States research shows that shareholder litigation is 'an infrequent experience'.[97] Romano's study found 'little evidence of specific deterrence' and concluded that 'it is virtually impossible to identify a general deterrent effect' from the prospect of litigation.[98] Similar results have been predicted for the SDA in Australia and the United Kingdom.[99]

---

[93]   G Dal Pont, *Lawyers' Professional Responsibility in Australia and New Zealand*, (2nd ed, 2001) 400. It is permissible for a lawyer to enter a speculative fee arrangement, whereby the lawyer acts on a 'no win, no fee' basis.

[94]   *Corporations Act 2001* (Cth) s 242.

[95]   For a discussion of these and other perceived disincentives, see I Ramsay, 'Corporate Governance, Shareholder Litigation and the Prospects for a Statutory Derivative Action' (1992) 15 *University of New South Wales Law Journal* 149.

[96]   B Cheffins, 'Reforming the Derivative Action: The Canadian Experience and British Prospects' [1997] *Company Financial and Insolvency Law Review* 227, 256.

[97]   Romano, above n 8, 59.

[98]   Ibid, 84 and 85.

[99]   For the United States see Romano, above n 8. For Australia, see Ramsay, above n 95, 175. For the United Kingdom see Cheffins, above n 96, 260.

These criticisms are significant if deterrence is assumed to be the only rationale for the SDA. If, however, we accept that it is the existence of the right to commence an SDA which is important in legitimating decision-making processes then low levels of specific deterrence do not present such a problem, provided that this is not a product of overly restrictive procedural rules, or unduly expensive or drawn-out legal processes. The SDA must have the potential to make the exercise of corporate decision-making power answerable to the interests of the corporation as a whole. This requires that there should be *some* evidence of specific deterrence, that there be *some* instances where the SDA is used to defend the corporate interest. But it does not require high levels of specific deterrence. As I noted earlier, compared to exit, voice is the subsidiary mode of reaction. By imposing preconditions which limit the use of the SDA we underline the significance and magnitude of those occasions when such actions are commenced. Hirschman notes that there is a paradox at work here: the ease with which the exit option can be used undermines the extent to which the voice option is used, but on the other hand the ready availability of exit can strengthen the effectiveness of the voice option when it is used.[100] As Fischel and Bradley concede, voice, in the form of the derivative action, has a 'limited, albeit important' function.[101]

The argument above supports the relative importance of the SDA. The SDA is *important* because it offers a legitimating device for corporate decisions through the mechanism of contestability, and because it offers an avenue for arguments about the corporate interest to be voiced by members. It is *relatively* important because the SDA should not be regarded as the centrepiece of an effective corporate governance and accountability system. Indeed, as Rostow warned three decades ago:

> [t]he stockholders' suit is not a uniformly effective remedy for the misdeeds of directors – indeed, it is not often an effective remedy for such misdeeds at all. Sporadic in its incidence, costly in its procedures, it has been, from time to time, a vehicle for extortion as well as for purification.[102]

Poor deterrence can be an outcome of over-use of the litigation option. Overuse of the voice option can diminish its effectiveness. If a purpose of using the voice option is to restore or improve corporate behaviour and performance then, as Hirschman argues, it is important to avoid reaching the point where discontented members become so harassing that their protests hinder rather than help the efforts at recovery.[103]

---

[100]	Hirschman, above n 15, 83.
[101]	Cheffins, above n 96, 287.
[102]	E Rostow, 'To Whom and for What Ends is Corporate Management Responsible?' in E Mason (ed), *The Corporation in Modern Society* (1960) 46, 49.
[103]	Hirschman, above n 15, 31.

The SDA and Corporate Regulation

Thus far I have considered three rationales for the SDA — compensation, deterrence, and legitimation — and I have argued that the latter requires more emphasis than it has received. There is a fourth rationale that I want to consider briefly: the SDA can also have a regulatory function. This suggestion stems from the discussion back in Chapter 3 about the state's role in protecting and furthering public values and, consequently, putting limits on the power of private organisations. From this perspective corporations are regarded not solely as private arrangements, but also as key participants in the public economic and social arena. In that argument I suggested that a system of corporate law should be concerned to enhance public values such as the avoidance of oppressive or unfair behaviour and improving the accountability of corporate decision making.[104] The SDA can play a role here by preserving the possibility that such values can be applied through the medium of judicial decision.

The question, then, is whether the SDA should be regarded exclusively as a private self-help mechanism or whether it also has a role in the public regulation of corporations.[105] Can the SDA, as Whincop and Keyes suggest, support the emergence of a 'new corporate law' based on public law-like standards of fairness and propriety, in which public review and regulation are emphasised alongside private ordering of affairs?[106]

There are some hints about this possibility in the history of SDA in Australia. The idea of introducing a derivative action into the corporations legislation was put forward by the Companies and Securities Law Review Committee (CSLRC) in its 1990 inquiry into the standards of conduct and performance of company directors and officers.[107] The CSLRC recommendation was driven partly by a concern about the unsatisfactory nature of the common law, but it was also prompted by the Committee's belief that a new regime of civil proceedings:

> ... might serve a useful purpose in the general scheme of regulation of corporate activity in the interests of investors and creditors. Civil proceedings brought by

---

[104] See Chapter 3 n 18, and accompanying text.

[105] See D Sugarman, 'Reconceptualising Company Law: Reflections on the Law Commission's Consultation Paper on Shareholder Remedies' (1997) 18 *The Company Lawyer* 226, 281.

[106] M Whincop and M Keyes, 'Corporation, Contract, Community: An Analysis of Governance in the Privatisation of Public Enterprise and the Publicisation of Private Corporate Law' (1997) 25 *Federal Law Review* 51, 92.

[107] Companies and Securities Law Review Committee, *Enforcement of the Duties of Directors and Officers of a Company by Means of a Statutory Derivative Action*, Report No. 12 (1990). The Committee used the derivative action provisions in the Ontario *Business Corporations Act* 1982 as the model for its recommendations.

members might provide enforcement in cases which the regulatory authorities are unable to prosecute because of competing demands on limited resources.[108]

Alongside the idea that shareholder-initiated derivative actions could play a part in a wider system of corporate regulation, the CSLRC also recommended that the Australian Securities and Investments Commission (ASIC) should have standing to seek leave to bring derivative actions. In this way the SDA would 'assist in the recognition of the Commission as a protector of the broader public interest in the orderly administration of the affairs of companies'.[109]

In the end this overt regulatory perspective was abandoned. The CLERP recommendations, which led to the resulting legislation, stated that the SDA was 'not intended to be regulatory in nature but to facilitate private parties to enforce existing rights'.[110] The CLERP proposal did not include ASIC in the list of persons who can apply for leave to bring a derivative action.[111] Nevertheless, the statutory provision of a right to seek leave to bring a derivative action retains strong public enforcement elements.[112] This is evident in the use of a model that depends on judicial leave, giving the court the power to grant or refuse leave and, within that, the power to override an express ratification by majority shareholders.

The SDA Compared With the Oppression Remedy

Of course, the SDA is not the only contestability mechanism found in modern corporate law statutes. There are other mechanisms that can have the same potential effect as the SDA. The most commonly encountered example is the statutory remedy for oppressive or unfair conduct.[113] As an example, the Australian

---

[108] Companies and Securities Law Review Committee, *Enforcement of the Duties of Directors and Officers of a Company by Means of a Statutory Derivative Action*, Discussion Paper No. 11 (1990) para [2].

[109] Ibid para [63].

[110] Above n 31, 35. CLERP relied on s 50 of the *Australian Securities and Investments Commission Act 1989* which gives the Commission power to commence proceedings in another person's name. This discretion only arises as a result of an investigation or examination conducted by ASIC, and the power can only be exercised if 'it appears to the Commission to be in the public interest'. One view is that Australian courts have implied a '*Foss v Harbottle* consideration' into the public interest pre-requisite by inquiring into the company's ability to make a decision about the proceedings: P Hanrahan, 'Distinguishing Corporate and Personal Claims in Australian Company Litigation' (1997) 15 *Companies & Securities Law Journal* 21, 32.

[111] The Commission's standing to seek leave had been removed from proposals for an SDA in the 1991 Lavarch Committee report: see above n 31, 202 (rec 26) and 194-195. It was then re-instated in the 1993 CASAC proposal: above n 31.

[112] See S Bottomley, 'Shareholder Derivative Actions and Public Interests Suits: Two Versions of the Same Story?' (1991) 15 *University of New South Wales Law Journal* 127.

[113] For example, *Companies Act 1985* (UK) s 459; *Canada Business Corporations Act*, RSC 1985, s 241.

Corporations Act 2001 permits a court to make a variety of orders where it is proven that the conduct of the affairs of a corporation or a members' resolution is either contrary to the interests of the members as a whole, or is oppressive to, unfairly prejudicial to, or unfairly discriminatory against, a member or members.[114] The court can make any order it considers appropriate, including an order that the corporation be wound up, that the corporate constitution be modified or repealed, or that a member's shares be purchased.[115] The court can also order a derivative form of action, authorising a member to institute proceedings in the name of the corporation.[116]

If, as many commentators contend, the remedy for oppression or unfairness ('the oppression remedy') will continue to be the main form of shareholder action,[117] then the question is whether it is necessary to preserve a separate derivative action in the statute. The oppression remedy clearly operates as a means for contestability, and it offers the opportunity for members to voice their concerns rather than simply exiting the corporation.

In practice it is often difficult to maintain a clear distinction between actions for oppression or unfair conduct and derivative actions. In Australian courts the primary method of distinguishing between derivative and personal actions is to examine the nature of the legal right or duty which is alleged to have been infringed.[118] Derivative suits are said to be concerned with breaches of officers' duties such as diversion of corporate opportunities from the corporation, the improper use of corporate information, self-dealing, or negligent management,[119] while personal actions are concerned with issues such as the wrongful expropriation of shares, or the deprivation or manipulation of voting or other rights of members. Even though a member's statutory right to bring an action for oppression is personal and is not derived from the corporation, the substance of many of these actions has a strong derivative quality.[120] For example, the oppression remedy has been used in cases where corporate controllers have exercised their powers for an improper purpose,[121] awarded themselves excessive remuneration,[122] or have made uncommercial loans to a director's company.[123]

---

[114] *Corporations Act 2001* (Cth) s 232. The UK Act refers only to conduct that is unfairly prejudicial: s 459.

[115] *Corporations Act 2001* (Cth) s 233.

[116] *Corporations Act 2001* (Cth) s 233(1)(g).

[117] J Poole and P Roberts, 'Shareholder Remedies – Corporate Wrongs and the Derivative Action' (1999) *Journal of Business Law* 99, 117; Cheffins, above n 96, 260; Sugarman, above n 105, 243.

[118] Hanrahan, above n 110, 34. An alternative approach, common in the United States, is to look at whether the direct effect of the wrongful conduct is on the company or the shareholder – see T Brandi, 'The Strike Suit: A Common Problem of the Derivative Suit and the Shareholder Class Action' (1993) 98 *Dickinson Law Review* 355, 359.

[119] These are derivative wrongs because the duties are owed to the company or the members as a whole.

[120] CSLRC, above n 107, para [251]; Hanrahan, above n 110, 38.

[121] For example, *Re Bagot Well Pastoral Co Pty Ltd* (1992) 11 ACLC 1.

[122] For example, *Roberts v Walter Developments Pty Ltd* (1992) 10 ACLC 804.

In a survey of Australian cases Ian Ramsay found that the most common ground of shareholder litigation was oppression (thirty five per cent of reported judgements).[124] In a separate study of oppression actions, Ramsay reported that twenty six per cent of cases concerned action for breach of fiduciary duties, twenty per cent concerned the misappropriation of corporate assets, and twelve per cent concerned excessive remuneration.[125] In other words, a significant number of oppression cases concerned the enforcement of corporate rights and duties.

The usual remedy in oppression actions is an order requiring another shareholder or the corporation itself to purchase the plaintiff member's shares.[126] So, although it serves the purpose of providing contestability and voice, in practice the oppression remedy 'has largely become an exit remedy'.[127] In the jurisprudence of the oppression remedy, the use of voice is oriented towards exit. In contrast, the use of voice in the SDA is tied to the plaintiff's wish to remain within the corporation and to improve the way in which it operates. The SDA thus operates as a dedicated voice — loyalty response.

There is another important feature of the SDA that is highlighted by the comparison with the oppression remedy. The derivative action is not and never has been intended as a personal form of action designed to yield direct benefits to the individual shareholder/investor. By definition, the derivative action presumes that a shareholder is willing to act as a 'corporate-interest plaintiff' in pursuit of a goal that will yield benefits for the corporation as a whole.[128] In short, the SDA is a mechanism for 'corporate-regarding' behaviour. It would, of course, be naïve to suppose that SDA applicants will always be devoid of self-interest, and there will be different degrees of corporate-regarding motivation. Actions such as the misappropriation of corporate property by directors, the foregoing of a corporate opportunity, or abandoning a corporate claim against a third party — any of which

---

[123] *Re George Raymond Pty Ltd* (2000) 18 ACLC 85. See further examples in E Boros, *Minority Shareholders' Remedies* (Oxford, Clarendon Press, 1995), 231-232.

[124] I Ramsay, 'Enforcement of Corporate Rights and Duties by Shareholders and the Australian Securities Commission: Evidence and Analysis' (1995) 23 *Australian Business Law Review* 174, 175.

[125] I Ramsay, 'An Empirical Study of the Use of the Oppression Remedy' (1999) 27 *Australian Business Law Review* 23, 33.

[126] Ramsay's survey shows that in nearly 49 per cent of cases the plaintiff sought an order for the sale of shares, and this was granted in nearly 31 per cent of cases: ibid 35-36. In Australia this is because the remedy is used primarily by minority shareholders in proprietary (that is, private) companies, where there is usually no market for the sale of shares. The research also shows that 70 per cent of plaintiffs are minority shareholders in proprietary companies: ibid 31.

[127] United Kingdom Law Commission, *Shareholder Remedies*, Report Law Com No 246 (1997) para 6.11, referring to s 459 of the *Companies Act 1985* (UK).

[128] The benefits of a successful derivative action may also flow to other stakeholders in a company, such as secured and unsecured creditors and employees: Hanrahan, above n 110, 30. A derivative action may also directly satisfy a plaintiff's non-financial personal goals, such as a concern to see that rules are followed, or a concern for fairness.

might be the subject of derivative action — will involve some element of personal grievance and redress on the part of the applicant shareholder. The point remains, though, that the derivative action is oriented towards collective outcomes. At a minimum it requires shareholders to consider how the pursuit of the wider corporate interest might also be in their own interests. This echoes the deliberative requirement that corporate decisions should represent a collective judgement about the issue at hand.[129] In this way the statutory derivative action symbolises an aspect or dimension of corporate law and corporate life that has been drowned out by the volume of wealth maximisation/managerial incentive arguments. In 1960 Eugene Rostow summed up the precarious status of this dimension in the following way:

> [O]ne would expect those concerned for the integrity and future of private business institutions to applaud the intrepid souls who ferret out corporate wrongdoing, and risk their own time and money against a contingency of being rewarded, if in the end sin is found to have flourished. Not at all. Such men are not treated as honored members of the system of private enterprise, but as its scavengers and pariahs. ... At best they are viewed as necessary evils, the Robin Hoods of the business world, for whom a patronizing word may sometimes be said, when they succeed in revealing some particularly horrendous act.[130]

Similarly, consider Kirby P's dissenting judgement in the New South Wales Court of Appeal in *Parker v National Roads and Motorists Association*:

> [The plaintiff's] cause was at no time one for personal gain or for his own financial profit. It appears to have arisen from an anxiety about unequal treatment of company directors. It blossomed into a concern about the lawfulness of the conduct of his fellow directors and the companies in their charge. It came to full fruit in a determination to seek out the shield of the law when his fellow directors (as he saw it) attempted, by oppression, to suppress his complaints and to get rid of him. The judges should not deny that shield of the law. They should support corporate gadflies when their cause is the correction of apparently unlawful and self-interested action by directors, defended by oppressive conduct.[131]

The statutory derivative action symbolises the importance of corporate concerns, rather than purely personal goals. It ties in with that dimension of corporate law that stresses the constitutional ties within a corporation, rather than the nexus of contractual relationships between individual corporators.

The risk that arises from the overlap between the oppression remedy and the SDA is that the effectiveness of the SDA in cases where the action is solely or largely derivative will be undermined by the easier availability of the oppression remedy. The oppression remedy contains none of the procedural prerequisites that

---

[129] See Chapter 5 above, n 15 and accompanying text.
[130] Rostow, above n 102, 49.
[131] (1993) 11 ACLC 866, 877-878. The case involved an action under the statutory remedy for oppressive conduct in which the plaintiff sought orders that he be allowed to conduct proceedings in the name of the respondent companies. See also *Wallersteiner v Moir (No. 2)* [1975] QB 373, 389 per Denning MR.

apply to the SDA. Even though 'there is room for doubt whether the Australian statutory 'oppression' remedy covers cases which only involve a wrong to the company'[132] it would be preferable for the legislation to be drafted to ensure that solely derivative wrongs are channelled through the SDA.

Conclusion

In this Chapter I have argued the importance of having clear and accessible mechanisms for shareholder contestation to ensure that shareholder interests are properly taken into account in corporate decisions, and to protect the corporate interest. In part — but only in part — this is important because of the compensation and deterrence effects that contestation can have. But I have argued that contestability also has a legitimating function: shareholders, knowing that action can be taken if their interests are not being tracked, can have a measure of confidence in the decision-making process and be more likely to view that process as legitimate. This does not require that there be lots of actual contestations, but it does require that contestability be a realistic option.

The two examples that I have used to illustrate this argument — the right to request an extraordinary general meeting, and the right to seek leave to bring a derivative action — reveal just some of the issues in trying to achieve this balance. Neither form of contestation has been widely used in Australia. Curiously this fact has led to different conclusions in the literature and policy debate. The relative absence of shareholder-requested general meetings has not placated concerns about abuse by shareholders and has resulted in more restrictive criteria. By comparison, the perceived under-usage of the SDA has been seen by some critics as proof of a legislative failure or the purely symbolic nature of this statutory provision. This may simply illustrate the point that there are no pre-determined thresholds or criteria that can be applied in all cases and contexts. The maintenance of effective mechanisms of contestability requires continuous debate — and deliberation.

---

[132]   R Simmonds 'A Summing Up and a Search for Solutions' in M Gillooly (ed), *The Law Relating to Corporate Groups* (1993) 239.

Chapter 7

The Prospects for Corporate Constitutionalism

Having spent the previous three Chapters exploring particular aspects of a constitutional perspective on corporate law and governance, it is useful to conclude by returning to the bigger picture that I described in Chapter 1 and spelled out in more detail in Chapter 3. In this final Chapter I re-visit the ways in which the principles of accountability, deliberation and contestability work together within a framework of corporate constitutionalism. I then look at where this might take us in approaching questions of corporate governance. I offer some suggestions about how corporate constitutionalism might allow us to move beyond the strict parameters of the shareholder primacy model, at least as it operates in large public corporations.

Reading the Principles Together

Notwithstanding the separate discussions in the previous three Chapters it is hopefully clear that the principles of accountability, deliberation and contestability are interrelated; they work together and should be read together. The three principles work together in two ways.

First, each has implications for the other two. Contestability, for example, has the capacity to enhance accountability if we insist that, at a minimum, corporate actions or decisions that are contested should be explained and justified, in an open forum where possible. In Chapter 3 I described this as explanatory accountability.[1] Where the contestation is escalated to a court or similar forum then we see a stronger dimension of accountability, in the sense of 'being held to account'. Conversely, mechanisms of accountability, such as the division and separation of decision-making powers within the corporation, can provide an internal system of contestability. An example is found in the many 'best practice' codes of corporate governance which encourage the appointment of outside directors to act as independent checks and monitors of executive directors and non-director managers.[2] The different roles of the internal audit committee and the

---

[1] Borrowing John Uhr's description: see Chapter 3 above, n 5 and accompanying text.

[2] See for example, the Australian Stock Exchange Corporate Governance Council, *Principles of Good Corporate Governance and Best Practice Recommendations* (March 2003) Recommendation 2.1; Financial Services Authority (UK), *The Combined*

The Constitutional Corporation

corporation's external auditor provide another example.[3] Deliberation can also enhance accountability within the corporation, in so far as it enhances ex ante explanations of proposed actions. Moreover, effective deliberation depends on the effective supply of information, and so a commitment to deliberation has the potential to encourage accountability through attention to the flow of corporate information and provision of explanations.[4] And, drawing on Tom Tyler's work, I argued in Chapter 5 that deliberation also has the potential to reduce the risk of needless contestation; members who feel that their voice has been given an adequate hearing in the processes leading up to a decision are more likely to accept the outcome of the decision-making process and will have less cause to voice their concerns through external means.[5]

A particular example of all three principles at work is found in the statutory right of members of a corporation to requisition a special general meeting, which was discussed in Chapter 6.[6] A special general meeting that is requisitioned in this way is likely to be a form of, and forum for, contestation in which, through processes of deliberation, the corporation's directors are required to account for their actions with regard to the matters on the agenda. The effectiveness of this particular mechanism as a corporate constitutional device depends, amongst other things, on how widely or restrictively the threshold requirements are specified. That will involve consideration of factors such as cost, which must be balanced against considerations of accountability, deliberation and contestability. I come back to these questions in a moment.

The second way in which the three principles can work together is that, in a given corporate setting, shortfalls in the operation of one principle can potentially be addressed and remedied by the other two. For example, it will not always be feasible for a corporation to implement particular separations of power. There may not be any available or suitable independent candidates for appointment to the board; the incumbent directors may be insufficiently qualified to form an effective audit committee; or the founder and chief executive officer of the business may insist on retaining control by also holding the position of chair of the board.[7]

Code on Corporate Governance (July 2003) principle A.3; OECD, *Principles of Corporate Governance* (2004) principle VI.E.

[3] See for example, the Australian Stock Exchange Corporate Governance Council, *Principles of Good Corporate Governance and Best Practice Recommendations* (March 2003) Recommendation 4.4; Financial Services Authority (UK), *The Combined Code on Corporate Governance* (July 2003) principle C.3.

[4] See, for example, Chapter 6 above n 147 and accompanying text, referring to the practice in some corporations of inviting members, prior to the general meeting, to nominate issues for discussion at the meeting.

[5] Chapter 5 above, n 24.

[6] See Chapter 6 above, n 37 to n 55 and accompanying text.

[7] A well-known Australian instance of this situation is the large retailer Harvey Norman Holdings Ltd. Faced with criticism of his dual role as CEO and board chair, company co-founder Gerry Harvey's reported response was: 'If you reckon I should piss off [as executive chairman] and get someone who knows nothing about my business, well, I

Situations such as these will require that greater attention should be given to mechanisms of deliberation or contestability, for example by ensuring adequate opportunities for questions from members at the annual general meeting or from directors at board meetings.

Read together, the arguments about accountability, deliberation and contestability involve descriptive and prescriptive claims. The descriptive argument, as I have indicated throughout this book, is that examples of these principles can already be found in current corporate law rules and doctrines. These expressions are not always clear, coherent, or consistent and perhaps for that reason they are often overlooked, being subsumed by other values such as efficiency or 'freedom of the market'.

The arguments are prescriptive because I claim that accountability, deliberation and contestability are principles around which a system of corporate law *ought* to be built. That said, these principles are not presented here as detailed blueprints for 'good corporate governance', or (to repeat what I said in Chapter 1) as part of a 'grand theory' of the corporation or of corporate law. Instead, they are broad criteria that should be taken into account by courts, legislators, business people and academics when they deal with corporate governance disputes, consider changes to corporate law, or conduct corporate affairs, in the same way that they already consider goals such as efficiency or profit maximisation. For example, while there are obvious efficiency arguments to be made in favour of amending the law to allow electronic or 'virtual' meetings to replace (rather than merely augment) face-to-face meetings, there are also significant implications for the quality of deliberation. While, as I argued in Chapter 5, we must allow for attenuated forms of deliberation, this should not outweigh the importance of directors being called to account in face-to-face meetings.

I do not suggest that greater attention to the ideas of accountability, deliberation and contestability would, of itself, have prevented scandals such as HIH Insurance or Enron. For one thing, these collapses were the product of unique sets of circumstances and personnel, and the impact of different industry settings (contrast insurance to energy) and different regulatory requirements must also be taken into account.[8] My sense, however, is that a legal and corporate environment that gives too much prominence to the economics of corporate life, and to the interests of shareholders as investors, certainly has encouraged a culture in which those scandals were more likely to occur. William Bratton's analysis of the Enron collapse bears this out, arguing that the collapse was the product of the 'pursuit of immediate shareholder value' which caused Enron's managers 'to become risk-prone, engaging in levered speculation, earnings manipulation, and concealment of

---

don't think my shareholders will be very impressed' – quoted in Fiona Buffini 'Directors Slam New ASX Rules', *Australian Financial Review*, 4 April 2003.

[8]   Commonwealth of Australia, The HIH Royal Commission, *The Failure of HIH Insurance* (2003) describes the background to the HIH collapse. On the 'maddeningly unique' features of Enron, see J Coffee, 'Understanding Enron: "It's About the Gatekeepers, Stupid"' (2002) 57 *The Business Lawyer* 1403.

critical information'.[9] So, while I do not presume that greater attention to accountability, deliberation and contestability will invariably lead to improvements in managerial or shareholder behaviour, or to responsible corporate decision-making, I am sceptical that sustained improvements are possible without addressing these three principles; they are, I suggest, necessary although not sufficient conditions for improved corporate governance and corporate behaviour.

The post-HIH, post-Enron legal reforms demonstrate a partial vindication of this claim. The CLERP 9 legislative amendments in Australia,[10] the *Sarbanes-Oxley Act* in the United States, and similar reforms in the United Kingdom,[11] are fundamentally concerned with improving corporate accountability, especially (though not exclusively) with enforcing separations of power in the audit function. These are steps in the right direction (leaving aside debate about the detail). But, as I argued earlier, mechanisms of accountability should not be left to carry the burden of reform on their own. In Australia the next major set of corporate law reforms to be considered after the CLERP 9 changes have focussed on amending and, in some respects, improving mechanisms for shareholder deliberation. The draft Corporations Amendment Bill (No 2) 2006 proposes, amongst other things, to facilitate the electronic circulation of members' resolutions and statements, and to improve procedures for the exercise and disclosure of proxy votes.[12]

Balancing the Corporate Governance Debate

Are these the only principles that might be assembled within a constitutional framework for corporate governance? Undoubtedly not. This book has presented an exploratory argument, not a definitive catalogue. There will be — and should be — debate about the relevance of these and other values. Should, for example, the ideas of representation and participation also have a role in shaping our system of corporate law and corporate governance? What about the idea of equal opportunity for input into corporate decisions? Consider too the importance of different corporate settings. It has not been the purpose of this book to investigate the implications of corporate constitutionalism for all types of corporation. I have concentrated on what is perhaps the easiest example: the widely-held public

---

[9] W Bratton, 'Does Corporate Law Protect The Interests of Shareholders and Other Stakeholders? Enron and the Dark Side of Shareholder Value' (2002) 76 *Tulane Law Review* 1275, 1283.

[10] *Corporate Law Economic Reform Program (Audit Reform and Corporate Disclosure) Act 2004.*

[11] *Companies (Audit, Investigations and Community Enterprise) Act 2004.*

[12] Against this, as discussed in Chapter 6 above, n 50, the draft Bill also proposes to restrict the threshold allowing members to requisition a special general meeting, removing the '100 members rule' and leaving only the 'members with 5 per cent of votes' rule. In the UK, the Company Law Reform Bill 2005 similarly addresses, amongst wide-ranging reforms, the right of shareholders to requisition meetings, and to circulate statements prior to a general meeting: see eg cls 279 and 290.

corporation. There is no reason to think that the principles of accountability, deliberation and contestability cannot apply in smaller, proprietary corporations or other corporate forms, although we should expect that these ideas will be played out differently in those different corporate contexts. In small closely-held corporations, for example, where there is no neat separation between membership and management, it is likely that decision-making involvement by members will extend beyond periodic voting at general meetings. Indeed, in these corporations voting may well be regarded as a mere formality, something that is done for the sake of the required corporate records. Exit options in such corporations are likely to be limited — indeed we may need to consider ways of fostering exit where the use of deliberation and voice have run its course (as in the case of a deadlock). Separations of powers and other accountability mechanisms may also be more difficult to sustain. The point is that with different corporate contexts decisions need to be made about the interaction and balance between the principles discussed in this book.

And, of course, there will always be criteria or desiderata drawn from other frameworks to be weighed up. This is part of the plurality of discursive perspectives that I referred to in Chapter 5.[13] As an example, I argued above that the right of a small group of members to requisition a special general meeting demonstrates the joint operation of all three principles. There are obvious competing concerns here, some of which come from an economic perspective: there can be considerable financial cost in calling a special general meeting,[14] along with the opportunity costs of diverting management's attention away from 'getting on with the job' of running the corporation. A related concern, owing as much to political as to economic considerations, is the risk that the right to requisition general meetings might be abused by sectional minority groups in the corporation's membership who are pursuing their own special interests (the 'tyranny of the minority' argument).

My concern, and one of the reasons for writing this book, is that while they deserve attention, economic or financial arguments such as these are too often assumed to have precedence over other considerations. Moreover, to the extent that more politically-oriented arguments have been taken into account, this has only been done within the parameters set by those economic arguments. For example, when it recommended the repeal of the statutory rule that allowed 100 members in a corporation to requisition the directors to call a general meeting, the Australian Parliament's Joint Committee on Corporations and Financial Services did so on the basis of arguments that the rule exposed large corporations and their members to significant costs and that it gave economically disproportionate influence to

---

[13] Chapter 5, above n 39 and following text.
[14] In a study of 217 Australian listed corporations in 2003, the median cost of an AGM was A$15,000: S Bottomley, *The Role of Shareholders' Meetings in Improving Corporate Governance* (Research Report, Centre for Commercial Law, Australian National University, 2003), 45.

174 *The Constitutional Corporation*

minority shareholders.[15] Again, my argument is not that these are irrelevant or inappropriate considerations. It is, rather, that they should not be assumed to be the *only* relevant or appropriate considerations; on a given issue they may 'win the day' but this should be in light of a serious consideration of other concerns such as those examined in this book.

But, it may be asked, do shareholders in public companies really care about the protection of accountability structures? Do they want to deliberate? When dissatisfied with corporate performance or managerial behaviour, would they prefer to contest improper decisions rather than simply selling their shares in the company? These questions require empirical investigation, but a safe hypothesis is that for many shareholders in many public corporations the answers are likely to be: 'to an extent', 'maybe', and 'no' respectively. Does this mean that the arguments presented in this book are irrelevant? Not surprisingly, I do not think that they are. I do not think that corporate constitutionalism fails in its job of assisting us to understand and promote better corporate governance even if, in practice, its ideas do not touch numbers of shareholders. I explain why under the next heading.

Shareholder Primacy Revisited

In Chapter 1, I explained that this book takes the shareholder primacy model as its reference point. This is for practical reasons: for better or for worse, the shareholder primacy model has proven to be resilient (notwithstanding its imprecision and malleability) and it seems to me to be a better strategy to work with it rather than try to overthrow it (in a single move, at least). But, as I also explained, it is important to re-visit the shareholder primacy model because often its adherents give it a very narrow reading. Too often, shareholder primacy is distorted by a pre-occupation — on the part of directors, managers *and* shareholders — with short-term profit maximisation.[16] This, in turn, translates into arguments about the need for greater managerial discretion:[17] shareholders are investors, their interests are directed at earning profits on their investments, and the

---

15 Joint Committee on Corporations and Financial Services, Parliament of Australia, *Inquiry into the Exposure Draft of the Corporations Amendment Bill (No. 2) 2005* (2005), paras. 2.6-2.10; see also Companies and Securities Advisory Committee, *Shareholder Participation in the Modern Listed Public Company: Final Report*, (2000) para 2.6 (pointing to the costs of calling a meeting and to the risk of giving small groups of shareholders 'undue leverage in negotiating' with the corporation).
16 On the impact of short-termism, see L Mitchell, *Corporate Irresponsibility: America's Newest Export* (2001).
17 Culminating, sometimes, in arguments for 'director primacy': S Bainbridge, 'Director Primacy: The Means and Ends of Corporate Governance' (2003) 97 *Northwestern University Law Review* 547.

best way to achieve this is to let corporate managers get on with the job (within basic fiduciary constraints) of keeping the shareholders happy.[18]

It should be apparent by now that, as I see it, the shareholder primacy model does not, as a matter of law, restrict the concerns of corporate managers to the financial interests of shareholders (short-term or otherwise).[19] The model permits attention to be given to shareholders' non-financial concerns (such as concerns for the social or environmental impact of their corporation's activities) and, through the medium of the shareholders, the model can also take account of the interests of non-shareholders.[20] By giving greater attention to the role of shareholders as members of (as opposed to their role as investors in) a corporation, by encouraging and then taking seriously their input through processes of deliberation, by investigating the use of corporate interest groups,[21] it is quite feasible that shareholders — of all types — can be a means whereby the concerns and interests of corporate employees, of tort victims, of consumers and others can be factored into corporate decisions. Corporate law should encourage shareholders to be active as members, to consider and make use of the options offered by deliberation and contestation rather than those offered by passivity and exit. In this way shareholders can act as conduits to introduce other ideas and interests into corporate deliberations.

There is reason to believe that at least some shareholders would respond to this encouragement. An indication is found in the growing interest in socially responsible investments (SRI) in Australia, the UK, the US and other countries. Institutional investors in particular have demonstrated a willingness to screen investment opportunities against ethical, social and environmental criteria.[22] According to one estimate, in Australia in 2002 approximately A\$2.18 billion was invested by institutions pursuing SRI strategies.[23] Another Australian study of shareholders' responses to ethical issues shows that a majority of shareholders surveyed would be likely to sell their shares in a corporation that was discovered to have engaged in certain ethically contentious practices (such as using child labour, causing environmental problems, or giving large bonuses to directors).[24] This

---

[18] See Bratton, above n 9.

[19] David Millon makes a similar argument in his response to Mitchell's book (above, n 16): D Millon, 'Why Is Corporate Management Obsessed With Quarterly Earnings And What Should Be Done About It?' (2002) 70 *George Washington Law Review* 890.

[20] Similarly, see Millon, above n 19.

[21] See Chapter 5 above, n 137 to 146 and accompanying text.

[22] Editorial, 'Corporate Governance, Institutional Investors and Socially Responsible Investment' (2002) 10 *Corporate Governance* 1.

[23] P Ali, G Stapledon, M Gold, *Corporate Governance and Investment Fiduciaries* (2003) 193.

[24] D Hanson and B Tranter, 'Who Are the Shareholders in Australia and What Are Their Ethical Opinions? An Empirical Analysis' (2006) 14 *Corporate Governance* 23, reporting that, given the choice of keeping or selling their shares, in a sample of 2087 shareholders 88.2 per cent of shareholders would probably or definitely sell in response to the use of child labour; 70.9 per cent would do so in response to a major environmental problem. The figure for payment of large bonuses to executives was 60.1

speaks well of the willingness of shareholders to bring ethical considerations to bear on their investment choices. On the other hand, it also demonstrates the continued orientation towards exit as the preferred response to dissatisfaction with corporate performance. But, as I argued in Chapter 6, while exit in such situations can send a clear message to the corporation, it is also important that our systems of corporate law and governance should give clear recognition and encouragement to the option of remaining and voicing one's concerns.[25] The Royal Commission of Inquiry into the collapse of HIH Insurance recognised this point, albeit in a limited context:

> Shareholder apathy can play a part in undesirable corporate governance. If shareholders as owners are unwilling or unable to exercise their powers or make themselves heard, directors and management will lack guidance or constraint from those whose interests they are supposed to serve. Shareholders have an interest in seeing that a board is properly constituted and in holding it to account for the company's performance.[26]

I would add, going beyond concerns with board composition and corporate performance, that shareholders can, and should, also be encouraged to take responsibility — in a moral sense — for the actions of the corporations whose shares they own.[27]

I do not want to overstate the case for greater shareholder involvement. There are questions to be asked about the capacity of shareholders (including institutional shareholders) to influence the course of corporate events. The passivity of institutional shareholders has been the subject of widespread comment.[28] So too has been the low success-rate of those shareholders in getting SRI resolutions passed at general meetings.[29] And it is true that some shareholders may use their deliberative options and their contestability mechanisms simply to pursue their own short-term investment concerns. But, as I have argued elsewhere in this book, we need not assume that self-interested investors are the only or the preferred inhabitants of the corporate world. There is no reason why the model should not, and cannot, encourage a different vision — of shareholders who, while mindful of their investments, also have other concerns and who take steps to bring them to the attention of directors and managers.

---

percent. Other scenarios were: producing military weapons – 58.2 per cent; investing in genetically modified food or crops – 67.5 per cent; and being prosecuted for racial discrimination – 48.5 per cent.

[25] See Chapter 6 above, n 15 to n 23 and accompanying text.
[26] HIH Royal Commission, above n 8, vol 1, 121.
[27] See, eg, R Warren, 'The Responsible Shareholders: A Case Study' (2002) 11 *Business Ethics: A European Review* 14.
[28] See, eg, I Ramsay, G Stapledon and K Fong, 'Corporate Governance: The Perspective of Australian Institutional Shareholders' (2000) 18 *Company and Securities Law Journal* 110.
[29] See, eg, M Haigh and J Hazelton, 'Financial Markets: A Tool for Social Responsibility?' (2004) 52 *Journal of Business Ethics* 59.

Beyond Shareholder Primacy

It is, of course, important to think about moving beyond the parameters of the shareholder primacy model. There are other corporate actors who lie outside these strict parameters, and who are clearly implicated in how the model operates and how it conforms with the ideas of accountability, deliberation and contestability.

There are two ways that this might be done. Read strictly, that model confines our attention to the relationship between shareholders and directors, mediated through the separate legal entity of the corporation. So we can ask, first, whether there are others outside the boardroom who ought to be subject to legal duties or expectations which might enhance the prospects of accountability, deliberation or contestability. Secondly, we can consider expanding, beyond the shareholders, the list of people to whom those duties are owed.

On the first point, there are already ways in which Australian corporate law looks beyond the boardroom. Auditors, as we have noted, have a statutorily mandated role in corporate accountability processes. The *Corporations Act* now requires auditors of listed companies to attend the company's AGM at which the audit report is to be considered.[30] The chair of the meeting must allow a reasonable opportunity for the members as a whole to ask questions at the meeting about the conduct of the audit, the preparation and content of the audit report, and the auditor's independence.[31] Moreover, members of a listed company may submit written questions to the auditor prior to the meeting about the content of the auditor's report or the conduct of the audit.[32] The role of non-board corporate officers has also been noted at various places in this book. In the wake of prominent corporate collapses between 2001 and 2002, attention has turned to the question of whether, and to what extent, legal duties and liabilities should be more explicitly imposed on corporate officers and employees who operate outside the boardroom.[33] In Australia the HIH Royal Commission made the obvious point that 'in larger companies many significant decisions are made by management without reference to the board', and found that many of the practices that formed part of the HIH collapse were undertaken by employees in 'middle management'.[34] The extension of duties and liabilities, similar to those presently imposed on directors, to other corporate officers is one means (but only one) by which processes of accountability, deliberation and contestability can be shifted from the board room into the wider corporate managerial framework.[35]

---

[30] *Corporations Act 2001* s 250RA.
[31] *Corporations Act 2001* s 250T (also permitting questions about the accounting policies used by companies).
[32] *Corporations Act 2001* s 250PA.
[33] See Australian Government, Corporations and Markets Advisory Committee, *Corporate Duties Below Board Level*, Report (2006).
[34] HIH Royal Commission, above n 8, vol 1, 121-122.
[35] This was recommended by the HIH Royal Commission: see ibid, recommendation 2. Similar recommendations have been made by Australian Government's Corporations and Markets Advisory Committee: see above n 33.

The second point — expanding the list of people to whom those duties are owed — takes us to 'stakeholder theory' and wider debates about corporate social responsibility. I do not intend to enter these debates here, but it is worth noting that, in Australia at least, there appears to be a loose correlation between periods of significant corporate collapse and a renewal of concern about standards of corporate social responsibility. For example, even before the spate of corporate collapses in the late 1980s had concluded, the Australian Senate conducted an inquiry into the social and fiduciary obligations of company directors (recommending that directors' duties not be expanded to include environmental and similar matters).[36] Some twenty years later, in the wake of the HIH Insurance and other collapses, simultaneous but separate inquiries into corporate social responsibility were conducted by the Australian Government's Corporations and Markets Advisory Committee [37] and by the Australian Parliament's Joint Committee on Corporations and Financial Services. [38] The Parliamentary Committee's recommendations echo the point made earlier in this Chapter: that is, the existing legal model does not preclude the consideration of stakeholder interests, and that attention should be given to various ways in which corporate responsibility can be encouraged on a voluntary basis.

It appears, then, that concerns about accountability failures and questions about broader corporate responsibilities are never far apart. My view, elaborated at length in this book, is that as important as issues of corporate social responsibility are, they must be built upon a robust and searching examination of the ways in which the role of shareholders can be revitalised. In Chapter 1 I expressed pessimism about the prospects for a serious consideration of broader perspectives on corporate governance and corporate responsibility by directors and managers until they can be convinced that a broader approach is consonant with the ideas that underlie the standard legal model. Put more bluntly, I wonder what hope there can be for stakeholders if corporate laws and practices do not take the roles and interests of shareholders seriously.

The Lens of Corporate Constitutionalism

I said in Chapter 1 that the purpose of this book is to use the lens of corporate constitutionalism to offer a fresh perspective on the way in which we view the

---

[36] Senate Standing Committee on Legal and Constitutional Affairs, Australian Parliament, *Company Directors' Duties: Report on the Social and Fiduciary Duties and Obligations of Company Directors* (1989).

[37] The Advisory Committee, established under Part 9 of the *Australian Securities and Investments Commission Act 2001*, operates as a specialized corporate law reform body. It released a discussion paper in November 2005: see Corporations and Markets Advisory Committee, *Corporate Social Responsibility: Discussion Paper* (November 2005).

[38] Parliamentary Joint Committee on Corporations and Financial Services, Australian Parliament, *Corporate Responsibility: Managing Risk and Creating Value* (2006).

processes of governance within public corporations. The metaphor of 'looking at things through a different lens' is appropriate. Corporate constitutionalism does not introduce us, to borrow Philip Pettit's expression, to 'a new-fangled idea'. [39] Instead, it reminds us of, and revives our interest in, some important principles that are already there to be found in our system of corporate law.

Through the lens of corporate constitutionalism we are able to emphasise aspects of, and issues in, corporate governance and corporate law that are otherwise likely to be overlooked or down-played in prevailing legal and economic analyses (for example, the importance of decision-making *processes*, the role of separations of powers in corporate decision-making; and the value of encouraging shareholders to voice their concerns).

The arguments in this book also remind us that the language we use in debates about corporate governance is important. When we choose to refer to 'members' rather than 'investors', our choice conveys a particular set of assumptions and expectations about the roles and interests of those corporate actors. The same is true when we choose between 'contract' and 'constitution' as the underlying framework for thinking about corporate governance. Having reminded us of these things, corporate constitutionalism then invites us to consider how we might re-think some core questions of corporate governance — questions such as: what is the purpose of the corporate endeavour? In whose interests should the corporation be run? And who should participate in deciding the answers to these questions? [40]

---

[39] P Pettit, 'Democracy, Electoral and Contestatory' in I Shapiro and S Macedo (eds), *Designing Democratic Institutions: Nomos 42* (2000) 105.

[40] I have adapted these questions from Lyman Johnson, 'The Social Responsibility of Corporate Law Professors' (2002) 76 *Tulane Law Review* 1483, 1494.

Index

an informa business

ISBN 978-1-138-24835-9

Routledge
Taylor & Francis Group

www.routledge.com

9 781138 248359

THE INTERNATIONAL ORDER OF ASIA IN THE 1930S AND 1950S

Edited by
Shigeru Akita and Nicholas J. White